2⁵⁰

The Laughton Story

Portrait of a genius. All things to all people. To himself, nothing but perfection.

The Laughton Story

By *KURT SINGER*

An Intimate Story
of Charles Laughton

THE JOHN C. WINSTON COMPANY

Philadelphia · Toronto

DEDICATION

To H. Who Stood Behind the Author

Acknowledgments

The author wishes to thank all who have provided assistance, advice, co-operation, interviews, files, clippings, letters and other source material for this book.

Among the individuals, special mention should be made of Harold Ornstein, New York; Ilse Lahn, Hollywood; Cecilia and Albert Rappaport, San Francisco; Lotte Fuld, Los Angeles; Dr. Lou Goldhaber, Los Angeles; James Lombard, Minneapolis; Roxanna Wells, New York; Max Pfeffer, New York; Helen Crosby, New York; Bing Crosby, Hollywood; Tallulah Bankhead, New York; Elsa Lanchester, Hollywood; Thornton Wilder, Connecticut; Somerset Maugham, France; Edmond Pauker, New York; Lilian Rudolph, Denver; John Mason Brown, New York; Merle Oberon, Hollywood; Marlene Dietrich, New York; Joseph von Sternberg, Japan; Lauritz Melchior, California; Alfred Hitchcock, Hollywood; Rose Pelwick, New York; Ingrid Bergman, Italy; Leonard Lyons, New York; Dr. Remsen D. Bird, Eagle Rock, California; Ezra Ellis, Glendale, California; Dr. Graham Hunter, Cathedral City, California; Maria Bazzi, Italy; Ethel Barrymore, New York; Seymour Peck, New York; the late Alva Johnston, New York; Scudder Middleton, New York; Richard Winston, Brattleboro, Vermont; Margot Schkeitzer, London.

The author is also most grateful to the following: University of Minnesota; Library of Congress; *Reader's Digest; London Observer; Theatre Arts,* New York; *Art Digest,* New York; *Atlantic Monthly,* Boston; New York Public Library (Theatre Collection); *The New York Times; New York Herald Tribune;* Decca Recordings, New York; *Time* and *Life,* New York; Faber & Faber, London; Harcourt Brace & Co., New York; Turnabout Theater,

Hollywood, California; *Denver Post;* Tucson Town Hall, Arizona; San Francisco Town Hall, California; *Current Biography,* New York; *This Week,* New York; Harper & Brothers, New York; *Collier's,* New York; *The Saturday Evening Post,* Philadelphia; Doubleday & Company, Inc., New York; *Variety,* New York; *New Republic,* Washington; and many members of the Motion Picture Industry in Hollywood, New York, Paris and London.

Charles Laughton
on Storytelling

BY CHARLES LAUGHTON

URING the recent war I was in Hollywood. I was not actively in the war and I was restless. I had a heavy contract at a movie studio, and apparently I was behaving badly around the house. Elsa, who understands me only too well, said, "You're an out-of-work man and a nuisance around the house; get out of here and work." I was angry—very angry—but as usual, after two or three days I knew she was right. I was being paid a lot of money, but movie acting is no complete job. In a year it will absorb only four to five months of your time, and a tenth of a man's energy. I was in a still department one day, up at Universal, I think. There were two wounded men there from Birmingham Hospital and I asked what the fellows did of an evening. They said, "Nothing," and I asked them if they would be interested in anybody's coming and reading to them a couple of times a week for two hours or so. They said they would, so I had a full occupation.

I read Dickens, Aesop, Shakespeare, Walt Whitman, Maupassant, James Thurber, Hans Christian Andersen, Washington Irving, and what all. One day I picked up a Bible, and they protested. They did not want to hear anything from a dull book. The Bible was not dull to me, but I had to prove to them that it was not dull to me, and I used every trick that I had learned, and they liked it and asked for more. We had a pleasant time.

There is something about reading aloud to a group of people, however scarred, that turns them into children. They would sit and listen to fairy stories. They found a reflection of their sufferings, which they thought to be unique, in the tragedies of Shakespeare, and felt better. I lost my actor's nerves. I taught dozens of them how to read aloud to their wives and children. The whole affair is one of the good memories of my life.

One evening when I went home to Elsa I said that I believed people want this thing that I am doing. We are all disturbed and unsettled, and they seem to like sitting down and hearing about the same things that have happened to people in the past which have been set down by great writers. I found that they all had—contrary to what I had been told in the entertainment industry—a common shy hunger for knowledge. I found that when I went home after one of these sessions I slept like a log—I am not normally a sound sleeper. I then began to read about reading aloud. I read of two famous tours of Charles Dickens; of Fanny Kemble and of the Chautauqua circuit; and learned that I had invented nothing but was carrying on an American tradition.

It is a friendly thing to read from great books to large numbers of people. I have always been a nervous actor and scared of appearing before audiences. I have never yet been scared when I have had a bundle of books under my arm.

I have been asked which of the great authors people seem to like best. I have read to audiences varying in size from several hundred to six thousand or so, and the main impression that I have taken away is that people have just liked hearing things out of real books. Sometimes they have said, "I liked Dickens best" (it may have been snowing outside—it was in Detroit); sometimes James Thurber (they wanted to laugh together); sometimes a psalm (they wanted to be solemn together); and sometimes Shakespeare's magic wood from *A Midsum-*

mer Night's Dream (they were indulging in magic together). There has been no preference. I have been moved by their acceptance of things particularly loved. And that is an interesting thing about people in theaters—doing things together. That is the beauty of being in a theater. That we all—fifteen hundred or so of us in a big room—do the same thing together at the same moment—laugh or wonder or pity—and we feel good and safe because the people around us are the same as we are.

I have thought about this a lot—what theater is—and I think this is a good part of what it is. And when we agree, as we mostly do, that a play is a good or bad play, what we are saying is that it had the truth or it did not have the truth to fuse us then and there. And the communion that happens in a theater is one of the best things we have in life.[1]

---

[1] Copyright 1950 by The Atlantic Monthly Company, Boston 16, Massachusetts.

Chapter 1

IT WAS NINE o'clock on a clear December night that I met this bewildering man for the first time. As I drove through the Hollywood hills to his house, the street lights seemed to grow dimmer and further apart. But the moon and the reflection from myriads of lights below in the Los Angeles valley helped me to find the place. The house and the grounds were bathed in an eerie and romantic effulgence.

I rang the bell with trepidation. The windows of the house were dark.

Suddenly, quite to my surprise, the house lighted up and the front door was thrown open.

In front of me stood a massive two-hundred-pound mountain of flesh. It wore only pajama bottoms and blue slippers. For a moment I was taken aback. I had expected a suave Hollywood butler.

Then an immensely warm and enchanting, almost hypnotic, voice greeted me.

As Charles Laughton ushered me into the house, he grabbed up an old shabby blue dressing gown. He must have outgrown it years ago, for when he put it on, it covered only a small part of his huge body.

"I was working," he apologized, "preparing my new television show, twenty-six programs to do; I really had no time to dress."

He led the way into a large living room, the wrinkled

1

bathrobe flapping around his knees, his hairy chest protruding ponderously.

Standing before a built-in wood-paneled bar, he poured our drinks. He was certainly a grotesque figure. The fabulously beautiful Renoirs and Utrillos on the walls around him only added to the incongruity.

It was hard to believe that this was the same man who, many times in the past, had cast his spell over me. Was this the man who had brought to the theater and the screen the thrill and exuberance of animal magnetism which are the roots of all great acting? Was this perhaps the greatest living actor of our time?

And I wondered, too, as I watched him, about the man himself. There have been all kinds of stories about him. I knew many people adored him and that many hated him with equal fervor. He had been called a spoiled, self-centered and arrogant intellectual. An outrageous nonconformist, who can't help it. I knew that it was generally agreed that in human relations he is difficult. He snubs people mercilessly. Yet he had, I was aware, on many occasions shown himself to possess true warmheartedness and understanding. All this was, perhaps, the contradictions of genius.

He passed me my drink and sat down on the yellow half-circle couch.

"Twenty-six television programs, every one different! You need variety; you need an enormous repertoire to prepare these. I wish I had the time to do all the things I want to do."

He spoke with energy that expressed itself in almost every muscle, in the slightest lift of his eyes and in the peculiar complexity of his smile.

"It is only here in America that I can do all these different things: films, theater, television, readings, radio. Now that I'm fifty-four, my only great ambition left is to portray David, Plato, Socrates—the dialogues. Yes, that's all I still want to get out of life. I'm not as young as I used to be." He smiled and began to pace up and down the room.

I was not surprised at his choice of roles: David, who stood alone against the world, as Laughton believes the strong man must; Socrates—what great actor has not wanted such a part?

When I mentioned Maxwell Anderson's new play, *Barefoot in Athens,* Laughton said, "Pooh—who needs all that? I mean to do the original dialogues—the original Socrates, the original Plato. I'll do them yet."

As we sipped our drinks he told me that for more than a decade he had wanted to bring the *John Brown's Body* poem to stage life. During his first years in America, in the early thirties, he had read this Stephen Vincent Benét work and was fascinated by its beautiful verse, its drama and human qualities. For years he thought of an adaptation and production. Now his dramatized version was touring all of America, with great actors reciting his own adaptation in the play directed by him.

Suddenly, as if compelled by an inner urge, he began to act out the memorable role of Melora in *John Brown's Body.*

There was no chorus, no music. He was dressed in the most grotesque costume. Yet he brought Melora vividly to life. He *was* that young girl becoming a woman, giving birth out of wedlock, waiting for her soldier who had left for the great war between the South and North.

> "Melora, in the room she had to herself
> Because they weren't white-trash and used to be Eastern, . . .
> She was changed, then. She was not a girl any more.
> She was the white heart of the birch, . . .
> Out of bronze air and light, on a wheel of light.
> Her sharp clear breasts
> Were two young victories in the hollow darkness . . ."[1]

---

[1] Lines from "John Brown's Body" in *Selected Works of Stephen Vincent Benét* published by Rinehart & Company, Inc. Copyright, 1927, 1928, by Stephen Vincent Benét.

Laughton seemed to be in an absolute trance as he went on. The man had forgotten that he was in his own living room. He probably did not care where he was.

> "The good girls sleep in their modesty,
> The bad girls sleep in their shame,
> But I must sleep in the hollow tree
> Till my child can have a name." [1]

Few male actors would have dared to attempt the portrayal of woman in childbirth. Yet Laughton did it that night with words—with gestures and a gracefulness which made one forget his looks, his heavy chest and his surroundings. It was in every way a great performance.

> "The pains came hard now, . . .
> She heard the roar of the tunnel, drowned in earth.
> Earth and its expulsive waters, tearing her, being born.
> Then it was yellow silence and a weak crying." [1]

Here he stopped, his hands reached into space;

> "After the child was washed, they showed her the child,
> Breakable, crumpled, breathing, swathed and indignant,
> With all its nails and hands that moved of themselves." [1]

And again his graceful hands reached forward, longingly. They showed how Melora took the newly born baby to her body. His tears were Melora's tears. He conveyed, visually, the sacred emotions of motherhood.

At that moment I did not know where I was. I was breathless, hypnotized by the actor's superb art.

I had not noticed until then that I was standing, too, facing the actor. Suddenly he recognized in me a stranger he had never seen before. The spell was broken.

"Another drink?" was all he said.

---

[1] Lines from "John Brown's Body" in *Selected Works of Stephen Vincent Benét* published by Rinehart & Company, Inc. Copyright, 1927, 1928, by Stephen Vincent Benét.

I shook my head, and he relaxed on the yellow couch. He began to talk of the actors in *John Brown's Body*. "Judith Anderson and Raymond Massey are just marvelous. But what do you say of Tyrone Power, a movie actor? Did you see to what heights he could rise, how tremendously he can develop if given a chance at real drama?"

Then Laughton's mind shot back to the subject of Socrates. He was miles away from his twenty-six television broadcasts and *John Brown's Body*. He was now—on the spur of a moment—living with *his* David, *his* Socrates: outlining scenes, sketching in dialogue, speaking, living parts in a play not yet written.

Words—all words—but what words. And how he endowed them with magic!

Finally he stopped. "Let me show you the house," he said abruptly.

From the French impressionist paintings in his house it is obvious that he is a romantic at heart. We walked over to the Renoir. "I bought it for $35,000. They offered me $150,000 not so long ago, but I wouldn't sell it."

There was great simplicity in this functional house, but the modern and pre-Colombian treasures revealed a man who had a catholic appreciation of beauty.

The most amazing room is, perhaps, his bedroom. It is almost monastic in its simplicity and consists of one very comfortable bed and hundreds of books around the free walls.

Then he showed me the swimming pool which Frank Lloyd Wright had built for him. It has all the functionalism and beauty that this great architect is capable of creating.

It was a few weeks before Christmas. The swimming pool was lighted under the water and hot vapors rose from the surface. It sparkled playfully in the moonlight.

"This is a tactile bath you have in your back yard," I said laughingly.

Laughton's face lighted up. He looked at me with astonishment, but said nothing.

After a short pause he turned to me and said:

"I'm not an actor; I'm really not. I don't want to be an actor. I'm a storyteller!"

It took me many months to find out what Laughton proposed by saying he is a storyteller. Storytelling to him means writing his own scripts, inventing his own plots, designing his own sets, directing his own vehicles, being his own stage manager and, of course, acting his role. If it were possible, he would also write his own reviews.

Confreres and fellow actors gasp and shake their heads when they see Laughton at work. Work means twenty hours a day, laboring over a script, reciting, rehearsing until he finally falls down on his bed, thoroughly exhausted.

"No one can handle this all alone; this fierce man is headed for collapse," they say, watching him. They stare at him in amazement and even awe—friends and veteran actors such as Charles Boyer, Tyrone Power, Sir Cedric Hardwicke, Henry Fonda and Judith Anderson. Before their openings of *Don Juan in Hell, John Brown's Body* and *The Caine Mutiny Court Martial,* Laughton carried on like a human avalanche.

"Storyteller?" It is hardly the term to describe Laughton.

But Charles Laughton, when he used the phrase, was never more serious in his life.

To his mind, the words an actor speaks are not harmless, empty sounds.

"Never speak of words as if they were minor weapons," he had said. "Words have accomplished more than all bombs ever dropped. Moses wrote the Ten Commandments on tables of stone from divine inspiration. The tables of stone have long been dust, but the words live. Men's greatest and noblest works of genius built from brick and mortar crumble and perish—but words do not die."

It was late. His wife, Elsa Lanchester, came into the room. His sharpest critic and favorite heckler is not especially impressed by these parlor theatricals.

"Just a gifted amateur, aren't you?" she said.

"Why not?" he smiled back. "After all, amateur means lover, doesn't it?"

Chapter 2

CHARLES LAUGHTON was born as unobtrusively as most babies, on the first of July, 1899, in the old-fashioned Victoria Hotel, a substantial building near the railroad station of the old town of Scarborough, England.

In the course of time he was joined by two younger brothers, Tom and Frank. Due to the constant switching from hotel room to hotel room as vacancies cropped up and seasons shifted, the Laughton home life was a little erratic. When their parents sold the Victoria Hotel and bought the larger Pavilion Hotel, very little changed for the boys. For the older Laughtons, however, the step represented something of a triumph. They had bought the Victoria early in their married life, on borrowed money. In not too many years they were solvent, and before Charles was quite grown up, they were the owners of three establishments and considered very solid people.

From his eighth year Charles knew that all he wanted in the world was to act. The Victoria Hotel at Scarborough had no charm for him. He used to put on little performances for the benefit of the maids—his stage was the linen room and he used pillows and sheets and towels for costumes. He took for his subjects the baleful lives of great sinners and the exploits of Britain's heroes.

Laughton's youth and early life were unhappy. He was handicapped by the good advice and misdirected opinions of uncles, cousins, brothers, teachers, parents.

He lost many precious years because of his family's opposition to his acting. He has thrown away time and emotion on foolish causes, projects and people because he never can bear to hurt or offend. He has committed many follies and wronged himself many times through this oversensitive nature of his.

His entire youth had been a struggle against convention and normality. He has experienced early man's uncertainties in regard to many major issues of life. Dozens of difficulties lay in his way. He had to harden himself against the appeals of his nearest and dearest whose plans for him were very contrary to his own desires. He was an unruly and headstrong child.

His parents were hard-working business people. They were unsophisticated and old-fashioned and couldn't understand the impulse that drove their oversensitive son to such antics. They made things worse by locking him in a dark room for a day with nothing but bread and water to eat. That would cure him, they thought. His chief crime had been running away from home to see a play: George Royle's *Folde-Rols*. In the dark room Charles sat composing a long monologue. He talked himself into such a rage that he stripped every bit of wallpaper off the walls. When the "prison" door was unlocked, the hotel owners had a redecorating job on their hands.

His family's final words were, "If you don't stop this nonsense you will wind up as an actor someday," which was about the worst fate this honorable family of hotelmen could think of.

Poor Mrs. Laughton, far from being a beauty, had been so plain a girl that her parents thought she would never find a husband. Yet find one she did, in Robert Laughton, a gentle, soft-spoken man, who one time reminded her:

"Didn't you, too, rebel and run away from home and work as a barmaid until I found you? He is your son, through and through. Let Charlie do what he likes. He may never have been cut out for a hotel owner."

Charles's mother couldn't see it that way. She had put her whole life into the hotel business, and her greatest dream was for Charles to take up where she had left off. For more than a decade she fought against his yen to go on the stage. In spite of this, Charles loved his mother and was always devoted to her.

Laughton himself has forgotten much about his early days, but his family remembers. They will reminisce about Charles's pathological fear of thunderstorms, ants, and various other things. From these stories you can gather that he was afraid of life to a large extent. In the religious family atmosphere he turned into something of a fanatic and a prig. He took the Sunday sermon to heart and worried about the sins on his soul.

This worry led to one of his most memorable childhood adventures. Young Charles secretly slipped into a hotel room occupied by a visiting bishop. When the bishop went out on some parish calls, Charles seized the opportunity to sleep in his room for an hour. Someone had told him the fairy tale that whoever sleeps in the same room as a bishop will be absolved of all his sins.

The next day Charles came down with measles. After several days, the bishop broke out in spots too.

The nine-year-old boy had seized desperately upon this chance to have his sins wiped away. His rigid religious instruction had scared him; his vivid imagination had reacted strongly to the threats of damnation and eternal hell-fire.

He still recalls this incident today. He also remembers how the meaning of eternity was explained to him. Suppose, he was told, that the earth was a solid globe of steel. If a hummingbird passed it every thousand years and brushed it with its wings, the period of time it would take the hummingbird to wear away the steel globe was "one grain of sand in the ocean of eternity."

Charles was a literal-minded child. He was quite convinced that he was a "sinner." He took it for granted
that the end of the world was near and that if he did
not get saved quickly, eternal hell-fire was waiting for
him. Taking all this together, there was nothing surprising about his sneaking into the bishop's room.

In this unhappy environment it was inevitable that
Charles should feel insecure, apprehensive, resentful,
isolated. It took him years to build up any adequate
self-respect.

His mother would introduce him to hotel guests with
a deprecating smile: "And this is my oldest son, Charles.
The poor boy is stage-struck—he has an artistic nature."

Most of his classmates in school were children of professional people. Few businessmen sent their sons to the
private school in Scarborough which Charles's mother
had selected for him. Here was another reason for his
feeling an outsider. Any chance he might have had to
mingle on easy terms with youngsters his own age seemed
doomed.

But in other ways Charles's school was as good a one
as could be found in Scarborough. His mother burned
with ambition to give her children the best education
money could buy. That was her greatest and most positive contribution to his life and one he has never under-
estimated. It was a superb school. The French classes
were outstanding, and Charles still speaks French today
with enjoyment and charm. In later years when he performed at the Académie Française the audiences were
amazed. They had never seen an English-speaking actor
who could play Molière without the slightest trace of
an accent.

Charles was too complicated a youngster to be a good
student, though he had an enormous capacity for concentration and seeing things through. He made just
about passing grades. The only subject in which he
showed any kind of brilliancy was mathematics, in which

he received a prize. Strangely enough, the prize was a beautiful leather-bound set of Shakespeare.

"This will be the most read and most famous Shakespeare set in England," the boy said. He meant it too.

Adults and classmates who heard what the mathematics prize winner said, thought him pretty swelled-headed. Who did he think he was, this queer-looking, queer-acting duck? He was genuinely proud of having won the mathematics award and rather overwhelmed by the Shakespeare. It was the first token of recognition he'd ever gotten in life.

In school he was an outsider, teased mercilessly by the other boys. "He was one of the most ungainly schoolboys I ever saw, very fat, with a huge head and a little cap. We should have dearly liked to kick him . . ." was the unvarnished description given by one of the neighborhood boys who later on was proud to have been Charles's classmate.

A glandular condition made Charles fat from infancy. He had no bent for physical work, sports or outdoor fun. Any abnormally fat boy becomes conspicuous and is the center of unwelcome attention. Thanks to his abnormal plumpness, Charles had an audience before he could crawl; he knew what it was to be stared at and criticized before he reached first grade. Even his walk was ridiculed, and his bearing today still shows traces of his early ungainliness and self-consciousness.

All this was a handicap of major proportions. Only iron will and inner strength helped Charles succeed.

When the school put on a play, *The Private Secretary,* there was the role of an innkeeper to be filled. Charles was given the part because of his close connection with the hotel trade. He did not steal the show, and no one in the audience was particularly impressed by his performance. However, the school magazine had this to say about his performance: "We hope to see some more of Mr. Laughton." This clipping he has never lost.

"About that time, too, I had a beautiful little book of Hans Christian Andersen's story, 'The Nightingale.' It had illustrations by Edmund Dulac. I have never been able to find the edition since. I remember thinking that I would like to spend months learning how to tell that story to large numbers of people, as if I were the author inventing the story for the first time. I knew very clearly that it would be a long, hard process. I knew that the smallest part of the labor would be the learning of these stories by heart."

In spite of such reveries, his imaginative nature and his obvious love of art, his mother kept hammering away at her great plans for him in the hotel business.

Laughton has recalled later: "I remember I was abnormally interested in pierrot troupes which I saw on the sands of Scarborough. That was when I was very young and had never been in a theater. Of course I always had to disappear when the velvet bag was handed around, as I had nothing to put in." He recalls as the most exquisite memory of his early youth a pantomime in which Mother Goose and her son Pimple went up in a balloon frying "sossa—a—ges" over a candle.

Then, too, there was Poole's *Mirorama,* a remarkable performance in which an endless painted cloth unrolled before the fascinated eyes of the audience, revealing a beautiful panorama voyage around the world.

He was so fascinated by these troupes that he built his own model theater with curtain, several changes of backdrops and puppets. His marionettes would talk, recite, play, sing, act—he memorized all their lines, made up all sorts of dramas with lovers and villains, knightly heroes and monsters.

But one day he had a terrible fight with one of his brothers, who was so furious that he bit off the heads of all of Charles's marionette performers. The guillotining put an end to Charles's career as a marionette stage director.

He was so hurt that he made himself a wordless promise never to hurt anyone—no matter what happened.

He was finally able to overcome his "ugly-duckling complex" and break free from its frustrations.

Though his marks in English and literature were never more than average, he used all his spare time reading and dramatizing scenes out of books, refashioning and retelling the stories he liked. He had more time for reading than most boys, for he had no friends. If asked what he read, he will say everything he could lay his hands on. But there were certain favorites.

Recollecting his childhood reading, Laughton said: "I suppose to an American child many European things seem romantic when he reads or hears about them: the beefeaters in the Tower of London, the white cliffs of Dover, the boulevards of Paris, the Mediterranean. But when I was a child in England, the most romantic place to me was the Mississippi River. There have been lots of good things written about that river, about the plantations and the cotton, the river boats and the city of New Orleans, the magnolia trees and the songs of the Negroes. The best of all, I have always thought, is Mark Twain's loving tribute to the river he knew so well as a steamboat pilot. . . . No boat could ever have been as plush as his nostalgic memory of a gilded river queen . . ."

So the lonely boy dreamed of the "gilded river queen" on the faraway Mississippi, of the men on the ship, of the Negroes singing, of the wooded banks and the wild forests of the New World. It was all intensely real to him. The world of Mark Twain was a wonderful place to escape to when you were a ridiculed fat boy with small eyes, living in a stuffy British town.

Today Charles Laughton recites these passages of Mark Twain to audiences of many thousands, to millions over radio and television.

What he read as a boy he seldom shared with teachers

or classmates. It was his own private world, and he kept it secret. But somewhere he got the idea of reading those magic words aloud. He did not know how this should be done. It was something he had to figure out by himself. "I have to teach myself," he said, and found the determination and strength to do it. He was fascinated by the beauty of Shakespeare's poetry, and he suffered at realizing that his own vocabulary was so ordinary and limited. His grammar was faulty. When he recited, he found he got out of breath, and his pronunciation was awkward. Besides, there wasn't much chance to practice reciting in the hotel. He used to go out into the country to fight his inner battles. The meadows, the sunlight and Shakespeare seemed to make a good combination.

Words can be tricky and dangerous. They can boomerang. An adolescent boy can easily be carried away by things that a grown man finds almost meaningless. In this respect Charles was an easy mark. His life was dull and narrow; he had no experience of the world. He found it very difficult to know and understand people. It was heaven for him to lose himself in literature.

At sixteen, when he left his school, he would compromise with his parents. "When I'm twenty-one, I'll go out on my own—I'll do what I want." Five years of waiting were ahead of him.

It was in 1917 he was sent to London's famous Claridge Hotel to learn the hotel trade from the bottom up. The war was on, but he was too young to go. From the vantage point of the Claridge he caught glimpses of the world—lords and ladies, barons and earls, industrialists, diplomats and Continental celebrities all stopped at Claridge's. Once in a while he saw famous actors and actresses of the London stage and he felt compensated for all the suffering the hotel job cost him. "My province was the office and there was little opportunity for gathering knowledge of glittering hotel intrigues, cork legs and secretly consumed liquor. A hotel clerk is a cipher, people in their dealings with him are off their guard and behave as though they were alone."

At Claridge's Charles had worked as bellboy, cashier, night watchman, kitchen clerk, desk help for ten shillings a week, and that was in the days when he didn't bother about his dress and went around in soiled shirts with soiled collars to save laundry bills. Charles used every available penny for going to the Drury Lane. He saw some revues a dozen times, *A Kiss for Cinderella* ten times, and any other play he could get into.

At the end of 1917 Charles was farther away from the theater than ever. He was just ready for the army.

As a young man of some education, Charles was entitled to apply for an officer's commission in the British Army. But Laughton, whose mind and heart were set on getting on the stage, was not in the least interested in taking a leading part in any theater of war.

"I did not want to command . . . I did not want to take the responsibility for other people's lives . . . I was a softy."

Laughton has always hated to discuss his war experiences. One thing we know for certain—he was gassed. It made him afraid that he would never have the physical stamina to be an actor.

His final word on his war experiences is this: "War had a toughening effect on me. . . . The best of it was, I saw Leslie Henson playing *Aladdin* in Lille. He was damned funny."

His family expected him back at the Pavilion Hotel in Scarborough. He was afraid his speaking voice was damaged permanently. But he still stuck to his ambition; he was going to be an actor.

Everyone at home tried to talk sense into him. Acting was the world's most insecure profession they told him. He knew that most actors rehearse more often than they play in a show, spend more time in employment offices and agents' waiting rooms than on the stage. But nothing could keep Charles from dreaming. He had to accept the work at his parents' hotel. His health was none too good—he had to be careful. But he also joined an amateur group—The Scarborough Players. For the time being, this was what he lived for.

His parents, seeing that the young man was chronically unhappy and indifferent to the business, again tried to reason with him. "You cannot sing. You can't dance. You have a poor speaking voice. You're not the least good-looking. How can you be an actor?"

Charles knew it was all true. It hurt deeply.

Long afterward, Charles said of those days, "We amateurs did *Trelawney of the Wells,* and I played the part of Sir William Gower. I must have been exceedingly bad. There is a photo of me in the part, pumping up emotion for the camera: a thing which I still do quite a lot of today, but I try not to let the camera see it quite so blatantly. We then did *Hobson's Choice,* and this was a real box-office success."

The circumstances surrounding this first "hit" are still very vivid in his mind. He remembers how the group backed the play with some advertising and publicity. The first night they played to an empty house, but word-of-mouth campaign helped, and more and more people came until they were sold out every night. Laughton played William Mossop, the part which Joe Nightingale took in the London production. After *Hobson's Choice* the group put on four one-act plays. It was wonderful fun for everyone.

Charles did act for glory. He did act for applause. He just had to act; that was life. Member of a miserable little dramatic group, he quickly formed habits and took on attitudes peculiar to the greatest of the great. He was in his dressing room two hours before the show.

Like Eleonora Duse, he wanted to absorb his role. He wanted to be a part of the atmosphere and the world to be projected on the stage.

Ironically enough, the small-town newspaper, in reviewing the plays, made no mention of Charles. He was not an especially good actor—at least not exceptional. His parents sighed at seeing their son persisting at this theatrical nonsense. In fact, he was getting worse and worse.

It became more apparent that Charles would not adjust himself to hotel work. He was rapidly becoming unbearable. His relationships with people became more difficult. He became more erratic and subject to whims, outbursts of tempers and tantrums. It was clear that there would never be peace in the Laughton family unless Charles was allowed to try his wings.

When his two brothers finally sided with Charlie, the battle was won. At last he was free to leave Scarborough and try his luck at the London Royal Drama Academy. His family agreed to give him an allowance of three pounds a week.

He was the happiest young man alive.

All through his youth he had dreamed of getting guidance and direction, of having friends with whom he could share enthusiasms and from whom he could learn what he so passionately desired to know. He was stage-struck as so many other young people are stage-struck; it was the darkened theater and the footlights that drew him. He was awed by the fact that actors could recite words to thousands and touch their emotions. That was for him the mystery and power of the stage. The sight of even an empty theater could stir him to the depths. He did not care for theatrical gossip, financial deals and box-office figures. That wasn't what he meant by the theatrical world. The theater was his temple, his church, his house of worship.

A childlike attitude? Perhaps. He has never outgrown it. It may be one of the secrets of his success. Even with the amateur dramatic group, he had loved rehearsing. The hasty meals between rehearsal and play, the camaraderie of the group—it was a foretaste of the life he wanted.

Naturally he had stage fright—but when the call of "curtain" came, a new man was born, a man strong and sure of himself in his own field where few could follow him and those closest to him found him unfathomable.

He was going to London now. He burned his bridges behind him without the smallest trace of regret.

When Tallulah Bankhead once jokingly predicted that Charles Laughton might go back one day to greeting guests in a hotel lobby, she was apparently wrong.

Chapter 3

Fter young Laughton finally had won the family's consent to attend the Royal Academy of Dramatic Art in London, there was still the entrance examination to be passed. For this he prepared a speech from *The Merchant of Venice*. He rehearsed it nineteen hours a day. He mumbled Shakespeare going through the London streets. On examination day everything went wrong. Charles was in such a dither that he sat down on the examiner's hat. But he passed his test. That was in 1925.

Alice Gachet, one of the Academy teachers, had heard his Shakespeare recitation and disliked it thoroughly. "I'll make an artist out of you, if I have to break you in the process," she declared.

However, Charles took to the Royal Academy as a duck to water.

The young fellow from the provinces moved into a small, cheap furnished room in London's famous Long Acre district. Early each morning he walked to the Royal Academy. His appearance had hardly changed. He still looked countrified, fat and ill-dressed.

He was now all of twenty-five. With all those wasted years behind him, he could not get enough of London. He was bound he was going to absorb everything. He was seen at art exhibits, in every small or large playhouse. He spent hours reading in theatrical libraries,

Elsa and Charles on the Newhall Rodeo Grounds. The place was sold out, and so they departed.

Alert in that split second before a performance.

Looking little like the land pirate he was soon to play in *Jamaica Inn*.

Two of England's finest. Laughton and Herbert Marshall take a lunch-time siesta on location.

Elsa Lanchester. Protégée of H. G. Wells — a charming wife, a distinguished actress.

visited museums and antique shows, looked in the oddest places for Moorish coins of Othello's times, hunted up swords and daggers of Richard III's day, studied the costumes of every Hamlet production since Shakespeare's era, examined Roman artifacts, historic rings and peacock feathers.

He imagined himself in every play he studied, and he read as many plays as he could get hold of. The green student lamp in the little furnished room burned far into the night. During that period in the early twenties he slept very little.

For years these interests had been repressed and starved. Now they burst out with abnormal force. He did not know himself from day to day—so many potentialities unfolded for him. He was like a house that was being basically remodeled—a wall of frustration was torn down here, new doors of courage were opened there, a new wing added, old windows widened, vistas cleared. He was an ever-changing scene. When the Royal Academy put on its student performances, Laughton was conspicuous for the vitality and power poured even into the smallest part.

He still believed he was cut out to be a great tragedian. It was to take almost thirty years for him to learn that he was at heart a comedian and storyteller. He got the first inkling of this other, lighter side of his nature in those early days in London, however. His new life was doing wonders for him. For the first time his natural gaiety, his lust for life and his great humor came to the foreground.

He was living on a shoestring, but he did not mind—there was so much to see and to grasp. "I'm so happy here—beyond expectations," he wrote home.

From Charles's very first roles in student plays his great talent was apparent to his teachers. It was all there—all it needed was some training.

He was nervous going on-stage. "I think I trembled,"

he admitted later. When his cue came he would hurl himself into the scene with almost comic intensity. One of his teachers once took him to task for this.

"Young man," he said, "I've been watching you for a long time. You're killing yourself. Give less. You've got some idea that you're supposed to be the greatest actor who ever lived. Calm down, relax. Read a newspaper, make a phone call, write to your mother, play poker, loaf around in the wings, but don't try to work yourself up to full steam before you are on-stage. It can't be done. No one ever did it. Just take it easy and wait for your cue. Then, when you hear it, go on the stage—*slow*—and act—and give it to them."

It was sound advice. But the flame burning in young Laughton was not the sort which could be turned up or down on orders.

Gradually Charles found friends among his fellow actors. Some of the older students had won their first real parts and were playing here and there in theaters in London. He went to see their shows, sat in on their rehearsals, heard their lines, made suggestions and discussed every bit of the play with them. He was well liked by everyone around the Royal Academy. Socially he was having a bit of a success, and not only among his fellow students. Older actors invited him to private parties at their homes. He was asked to backstage celebrations and was a frequent guest at the homes of theater lovers who took pride in showing their other aristocratic friends the brilliant young man from the Royal Academy.

The once shy, tongue-tied hotelkeeper's son was impressed at being presented to Lord So-and-So and Lady So-and-So. He never had been inside the huge parks of country estates. He was not used to flocks of servants wearing black uniforms, white caps and aprons. He found it enchanting to lie in a four-poster in an ancestral establishment.

"Dear Mother," he wrote home, "I feel no longer

empty and blank in my life—everything takes a new and bright color."

Then came the day when the celebrated Russian director Theodore Komisarjevsky, who was one of his teachers at the Academy, took Charles aside to tell him:

"Your time will come soon, Laughton. You are doing fine."

But it took months of waiting before Komisarjevsky took his star pupil to Philip Ridgeway at the Barnes Theatre. The result was Charles's first paid part: he played the drunken servant Ozip in Gogol's *The Government Inspector*. It was not an entirely successful performance. Charles fell prey to terrible stage fright. He was obsessed by the idea that all his clothes would fall off him while on-stage and he would stand there naked, helpless and scared as he had been throughout his childhood in Scarborough.

Still, the audience discovered Laughton's remarkable voice. It had a peculiar quality, still harsh, far from mellow and fully experienced, almost hoarse, but with definite individuality.

Producer Ridgeway could see how nervous Charles was, for the young actor was actually trembling when he came on the stage. But he also saw how the audience liked Charles's voice. And as the play progressed, both Ridgeway and Charles gained confidence and relaxed. At his curtain calls Charles was stiff, shy and hesitant, as though he did not quite believe the applause. Still, the reviews were very favorable and Charles proudly sent them to his family.

Mother Eliza Laughton must have been very pleased, but she said nothing.

Alice Gachet, the teacher who had once promised Charles to break him or make a star of him, now became his main teacher. She was to be a decisive influence on Laughton's entire career. Alice Gachet laid the foundation for his art and technique. She introduced him to the French and British classical drama, and although these classics were never to be the mainstay of his repertory, he learned enormously from them. Komisarjevsky drew him into the labyrinth of the Russian drama, with its knowledge of the depths and heights of human nature. Chekhov, Dostoevsky and Gogol opened up new fields of dramatic possibilities.

Thanks to Alice Gachet and Laughton's success in *The Government Inspector,* the Royal Academy gave Charles the role of Higgins in Shaw's *Pygmalion.* These student-workshop productions attracted a lot of attention. Laughton applied himself to the part, trying to make something new of it and disregarding previous interpretations. In the stage directions the dramatist had laid down his rules as to how the energetic scientist was to be played. His moods were to range "from genial bullying to stormy petulance." Shaw made his Higgins "void of malice" and insisted that Higgins remained "likable even in his least reasonable moments."

But Charles made Higgins a real tyrant, a heartless, inhuman monster. George Bernard Shaw was one of the audience, and he was quite annoyed.

The dramatist went to Charles's dressing room to give him a piece of his mind.

"All you wanted, Laughton, was to make the audience believe that it was witnessing a magnificent display of acting by a great actor. To you the play does not exist except as a steppingstone."

Laughton was almost paralyzed—the great Shaw had come to see him. He had not time to compose a speech, because Shaw, cynical and condescending as only he could be, said, "Young man, whatever your name is, you were horrible as my Higgins, but nothing will stop you from getting to the top of the tree in a year." With these words Shaw banged the door and left.

Shaw proved to be right. Twenty-five years later when

the two met again in England, Shaw remembered the early encounter. They began reminiscing. Laughton still defended his Higgins, saying, "I played it the way I saw the character then and I was very young."

Shaw was delighted with Laughton's uncompromising stand. The stubbornness and coolness of the novice Laughton still intrigued him.

"I did the same at your age and later. I did it all my life. I wrote novels they did not like; I wrote plays they were scared of and did not like. The editors and producers are always so sure of what the public wants. But finally they had to take me anyway, the way I am and the way I wrote."

Shaw's final comment was, "Laughton, you are the born comedian."

The young Laughton who stood up to G.B.S. in a student production has gone on being pigheaded in all artistic decisions whenever he believes that he is in the right.

When working on a part, Laughton always has forgotten himself. His personal ambition does not count, except in so far as he is dedicated to doing the very best with any part he is assigned. Even through his annoyance, Shaw must have seen something of this. Otherwise he would not have added his prediction that Laughton would someday reach the top.

Laughton might not have played Shaw's Higgins, but he had given a magnificent performance. It won him the Bancroft Medal, the highest award the Academy had to give. Charles had been enrolled in the school only a single year—no student actor in the entire history of the Royal Academy had been so honored after such a short period.

That was in March, 1926.

London now noticed him for the second time. The newspapers carried the story of Laughton's winning the Royal Academy Award. The elder Mr. Laughton went around showing the *Times* clipping to guests, and Mrs. Laughton wrote Charles to come home and visit whenever he had a chance. She seemed to be very proud of her "prodigal son."

When he did go home, he struck his family as taller and heavier. The strong lines of his jaw and the bold carriage of his head spoke of the assurance born of success. There was a fiery gleam in his eyes as he cast glances around restaurants, living rooms or parties. He was no longer shy in large gatherings.

His mother recognized how much the one year in London had changed her son. The lines of his face were sharper and stronger. He had found new self-confidence, or at least he put on a good show of it. He appeared to have friends and to enjoy people's respect and even admiration. No longer was he the ugly duckling, the queer fish or the weakling. He had found a style of his own, a strange combination of provincialism and undigested sophistication. He seemed a stronger man. His studies and hard work had started to pay off. His acting displayed definite individuality. He had developed a stage presence and a private personality at the same time. George Bernard Shaw's prediction that he would be on the top of the tree in one year rang constantly in his ears.

His visit home was brief. London seemed the metropolis of the world, and his new-found actor friends undertook to teach him the ropes of this huge city with its glamour, culture, poverty, wealth and temptation. He saw London, all of it, from Mayfair to Chinatown and the docks—its parties, its fashionable races, drinking, women, narcotics, sexual perversion, crime, politics and prostitution.

It was a new world again, but it presented no temptation to him. Actors have been accused of falling for everything that is wild and stimulating, from sexual aberrations to drugs to revolutionary politics. In Charles's

case, he did not give these vices a second thought. He
wanted to see everything there was to be seen, but far
from being fascinated, he was bothered by what he saw.
Again and again he returned to the refuge of his furnished
room to study his next role.

Those who remember Laughton from those days in
London remember him as a young actor who was
possessed by his own powers. His personality seemed to
give off some magnetic radiations. He was much sought
after socially, and there was seldom a party where he was
not asked to recite.

There was not the slightest trace of shyness left in him.

"You want to see real acting?" he would say impishly.

Without waiting for an answer he would begin to
do a bit from some Russian drama—Gogol, Chekhov,
Tolstoy. In those days he still believed that tragedy was
his forte, as did everyone else. As he spoke his lines, tears
would pour down his cheeks. It would not be long before
his audience, still holding filled glasses in their hands,
would be weeping too. His power to move was amazing.
There was no party that Laughton could not hold spellbound with tears and Shakespeare. It is the same today—
though now his stock in trade is laughter and he does
without the Russians and Shakespeare.

"Play Hamlet, play Macbeth, play Lear, play Gogol,"
people would clamor at parties. Finally a joke sprang up
in acting circles—it was attributed to Laughton, but it
had a venerable history, the words having been put into
the mouths of several famous actors already:

"Play Lear, Laughton."

"What do you you mean, sir? I do not play Lear. I play
Hamlet, Shylock, any Russian tragedian if you please—
but, friend, don't you know, *I am* Lear."

Laughton probably never said this. Still, he was much
quoted as having said it. His improvisations were quite
famous. "He is a little mad," people said, "but what a
fiery actor."

The cold facts of life, however, were knocking at the door of his furnished room. Though he acted day and night, he had scarcely made any money. He was feeling acutely the need to be independent of his family. He would not feel himself vindicated in their eyes until he could support himself. Reviews in the *Observer* and the *Times* were not enough.

Again Komisarjevsky, the guardian spirit of his early career, came to his aid. He asked Laughton to take the part of the soldier in Chekhov's *The Three Sisters*.

"I know you are not handsome, Charles, but I still want you for the part. You can do it."

Komisarjevsky, who was steeped in the tradition of the Russian theater, always preferred a real actor to a good-looking mediocrity. But Laughton was scared of the part. He was afraid to play the role of a lover. "Not with my looks," he objected. But Komisarjevsky insisted and won the point.

Before Laughton's great success came, he was obsessed by the fear of being turned down as leading man. Actresses used to young, dashing costars would not want to be teamed with him. He could not compete with tall, handsome stage lovers. All he had to fall back on was his acting.

While he was still working at the Royal Academy of Dramatic Art, he overheard the mother of a student actress whispering to her pet: "Be careful, dear; there's that dirty old man with his filthy habits. I hope you won't catch anything from him."

For years Laughton contended, "It would be ridiculous to cast me in the part of a lover."

But he gave in, although he was in agony.

Actually he put some very hard work into the new role. He rehearsed it at least a hundred times, but more than this, he read Russian novels and played the "soldier on- and off-stage until he got the part in his bones. He went about in a kind of trance—he so lost himself in his new character that he ordered his afternoon tea with a Russian soldier-like accent. The other actors smiled at this "nut." The saying went the rounds that if Laughton were to play in *The Merchant of Venice* instead of *The Three Sisters*, he would not eat a ham sandwich all day long so as to be in the proper mood to play Shylock at night.

But in spite of all these jokes and good-natured professional teasing, they admired his ambition and intensity. It was obvious that Laughton gave himself completely to the part. His private life was in complete abeyance. He lived Chekhov and his soldier and was not interested in anything else.

Laughton was to play opposite the beloved and admired Beatrix Thompson—this was a privilege for any actor of the day. On opening night Laughton proved himself equal to it. The reviews were unanimously enthusiastic. Komisarjevsky was glowing with pride in his protégé.

Still, there it was again, the stage fright, the pathological, ridiculous fear of his clothes falling off and leaving him naked on the stage. The neurosis got worse with every performance. When the final curtain fell and the applause ended, Laughton would be sweat-soaked, almost sick, fit for nothing but going home to his bed in the same furnished room in Long Acre.

Komisarjevsky wanted Laughton in his next production. It was to be Chekhov's *Cherry Orchard*, for Chekhov was enjoying an unparalleled vogue in Europe during the late twenties. Charles was to portray the unhappy clerk Yepikhodoff. It was the largest part he had yet had. He handled it with such mastery that the seasoned actresses in the company came to him to say, "Laughton, you were magnificent." Flattered as he was, he summoned up enough wit to answer, "Don't you know, I did it all just to please you." It was for such well-turned remarks, as well as for his talent, that they loved him. And Charles returned their feeling. He was gallant and respectful. All his life Laughton was more attracted by older women than by younger ones. They were people who could teach him something.

It was a first-class company that Komisarjevsky assembled for *The Cherry Orchard*. The director had transplanted the best elements of the great Moscow Art Theater—now scattered and disorganized by the Revolution—to the London scene. Laughton seemed to thrive in this atmosphere. On-stage, he outdid himself; but there was still his horrible stage fright which he did not dare tell anyone about. Nowadays he was haunted by the fear that his vocal cords would suddenly be paralyzed, or that he would faint in the middle of the stage, or that his legs which held up his heavy body would be attacked by sudden cramps such as he had experienced when going swimming as a boy.

But his most dreadful, most agonizing fear was that with all London watching him, even royalty, he would be exposed in all his nakedness in the glare of the footlights.

It had become a real obsession. Laughton did not know what to do about it. Worst of all was the fact that he had to keep it a secret. His colleagues and friends would only laugh at him. Above all, his family must not know anything about it.

His brothers had gone to London to see Charles in *The Cherry Orchard*. The unimaginative Laughtons did not make much of the play, or see anything special about the part their brother had. They went back to Scarborough to report that all was well with Charles. He wouldn't ever startle the world, but he seemed to be doing fairly well for himself. Soon he would be able to get along without the family allowance.

What they told their mother about this strange play made her wonder. She still had grave doubts about acting as a serious career for Charles.

The performance was also witnessed by such articulate

people as Somerset Maugham and Arnold Bennett. Maugham has set down his reaction to the play in one of his essays in *The Vagrant Mood*. He was apparently rather bewildered by the play as a whole and he took no special notice of the young man who played Semyon Panteleievitch Yepikhodoff. Laughton had no more than twenty-five lines—his most striking one being:

"Every day some misfortune's sure to happen, but I've been so long accustomed to it that I look at life with a smile."

Maugham did, however, have something to say about the actress who played Chekhov's "feckless heroine— moody, neurotic and emotional."

At any rate, the play was a smash hit. It was attended by everyone else who mattered. The London papers all hailed Komisarjevsky as a truly great director. As his protégé, Laughton came in for his share in the glory. Komisarjevsky told everyone about his ex-pupil at the Academy, the fat boy who was such a brilliant and sensitive actor.

When the successful *Cherry Orchard* finally closed, the Russian director gave Laughton a chance at a real part. From then on, no more twenty-five-line roles for Charles.

A certain amount of good luck entered into it, too. It happened that Komisarjevsky decided to produce Ferenc Molnár's immortal *Liliom*, the Hungarian playwright's greatest play. Fay Compton and Ivor Novello were the stars, and a very small part was being reserved for Charles Laughton. But since the fickle Goddess Luck was shining on young Laughton those days, it happened that the role of the thief Ficsur fell vacant suddenly and Charles begged Komisarjevsky to let him have it.

The Russian producer was taken aback. It was a large and very difficult role to play, more complex and demanding than Laughton perhaps realized. But Komisarjevsky was a man of whims and impulses. He looked at his "discovery" and exclaimed, "Charles, by Jove, I think you could do it. I know you can do it." The part was his.

The character of the pickpocket in *Liliom* was a natural for Laughton. He put in weeks of study to get the feel of the role—made tours of Whitechapel, the docks, the slum quarters, haunted low pubs to watch London's shady characters and to rub elbows with small-time crooks, pimps and ne'er-do-wells. On opening night the almost unknown Charles Laughton, in his mere supporting role, practically stole the show. Every newspaper agreed on that. His Ficsur was remembered for a long time—his hoarse voice, his furtive and criminal air.

Laughton's high moment in the play was when he solemnly asked Liliom, "Do I look like a cheat?" That line always brought down the house. He then proposed to Liliom that the two of them do a hold-up on a Budapest bank cashier and get themselves 16,000 kronen. Liliom agrees. But the cashier does not turn up according to schedule and the two toughs while away the time with a game of twenty-one for high stakes. Liliom loses 8,000 kronen—his share of the money they haven't laid hold of yet. Hoarse-voiced and cunning, Laughton sings the famous pickpockets' song:

> "And when you are in the prison cell
> They'll feed you bread and water,
> They'll make your little sweetheart tell
> Them all the things you brought her.
> Look out, here comes the damn police,
> The damn police,
> The damn police.
> They'll get you every time." [1]

The playwright Molnár went all the way to London to see the Komisarjevsky production. All eyes were turned to the author's box, which in London theaters

[1] From *Liliom*, by Ferenc Molnár. Used by permission of Edmond Pauker, New York City.

is next to the one reserved for royalty. There he was, the famous Molnár, with his oversized, pink, smooth, almost pudgy face. The face was almost childlike in its expression. Only the glint of humor in the dark, alert eyes betrayed him as a shrewd student of humanity. And the patrician monocle worn over the left eye. Afterward, Molnár heaped praises upon Komisarjevsky for the beautiful staging, the sensitive direction and the marvelous cast. We do not know whether he was particularly struck by Laughton's presentation. But as *Liliom* became the latest London hit, Laughton came in for his share of recognition, too. Impersonators in London's swanky cabarets began imitating him. He started being mentioned in the press in all sorts of connections. Yet with success seemingly in his grasp, a dark shadow of disaster hung over him. He was more unhappy, more anxious than he had ever been. There was still this pathological panic of being exposed naked on the stage. The neurosis was getting worse and worse.

He did not know that the spur of this fear was an important component in his style of acting. He was bringing to the Ficsur role something of the same intensity that the Barrymores, Booths and Irvings used to throw into their great heroic parts. But Laughton was reaching the breaking point. The hard stretch he had put in preparing the part and rehearsing had sapped his strength. Added to this was the mental strain he worked under. He came down with a terrible case of flu.

But it took more than flu to make him abandon his part in *Liliom*. Not now. Not when fame was in his reach. Now, when he was close to the top, he simply had to hold up.

What could he do? He tossed in fever all night and all day, took a cab to the theater a little before curtain time, got through the play somehow and went back to bed. Sometimes he doubted if he'd be able to keep on his feet until the final curtain. He finally learned to split himself in half—one part of his brain preoccupied with his phobia, the other just reciting, concentrating on his part and never permitting itself to think of his obsession.

He got over the flu by himself, without any doctoring and not losing a day at the theater. Then he gathered up his courage and his money and went to the most prominent psychiatrist in London's Harley Street.

Years later in Hollywood Laughton told how he was cured of this terrible obsession. It makes one of the most amazing stories of modern psychology. Laughton's psychoanalytical sessions lasted only three days. He talked and talked and talked. He told the physician of his youth and all the fears he had had—how he'd been afraid of other boys, how long it had taken him to break away from his family and try for an acting career, and now of his stage fright and the ridiculous form it took—the phobia of losing his clothes on the stage and being laughed at by every shopgirl in town.

All through those sessions he did not see his doctor, whose practice it was to sit listening behind a screen. Suddenly, in the midst of his recital, Laughton heard a wild animal yell:

"Out with you, out. Go. Run. Out with you; I've had enough. Go and be quick about it . . ."

Laughton did not know what could have happened. Had the doctor gone crazy? Was the famous psychiatrist a madman? Laughton hastily took his hat and coat and left. "Go . . . out with you . . . go . . . go," he heard the doctor puffing and shouting behind him. Laughton hurried out of the office. The doctor was running after him, rushing past his secretary and the patients in his waiting room. Laughton, certain now that the doctor was dangerous, began to run faster. The doctor was still pursuing him. "Go . . . go! Run!"

Laughton was really running now. The world-famous psychiatrist ran after him all along Oxford Street. Laughton reached Piccadilly Circus with the doctor in hot pursuit. He thought to escape by dodging into a pub on a small side street.

Laughton was sitting at a table trying to catch his breath when the doctor came through the door, also panting. "Two double Scotches," he ordered the bartender, and sat down beside Laughton, who was more disconcerted than ever.

But the doctor seemed calmer now and started to explain:

"Laughton, I don't know whether I can cure you, but you have just cured me of a complex I've had for more than twenty-five years. I have been through two and a half decades of an unhappy marriage, but when you told me of your fears of standing naked on a stage facing a full house, a block inside of me was removed. I saw my own wife in your position. She, too, is on the stage. For the first time in our life together I've been able to cut my actress wife down to her real size. I just had to cry out what I did . . . I said it to you, but it was really to my wife I was saying it. For twenty-five years I have not dared to say it or even to think it. Laughton, you have cured me. You are a great man."

Hours later the two left the pub arm in arm. This dramatic and bizarre incident not only cured the psychiatrist, but Laughton too. He was never again troubled by his obsession.

The two men remained friends for many years.

From those days early in his London career, when he went on with his part in *Liliom* in spite of flu and severe psychotic symptoms, Laughton made it a rule never to cancel a performance. The good old slogan, "The show must go on," is in his blood. Nowadays he will sometimes cancel one of the dates of a reading tour—taking advantage of the convenient clause in his contract—but these occasions are very rare. I remember one night in February, 1953, when Laughton was due at the Denver

City Auditorium. A capacity crowd had come to hear him read. During intermission, when Laughton went backstage, he had to sit astraddle a chair. He was suffering from a badly strained back and needed a special brace in order to make his Denver appearance at all. Shortly before that date, he had been hospitalized in San Francisco, and in his concern over keeping his California engagements he had a special "cradle" constructed in his car so that he could ride every night from the hospital to the theater. After each performance he was brought back to the hospital for more rest and treatment. For weeks he alternated between the hospital bed and the theater. The show had to go on.

This attitude was a carry-over from his struggles in the time of *Liliom*. When *Liliom* finally closed down, Charles found himself a successful actor, but unemployed. For days he did not leave his room. He was certain the phone would ring and someone would offer him a better and bigger role. It simply had to be. Hadn't his London notices been everything an actor could have asked for? But no phone call came. He went on waiting.

Critics had commented that Charles was someone who would go far if he continued along the lines he had started. He himself knew that his style had grown steadily. He seemed less flamboyant, more himself, more natural and less artificial. Audiences were captured by the timbre of his voice. His flaccid face could do anything —he could look like anyone and anything—and look it to the life. He was an actor burning with ambition, lost in reverie, a romantic, rebellious, wild, imaginative "youngster" who thought that the only thing that mattered was "work and what *I* thought about it."

But he was a lonely man. He had tasted fame and found it ephemeral as it always is. He was no longer the young man burning just to get on the stage. He had passed the baptism by fire. But where would he go from there?

Though he is admittedly no authority on ecclesiastical matters, Laughton reads the Bible superbly.

Do what I say

"Joy to the world"

Fire and brimstone

You better be good!

A merciless Lord Justice whom everybody feared. Charles Laughton in *The Paradine Case.*

He was still waiting by the telephone when an agent called up. He offered Charles £30 a week to play another pickpocket in a comedy. Laughton's answer was a polite but firm negative. "I don't care to be typed. I'll not play servants or pickpockets for a while."

He needed the job. He had sufficient faith in himself to hold out for a better, more interesting opportunity. And sure enough, the telephone did ring again. Would he play an old, fat general in the Lewis Casson production of Bernard Fagan's fine play, *The Greater Love?* "Yes," he said, "emphatically yes."

Sybil Thorndike and Basil Gill were with him in the play. Charles had known Gill for some time, having met him at parties. Basil had sometimes cheered up Laughton when he was depressed over the great difficulties ahead of him. Now a firm friendship developed between the two actors.

The opening night was the first one Charles had experienced without fear. He found the whole affair intoxicating. The psychiatrist—the man who had effortlessly cured him—was seated in the front row. The wildly enthusiastic audience clapped for the author, Bernard Fagan. In his excitement Charles found himself taking a curtain call along with the author. The mistake brought a big laugh.

Charles's destiny always seemed to throw him into plays where he was teamed with famous actors. When, much later, he was asked by his wife how he felt as a mere beginner playing opposite those seasoned veterans, he had to think about the question a little, for he had never precisely formulated what the experience meant. His considered reply was:

"It was exciting to find myself in the company of people I had admired for so long. I used to watch them night after night through cracks in the scenery, and wonder how they got their effects—they always seemed to be so sure. I don't know any more now than I did then."

After his successful shot at being an old general, producers were again after Charles to repeat himself, but again Charles declined. The producers' way of reasoning made him angry. He felt they had no imagination and were always trying to cash in on the success of a previous production. He had made up his mind—no more servants, no old pickpockets, no old generals. He wasn't going to be bored. He had already run through those types for his general's role; he had studied many specimens of Colonel Blimp. Now he wanted to do something fresh and new. He was at that stage of his development when each new role he played had to present a bigger challenge than the one before.

Sad to say, he was still living on his family allowance. He had made up his mind that he just had to be independent, and that meant getting bigger and better roles.

There was no question but that he had made his mark. His acting had taken on new values, progressed in depths. He had control of his voice, but his overemotionalism was still untamed. That wasn't altogether a curse. Audiences seemed to like that quality in Laughton. Some American tourists visiting London saw Laughton for the first time and called him a "tear-jerker," but fortunately that name never reached his ears. All through those early years Charles did not realize he actually did best in comedies, especially in lurid and slightly mad roles. As time went by he stopped being considered as a promising young actor; he had established himself, had his own style and method. He still struck people as a bit unpolished— crude, rude, wild, untamed, funny, boisterous, but always natural and original and human.

The year was 1928. Basil Dean, the successful London producer, needed an American for the title role in *The Happy Husband*. There was none available in London. It would be too expensive to get an actor from Broadway. Dean had casting worries.

When Laughton turned up, looking for a job, Dean said:

"Wait, can you speak with an American accent?"

"Sure I can, mister."

Charles got the part, although he had never so much as spoken with an American. Now he set his mind on learning the American lingo, and doing it thoroughly. He went to the nearest music shop and bought American jazz records.

"Have you other recordings?" he asked.

"American?"

"Yes, any speeches, recitations, verse?"

"Not much," replied the salesman, "unless you'd care for an old speech by the late President Woodrow Wilson, addressing the farmers in the Midwest. It's been around for years and we can't sell it. You can have it at a reduced price."

Laughton bought the record. President Wilson was one of America's greatest speakers. His talks were always masterpieces of factual, rational, unemotional oratory. So it was that an American President became the speech teacher of Charles Laughton.

Charles made a great hit. His Wilsonian accent, his cold portrait of a nonchalant American, brought huzzahs from all quarters. The play was so successful that Broadway producers cabled Laughton, offering him parts in New York. But Charles had already taken on other commitments in London.

He had achieved enough prominence for the *London Era* to write of him:

". . . Mr. Charles Laughton, whose American husband was a really comic creation, as rich in humor as it was in heightened sense of character. This adds another to the half-dozen extraordinary performances given by this clever young actor in the last year or two."

Now destiny was to throw a second "American" part into his lap. It happened by sheer luck. Edgar Wallace, the king of the mystery writers, had seen Charles in *The Happy Husband*. Wallace was a fantastic figure in the literary world—in twenty-seven years he had written one hundred and fifty separate works. He had a greater reading audience than any man living or dead—readers could not get enough of his mixture of his "suspense, action and excitement, humanized by a deft touch in characterization and an easy humor."

Edgar Wallace wrote Charles asking for a meeting. Laughton's voice was giving him trouble—the doctor's verdict was that his tonsils had to be removed. He was in no mood to pay calls just before an operation, but he went, certain that little would come of the meeting. After all, authors weren't the ones who hired actors.

Laughton was impressed by Wallace's luxurious mansion. He was shown into the tremendous study where the author sat waiting for him. The writer was at his desk surrounded by screens, and wearing a heavy silk dressing gown with a white scarf tucked in at the neck. Wallace gestured with his famous outsized cigarette holder.

On the desk stood three dictaphones—brand-new devices in those days. In this impressive setting, Wallace said: "I like your style, Laughton. Now I have just written a play for you—it's about an American racketeer. There's everything in it—adultery, gun fights, funerals, a kidnaping. And what is more, there will be plenty of dead bodies. I'm giving him a marvelous mistress—for a change we'll make her Chinese."

"Will the racketeer live in a house with purple carpets and have a golden organ to play Italian opera on?" asked Laughton.

"Fine," Edgar Wallace agreed enthusiastically.

The two understood each other immediately. The part of Tony Perelli, the American racketeer in Wallace's play *On the Spot* was hand-tailored for Laughton. There was only one incongruity. Laughton, who was no musician, was supposed at one point in the play to perform

Gounod's "Ave Maria" on the organ. One night in Manchester Laughton miscued, and the organ began to play too early. This brought a big laugh from the audience. At the end of the play Laughton came out in front of the curtain and addressed his hall:

"Ladies and gentlemen of Manchester, you are the only people in the world who know that I cannot play the organ. Will you please keep my secret?"

This was Laughton's biggest success so far. Overjoyed, he wrote his mother of the new play. She only replied, "And who is this Mr. Edgar Wallace?"

Her answer gave him something to think about.

When Wallace offered Laughton his next play, *The Mouth Piece,* Laughton read it and disliked it. He was faced with the choice of being loyal to Wallace or to his own artistic conscience. Laughton did not want to be in a poor play. He did not care to be typed eternally as a gangster. He turned the part down. It was the end of a glorious friendship. Wallace never forgave Laughton.

Chapter 4

IN HIS YOUTH Laughton had dreamed of playing Macbeth—the prototype of all guilt-laden men. But Macbeth did not come his way. With the Edgar Wallace play he had a chance at portraying the modern ruffian. But he was determined to do it without compromise. Instinctively he had decided at a very early point in his career never to be "typed." He would always interpret his roles the way he saw them and thought was right. The results were baffling to authors, directors and producers.

Komisarjevsky had returned to the Court Theatre. Laughton was in another play. He portrayed Count Pahlen in *Paul the First,* a drama of brutality, terror and strong emotions. It was another role close to his heart—he had a special gift for portraying scoundrels and his own idea about them.

He always wanted to bring out what was simple and stupid about brutality, so that people could laugh at it. Laughter always seemed to him a better reaction than shock and fear in the face of murderous brutality.

Laughton thought that people ought to laugh at brutal monsters like Hitler and his ilk. This conception underlay his portraits of Captain Kidd, Henry VIII, Herod and Nero.

While acting in *Paul the First* he began rehearsing for Arnold Bennett's new play, *Mr. Prohack.*

Bennett was difficult both as author and man. Shaw

was not the only great name the young Laughton ran afoul of. Arnold Bennett, like G.B.S., did not recognize his own character. He was terribly upset. He wanted to have Laughton removed, but things had already gone too far and opening night was close.

The final rehearsals were dreadful. Laughton appeared not to understand what Mr. Bennett wanted. He even talked back to the author. On opening night Laughton carried his mockery of Mr. Prohack even further than he had done previously. The audience was flabbergasted. The young and almost unknown Laughton emerged as the spitting image of author Arnold Bennett. He modeled himself on Bennett completely, even to Bennett's mustache, his way of wearing his hair, his way of talking.

Everyone saw the joke but Bennett. The newspapers spotted it. There were rave reviews, and Laughton became the talk of London's theater world.

After reading the reviews, Bennett phoned the actor. He was beside himself with indignation. "Who do you think you are, young man? Are you out of your mind? How dare you do such a thing to me! What infernal cheek!" He hung up without waiting for Laughton's answer, which no doubt would have been hardly conciliatory.

The furious playwright, however, calmed down considerably, when thanks to Laughton, the play became a success. He finally forgave Laughton his interpretation.

As a gesture of friendship, he confided to Charles that he had a mistress with whom he spent two nights a week. Another gentleman was spending two more nights with her. If Laughton cared to, he could have her for the remaining three nights.

Laughton bowed out graciously. He never knew that Bennett made this proposal to all people he wanted to impress. Only a few months before he had made the same magnanimous offer to Somerset Maugham, who, like Laughton, had declined it somewhat less gracefully.

Arnold Bennett, who became a close friend, actually changed Laughton's life quite fundamentally. At the first rehearsal of *Mr. Prohack* Laughton saw a striking-looking young woman. She was quite tiny and had fiery eyes. Her red hair was uncombed. She stared with fascination at Laughton. Finally she asked a stagehand, "What is his name again?"

When she learned it, she just nodded and went on watching the rehearsal.

Finally Bennett and the director introduced the shy-looking actress to Laughton, who smiled sheepishly.

"Miss Lanchester," he said, "I have admired you many times. I saw you on the stage in *Riverside Nights*."

But Miss Lanchester did not say a word. She had a peculiar feeling in the pit of her stomach. "What an odd-looking man! But what a voice! And how sensitively he spoke his lines."

Laughton did not notice her confused look and went on, "Miss Lanchester, I was almost your leading man in *The Pool,* but then I had another commitment and could not sign a contract."

Elsa Lanchester still looked with fascination at this man. Then she said rather curtly, "There will be other chances, Mr. Laughton, I hope."

Now Elsa Lanchester was to play Mr. Prohack's small and vivacious secretary, Mimi Winstock. It was not a big part, but she received the same salary as Charles, for she was a well-established actress, perhaps better established than Laughton was in those days.

"I knew automatically that he had this great and wonderful talent," she said later.

On the third day of rehearsals Charles said, "Miss Lanchester, we worked so hard and I think you are wonderful—you and your performance—what about a cup of tea?"

In the days that followed they had many cups of tea. Soon they went to matinees and dinner together, met friends—and the whispering began: "Elsa is sweet on him."

It was the typical courtship of two very busy people who had time to meet only after shows and between rehearsals. There was really very little chance for hand-holding and kisses.

Charles began to tell her about himself. He admitted he was a lonely man and knew little of women. But he did not want to be mothered. Elsa rushed nothing, promised nothing and said little. She was the best listener Charles ever had.

He felt peace with her and comfort. Her slowly growing devotion was so new and so soothing that often he waited impatiently to see her, to talk over his roles with her, his agents and other problems. Many a foggy night they strolled hatless through the London streets, he talking, she listening.

They showed up at actors' parties together; were seen at concerts. It was the most animated, stimulating and happy time Charles had ever had.

Elsa admitted she loved her independence and was afraid of permanent attachments. She also confessed finally, "If you do not know much about women, I do not know much about men." This tiny woman, with a beautiful body and a fascinating face, was almost afraid of men. Not that she could not put them in their place with her sharp tongue. However, she had always tried to keep them at a distance.

When Charles finally asked the fateful question, he saw there were tears in Elsa's eyes. She only nodded. Her ability to keep silent in important moments was, and still is, one of Elsa's greatest virtues.

The romance between them was never of the breath-taking variety. One thing is sure, that Elsa admired him from the first minute they appeared together on the stage. They fell into talk, discovered that they had much in common, and started going out together. Charles could sense the character of this young woman—her determination, strength and enormous will power. She spoke the same language as he in the field of art and beauty. She struck him as the first person in his life who understood him on many levels, who showed sincere interest in his work, life, ambition.

In her "elfin" book *Charles Laughton and I*, Elsa Lanchester never bothers to explain why she wanted to marry Charles. But anyone who has watched the two during the twenty-five years of their marriage knows that even today—after many marital storms—Elsa finds Charles the center of her life. She has never boasted of it, but their closest friends realize how much Elsa Lanchester has contributed in the way of support, advice, patience, friendship, companionship, criticism and ideas toward Laughton's great success in later life. But as she remarked in her memoirs:

"If I had been full of a sort of respectful awe, we should not have had any relationship at all. . . . It was a routine courtship. On the first day that we decided to walk in the country we met at Waterloo Station and Charles was wearing a loud checked cap. I screamed with laughter and he put it away in his pocket . . ."

"We had our romantic excursions and oodles of fun," added Laughton.

Elsa Lanchester repeatedly said of herself, "I know I'm not pretty." This statement, coming from a Hollywood actress, is a remarkable thing to say. But there is a wonderful charm and great humor about this real lady of the theater. Perhaps, by her absolute high standards she is not pretty, but she is exceptionally attractive. Like Charles, she makes no particular effort to look alluring. Like Charles again, she seldom looks the same way twice. They both are constantly experimenting with their expressions. In this respect they are both born actors.

Elsa has a large, deeply lined and thoughtful forehead.

She has great, impish-looking, laughing velvet-brown eyes, a tiny, uptilted nose, an upper lip which can do practically anything. The general impression is of great determination softened by pretty dimples. She is red-headed and has a flawless complexion. She has a very mild and friendly voice, but she has achieved her greatest successes in roles calling for a display of aggressive and ferocious traits, as in Shaw's *Androcles and the Lion*.

She was born into a pacifist, vegetarian and socialist family at Lewsham, near London, and spent her early youth at Clapham Common. She was one of twenty girls to be hand-picked from the seven corners of the world to develop her dancing talent at the famous Isadora Duncan Dancing Academy in Paris. She was very unhappy at the school, but she always loved dancing and still does. In her memoirs Elsa Lanchester has written: "I supposed Isadora Duncan's teaching . . . was always picturesque. I remember once during a lesson she drew us children toward a huge window which looked out on a rose garden—beyond was the Seine and Paris—and shepherding us in a Raphaelite embrace she pointed to a falling rose petal and said, 'They dance—now you dance!' "

Isadora Duncan considered herself the apostle of the New Light. American-born, she had taken farewell of her native land with the words: "You know nothing of love, food and art. I shall never see you again." She contended that the dance was the highest expression of the human spirit. Enemy of formality and convention, she pioneered in modern, spontaneous dance. Her recitals electrified the world. In her private life she was a fervent advocate of free love. One of her projects was buying a hill near the Acropolis and building a temple of dancing there. In her Paris academy she gathered together young girls of all countries who were to be taught dancing and brought up on the most advanced principles.

Little Elsa Lanchester was not at all happy in those inspired but unstable surroundings. It was a relief when her pacifist father arrived to take her home to England at the start of the First World War. Elsa Lanchester must have been quite a sight in Clapham, dressed in Grecian garments of hand-loomed cloth, sandals on her feet and a "hatless red head."

Eventually Elsa went to London and organized the famous Children's Theatre, where underprivileged children of talent were taught dancing, acting and music. The venture was fairly successful. However, the performances by child artists provoked complaints. The police intervened and claimed Elsa Lanchester had violated the child labor act, the white slave act, and had offended against minimum standards of literacy by putting on a play entitled *Love and Freindship*. The misspelling alone proved that she was completely unqualified as an educator. The constable could not believe that the misspelling was deliberate and had the sanction of Jane Austen.

There was nothing else to do but to suspend the Children's Theatre. The school had been almost self-supporting and Elsa Lanchester regretted giving it up. However, since the case received much publicity, her name had been aired all over London. The late Sir Nigel Playfair who loved balloon flying had seen her at work. He asked her to be his leading lady in *The Insect Comedy*. She was associated with Sir Nigel for several years, playing in *The Duenna, The Way of the World* and *Riverside Nights*, which ran a full year.

During those years she did everything an actress of great versatility could do. She acted, danced, sang and established herself as a gifted *diseuse*. She was a brilliant figure at fashionable parties in London, and people still remember Elsa Lanchester teaching Lady Astor old-fashioned temperance songs, which they both sang in the style of the Salvation Army singers.

PLEASE SELL NO MORE DRINK TO MY FATHER

> "Please, Sir, will you listen a moment,
> I've something important to say.
> My mother has sent you a message.
> Receive it in kindness, I pray.
> 'Tis of father, poor father, I'm speaking.
> You know him, he's called Ragged Gore.
> But we love him, and hope we may save him,
> If you'll promise to sell him no more.
> Please sell no more drink to my father,
> It makes him so strange and so wild.
> Heed the prayer of my heart-broken mother,
> And pity the poor drunkard's child."

As a wonderful comedienne, Elsa was a great hit. Her main interest was still in the dance, but she had a real actor's temperament, so that there was hardly a role she could not carry through with enthusiasm. She even ventured to play Little Lord Fauntleroy!

While playing in *Riverside Nights* she also took on a part in the show at the Midnight Follies—the interval between the two shows being so short that she had a taxi waiting for her at the stage door every night to drive her to the Follies. She also managed to change costumes in the taxi. Since then this sort of rush has never bothered her.

Being married to Charles Laughton has never been a restful kind of life. Elsa Lanchester might well say with Mrs. Walt Disney that life with her husband is "like being bound to the tail of a flying saucer."

When Elsa Lanchester fell on an octopus eight times in the course of filming *The Beachcomber,* the joke arose that after this ordeal even being married to Charles Laughton must be bearable.

Elsa was well on her way up when she met Charles. She was that well thought-of that the great H. G. Wells wrote three one-act plays especially for her—an honor any actress of the day could be proud of.

When Charles took Elsa home to meet his family in Scarborough, Elsa and her future mother-in-law were attracted to each other from the start. It was the beginning of a wonderful relationship between the two women which lasted until Eliza Laughton's death in March, 1953, at the age of eighty-four.

Charles introduced his mother to his future wife with the words, "She is a wonderful woman—tough as they make 'em." It must have been an odd scene, and people must have thought they were a far from perfect couple. Charles Laughton was five feet ten and weighed over two hundred pounds—a big, ungainly figure, dressed casually and even untidily in "sandals, a faded blue denim shirt [Charles loves baby blue] and a baggy pair of tattered pants." Elsa Lanchester, tiny and trim, shyly apologized to her mother-in-law, "I think he needs me."

Old Scarborough friends, looking at the unmatched pair, took him aside to say, "Charlie, we always thought you would pick out a nice big girl for yourself." Charles took these comments in good part. He laughed and recited Dickens to them, describing his imaginary bride:

> "She had a broad unfeeling bosom—
> Not a bosom to repose upon
> But a capital bosom
> For hanging jewels upon."

But it was some time before the wedding finally took place because, though they had some casual plans for getting married, those plans were completely upset by one of Charles's inner crises. He had played Crispin in *The Man with the Red Hair,* moved on to the Haymarket Theatre to perform in *Alibi,* and with the Christmas season drawing near, was cast as Mr. Pickwick in a play based on Dickens' *Pickwick Papers.* The part almost drove him to desperation. He hated the way he was doing it; he felt unequal to the part and fretted so over his work that he was too nervous, too irritated and too restless to go through with the marriage.

"Forgive me, darling," he said to Elsa. "I'm not good for anybody now. Let's wait until this mess is over."

Elsa was silent again and only nodded. She knew only too well that Charles was terribly upset about his role. He could not find the right way to do Dickens. The words were too monotonous, he thought. He began to look sick, and was so nervous he argued with everybody he met, even with waitresses.

Elsa did not press him. Let him have it his way, she thought. She was sure he would come back and set the wedding date. It never occurred to her that he would leave her.

Friends who visited him in those days often found him running around his bedroom, half naked, with towels around his neck and over his head. He looked "like a mad Turk."

Strange as such a situation might seem to the average young woman engaged to be married, Elsa Lanchester took it in her stride. She had been all set to move out of her apartment on Percy Street, Tottenham Court Road, but she patiently settled down again to wait until Charles had straightened out and "found himself."

Charles Laughton revealed something about this crisis in their courtship twenty-five years later in an article for *The Atlantic Monthly*. He wrote: "I was rehearsing Mr. Pickwick, founded on Charles Dickens' *Pickwick Papers*. We were rehearsing the famous Christmas scene at Dingley Dell farm—the scene of the mistletoe and the wassail and the old lady and the fat boy and blazing log fire and the dancing—and I found that I and it were dull and spiritless. Over the weekend I went to visit my home town and during the train ride to Scarborough and back I read Dickens' book, and the language jigged and swirled and was breathless and peaceful by turns, and I remember that Dickens' text was complete of itself and that the mistake of our play was that it could not be transferred to any other medium without taking away its excitement."[1]

Laughton had spent weeks trying to improve things. "This horrible speech," he moaned. "I've been practicing it all week. I've shouted, I've whispered, I've done everything I know, from screeching to roaring and mumbling, and it still does not sound right."

"Have you shouted enough now?" asked Elsa the next time they met.

Charles looked flabbergasted, but smiled. Elsa kissed him silently. There were tears in his eyes.

Elsa was confident that if he worked at it more it would come right. Mr. Pickwick taught him a lesson—there was another proof that Charles's talent was not a free, natural gift. It meant very hard work and painstaking self-development.

A few weeks later Charles had licked the Mr. Pickwick part and was in a far calmer state of mind. Someone had tipped off the papers, and their "engagement" was announced.

The cast of Mr. Pickwick wanted to celebrate, but Elsa and Charles preferred to be left alone. The final marriage date was still not set. Newspapermen were sure they would marry on the Saturday after the closing of Mr. Pickwick. But Charles and Elsa fooled them. Elsa did not leave the house, in order to avoid questions, congratulations and the bother of giving answers. "I only had two eggs, a piece of bread and half a pint of milk, so it was quite a hunger siege," tells Elsa.

They fooled the press and were married secretly early Sunday morning. The date was February 10, 1929. It rained hard when they started out for the Registrar's office. They had terrible trouble getting a taxi at that early hour. They had previously made special arrangements to get the Registrar out of bed on a Sunday when the office was usually closed. If they were late he might not wait and they could not be married that day.

"I'm completely wet," Elsa said. "I surely do not look like a bride."

"No," laughed Laughton, "this is not like a wedding; this is more like a funeral!"

But the two young lovers thought it was all great fun and didn't care.

They finally arrived at the Registrar's office. The clerk was still waiting for them patiently. And so, both dripping wet, they were married.

Charles has never regretted that day. He openly admits that his career, his success, his art would not be what it is today without Elsa Lanchester. On her side, it has meant sacrificing much of her own life and career to stand in the shadow beside this overpowering personality. It is not easy to become the wife of a great man.

Elsa is a remarkable woman—a great artist. Many an observer has wondered how much further she would have gone in her own career had she not taken on the extra job of being a great man's wife.

Elsa lets fall an amusing detail about their early days:

"Perhaps the beginning of our interest in each other was first shown by the fact that although we are both the kind of people who can usually express ourselves and our ideas with great ease in conversation, we were practically dumb when we were alone together." This may not sound like great romance, but perhaps it was something deeper.

All in all, Elsa Lanchester has performed miracles in building up his self-confidence. Laughton admits that his debt to his wife is enormous. His unusual looks never disturb her.

Today at the height of his career, it is most amusing to hear Laughton tease his rebuilt ego with such remarks as, "I have a face like the behind of an elephant," or

"I am modest regarding my appearance and talents because it is especially easy to be modest when you look like I do."

However, Elsa has spoken her mind on this once and for all:

"How dare you presume you are unattractive? Hold your shoulders back, keep your head up and smile so that I can hold my head up with other women."

Their honeymoon took them to Switzerland where they went sleigh riding in Arosa. They were breathless and overwhelmed by the majesty of the high mountains. Charles was pretty good at skiing but it was new to Elsa. Both spent much time "sitting and falling" in the snow. His thought that, as she had been a dancer, she would properly balance herself on skis, was quite wrong. "Being double-jointed," Elsa said later, "when I fell, I practically fell to pieces. I went down like a daddy longlegs." But both enjoyed the sleigh riding on the famous two-mile downhill run.

Elsa had the time of her life. She was really happy and in love. But Charles did not always laugh at the fun of falling in the snow or enter fully into the parties and hotel life. There seemed to be something on his mind. Elsa did not take this mood seriously. She thought, "He always loves to brood." She noticed that he was very moody when they visited one of the small village churches in the snowed-in idyllic valley. But Elsa brushed the mood off. It wasn't important, she was sure. And then they made plans to go to Italy, where the beauty of the country completely carried away the young couple. Elsa was particularly struck by Naples, where Vesuvius was still smoking after a recent eruption. Charles, however, was not particularly interested in volcanoes.

What was he brooding about?

Elsa felt that something he did not want to talk about was bothering him. He seemed worried. This shadow on the trip grew worse. Quietly and tactfully Elsa began to make hints about the future. Perhaps he wanted to get back to work. Elsa sensed that, with the wedding trip drawing to a close, Charles was beginning to be worried about the days to come. His last plays had had only short runs. Now he had a wife, and would have additional responsibilities. His voice was giving him trouble—the doctor said a minor operation might be necessary. They had hardly any savings. The future did not look bright at the moment, but Elsa did not care. She loved Charles and Italy and was sure the future would take care of itself. After all, they were both hard workers, and things generally turn out well for people who work hard. With a sixth sense, she could look ahead into the future Charles was so fearful of. Her intuition was right when she predicted, "Charles's career will be rocketing ahead, but mine will not. I think it will be just as well, as I would not like it if I were to succeed and Charles were to have a bad time."

As she saw him, Charles was a man of great talent—possessing remarkable wit and charm and magnetism. He was an amazing actor and even in ordinary life affected everyone as a superior being. She was deeply under his spell, devoted and completely in love. She was also aware that his love for her had a touch of the unusual about it—she never was fully sure when Charles was living in the real world and when in a world of his own creation. Actors were funny people that way, and she herself sometimes found that she was under such an autosuggestive spell.

Later on in their marriage when Charles "acted" at home a few times too often, she was as temperamental as he. She would shout at him, "Lay off!" And it was a favorite joke of hers, when he stumped around the living room as Captain Bligh or King Herod, to remind him that she had once played "the bride of Frankenstein." That would restore him to normality.

Before they married, Elsa knew little of his peculiarities. There was no way of telling that he would become an addict of the Sunday comics, or insist that they should get two Sunday newspapers so that each of them could read the paper without disturbing the other. She did not know that he loved to go to bed late and to get up late or to have a cocktail in his bath. She never dreamed that he would blossom out as a wonderful cook, a collector of cookbooks and a disciple of Escoffier. She did not know that he had a passion for bees and was as proud of being a beekeeper as of owning priceless Renoirs and Dufys. She did not know that he loved white pajamas or that he would require a double bed strictly for himself.

Their marriage has been a kind of corporation: Charles Laughton, Inc., with very few shareholders outside the two of them. Their separate careers in theater, film and coast-to-coast tours have sometimes kept them apart for long periods of time. They have known days when they could not bear each other, and days of supreme happiness together. There have been occasions when Elsa has given her spouse many "a caustic wifely wallop," but Charles has always known that Elsa is his best and most honest critic.

Her loyalty, friendship and love, and above all her unselfishness, have soothed him and helped him realize the great potentialities he knew were in him.

Chapter 5

"**N**OBODY LEARNS to take it on the chin from life," Laughton once said, "like a big, fat, roly-poly guy who thinks he wants to be an actor."

He certainly did. During his apprenticeship at the Claridge Hotel, he had been lodged in an obscure room with an Italian who was providing Charles with at least fifty per cent of the mannerisms employed in his characterization of Tony Perelli in *On the Spot*. It was so real, so perfect, so amusing that Charles was about ready to admit that his days as a kitchen clerk at Claridge's might not have been wasted—he had absorbed so much from his roommate that the whole experience was paying off now.

Laughton had cast the actor's spell on his audiences. Playing in Edgar Wallace's *On the Spot* for a full year, he still had the crowds coming in spite of the weather, frost and fog.

It was no ordinary fog that plagued London during the winter of 1929, but a real pea-souper, a "London particular"—fog that refused to stay out on the streets, but followed the theatergoer into the theater. There seemed no way to keep it out, and it brought chill and penetrating damp with it, so that no comfort was to be had even there. But dampness or no dampness, Londoners flocked to see Charles in *On the Spot*.

Then Laughton took *On the Spot* on tour. When it came to an end, Charles's relations with Edgar Wallace had deteriorated completely. The King of the Mystery writers was putting on his new play, and Wallace's letters no longer began "Dear Charlie." The salutation became more and more formal, ranging from "Dear Laughton" to "Dear Mr. Laughton" and finally to "Dear Sir."

Charles was not hurt. He had behind him a mere three years on the professional stage, but in that time he had played in twenty-one plays from *Everyman* to Ibsen's *Pillars of Society*. He had been Cantaville in *Naked,* Sir James Hartley in *Angela,* Creon in *Medea,* Ben Jonson in George Moore's *The Making of an Immortal,* Hercule Poirot in *Alibi,* Jacques Blaisse in *Beauty.* Most of these were short runs, but Charles had become an integral feature of the London theatrical world.

While he played Edgar Wallace's superracketeer, London theaters were putting on Pirandello's *The Mock Emperor* and *The Devil,* written by Laughton's old friend Benn W. Levy.

Hitler's shadow was already darkening Europe, and London showed Ernst Toller's revolutionary *Hoppla.* Since no season could be complete without George Bernard Shaw, *Major Barbara* and *Man and Superman* were both enjoying successful runs.

Laughton took in a matinee of *Man and Superman* and was quite upset to find the witty, philosophical dialogues omitted from the play. As was usual, it was a cut version that was being presented. Right then and there, in 1930, Laughton decided that he would someday play the Devil in this Shaw play. Some twenty years later he carried out this pet project and put on his famous reading of *Don Juan in Hell.*

"The literary salons were starting to play up to me." He and Elsa were on the invitation lists of Lady Colefax, at Argyll House, Chelsea. Lady Hamilton, another distinguished hostess of the day, welcomed him to her gatherings. Arnold Bennett noted in his journals: "Charles Laughton came to see me on intimate matters."

London in 1929-30 was the great cultural center of Europe. It outshone Paris, Vienna and Berlin. At dinners and banquets one could meet H. G. Wells, G. B. Shaw, Hugh Walpole, John Galsworthy, Somerset Maugham, J. B. Priestley, James M. Barrie, Ashley Dukes, Marie Belloc and many others. After such affairs, the guests went to smart night clubs, such as the Kit-Kat, the Gargoyle and the Cave of Harmony, where Elsa Lanchester and Harold Scott were entertainers.

The innkeeper's son who only three years before was slaving as kitchen clerk at Claridge's fitted perfectly well into those circles. He was accepted even at some of the midnight sessions which included Lord Beaverbrook, the late Dean Inge, Dr. Archibald Fleming, and an unemployed statesman by the name of Winston Churchill. With such cronies he would from time to time take tea at the Savoy. Claridge's, however, was a place Charles avoided for several years afterward.

He no longer tended to brood off in a corner at those brilliant literary parties. His wife had the gift of bringing him out, of subtly encouraging him and making him feel at ease among such people. Only Charles did not fully believe in his own social success.

"I was now worrying over an operation I had tried to stave off for almost eighteen months. I had been bothered by voice trouble." At first he thought it was a psychological block, a recurrence of the trouble he thought he had overcome. He was again frightfully nervous before every entrance. His acting colleagues still recollect jokingly how he used to raid the candy boxes of his fellow actors and stuff himself with sweets before he made his temperamental entrances on the stage.

However, the doctors were convinced that all Charles

had to do was to take some time out and have his tonsils removed. And this is just what he finally did.

Thereafter his voice difficulties vanished. He made a fast recovery and was back in the play before he was even missed.

The doctor had told him to try to get as much country life as possible—it would do him good, especially his throat, which was still tender after the operation.

He wanted to do something new, something different. He had had enough of Wallace's gangster and was rather fed up with constantly playing monsters and villains. Observers of his career also wondered when he would break away from morbid roles.

In an article in the *Theatre Arts Monthly* Edith Shackleton asked: "Can he escape from the long queue of murderers, sadists, drunkards and maniacs that are waiting for him to give them stage life? Can we give a fair stage reception to a Lear or Hamlet who is not handsome? Will he try Macbeth?"

That was a well-meaning question raised by a sympathetic theater critic. But when had Hamlet been played by a fat man no longer boyish-looking, even though he might command the warmest and most hypnotic sort of language? To play Lear—as all great actors had done in the history of the theater since Shakespeare—well, who would let him? "To really portray King Lear," Charles said, "an actor should go into retirement for six months, studying and living the part. Then he should come out, give two performances, and return to retirement."

The last thing on earth that Charles, still struggling for fame and recognition, could have afforded during those years would have been retirement.

Elsa and he were ready to buy a house in the country. The Laughtons were still living in the little flat off Tottenham Court Road which they had rented after their marriage. Now, with both earning good incomes, they made up their minds to take a deeper plunge. They went hunting for a place in the country, "a hut," anything that would give them real country life, fresh air, greenery, woods and freedom from the metropolis.

This country house of their dreams was an important milestone in their lives. Today, when earthly goods have come to the Laughtons in overwhelming bounty, the two have never forgotten that place in the country which meant so much more to them than a show place with a heated swimming pool in Hollywood's most exclusive neighborhood.

They were then the proud possessors of a very old jalopy. "We combed Surrey, Kent, Essex, the Chiltern hills and upper Thames Valley, but didn't find anything that suited us," writes Elsa Lanchester. Finally she—alone—found the "one and only cottage" in Surrey which was untenanted and for sale, and which she decided was what they wanted.

"We did not have much money then," told Laughton, "but we wanted to have at least a little cabin away from the great traffic."

They had gone house-hunting for weeks, but no agent had produced anything they had liked. Then one day the architect, Clough Williams-Ellis, and his wife, Amabel, gave a party to which the Laughtons were invited. Charles could not go, so Elsa went alone.

During the evening Elsa told about her house-hunting and how she had seen the world's oldest and most ramshackle dumps. The Ellises looked at each other, and Amabel nodded. The architect said they were selling their own country place, which was too small now that their family was larger. Their cottage in Surrey was seldom used. But they only wanted to sell it to someone whom they knew and who would appreciate it.

Elsa looked at it and wired immediately to Charles:

COME AT ONCE CLOUGH'S PARTY THATCHED LOG
CABIN 28 MILES LONDON 625 FEET UP HEART OF
WILD WOODS BRACKEN UP TO FRONT DOOR TWO
MILES NEAREST VILLAGE NO WATER NO LIGHT
PINE TREE BLUE BELLS. ELSA

Charles went and was astonished. He could not grasp
how so much untouched woodland had survived so close
to the large city of London. It was not an easy financial
transaction. But the die was cast.

Elsa wrote later about the place: "Paths had to be
cut in the wood, logs chopped for the fire, drinking
water fetched half a mile from a farm—and the ants had
to be got rid of." But it was there they had their real
honeymoon.

The two kept this idyllic spot for many years, even
after they had made their great success in America. It
had been the scene of their brightest and most carefree days. It was consecrated to a happy part of their
youth, and all the dreams for the future which had
been dreamed there. Even after great fame and wealth
and a hundred-thousand-dollar movie contract, Charles
Laughton still spoke ardently of their country place in
Surrey.

"It's heavenly," he said. "Absolutely in the heart of a
wilderness. Thirty-two acres, all trees, undergrowth and
wild flowers—a regular Garden of Eden and so secluded
that if we liked it, Elsa and I could go about in the attire
generally associated with that delightful spot. I'm long-
ing for the spring there; it's so beautiful. That's one
thing we can put over California, our fresh, green
countryside. The hills of Hollywood often look very
brown and arid through too much sun."

He was patriotic about the beauty of English nature.

Country life agreed with Charles and Elsa. They spent
every available day in their retreat. By and by Charles
and Elsa had new parts at the St. James Theatre in *Pay-*

ment Deferred. This was a grim and morbid play, a psychological study of murder. Elsa played the twelve-year-old daughter of the murderer, William Marble, who was portrayed by Charles.

From its first night it was a tremendous hit. Charles made his part so convincingly real that people in the audience were frightened. No one wanted to be quite that close to hate and murder, crime and disaster. People would exclaim or cry out—the play had an altogether extraordinary effect on its audience.

"I knew it was a most dangerous play. When you come to consider that it is really necessary to play the love scene with the Frenchwoman as you imagine a Senior—someone in the audience on his leave in Paris—you will realize that a fellow is not going to like you very much for it. . . .

"The play has a most searching element of how people lie to their wives. The scene when the wife says: 'Oh, Will, if I found out that you were not true to me, I think I should kill myself,' is really about the most horrible I have ever known . . . but I enjoyed it.

"Poor, rigid, hidebound Mr. Marble, the laugh is with him and on the audience. They crucified him, and by the end of the play they know they did in secret fear of their hidden lives under a mask of virtue. By that time they naturally want to crucify you for telling them so. I played it as if I had intimate knowledge of everyone in the audience's meanness and their secret desires."

Charles outdid himself in this role. He was even more powerful than in his successful *On the Spot* performance. It was based on the famous novel by C. S. Forester and had been widely acclaimed as soul-searching and profound. It was a good old melodrama, too, in the best British Jack-the-Ripper tradition. Charles's remarkable realism left little for the audience to desire. Playing the murderer, he carried the part off so well that it would seem even an audience of deaf-mutes would have understood him. By that time everyone knew that the more complicated and diabolic his villains were in the play, the more marvelously Laughton acted them.

One night H. G. Wells came to the theater to see the play. He was interested in Charles, but above all in Elsa Lanchester, a pet of his, for she had played in three one-act plays which he had explicitly written for her. The great novelist was shocked when he saw Elsa in the role of Charles's daughter. He called it a "recessive relationship." Elsa had known H. G. Wells before her marriage to Charles. Wells, a Nobel prize winner, was then at the height of his fame. He had been much taken by Elsa Lanchester's talent. Everyone in London's literary world knew Elsa Lanchester, the *diseuse,* and now Wells was smitten by Elsa's French manner in interpreting ballads and songs.

Wells was sharp-witted, proud and often highhanded. People who did not agree with him, or those who would not grant that he was a world reformer, he lumped together as "stupid." But Elsa was an amiable listener—and Wells could be very witty at the expense of others.

Those who knew H. G. Wells intimately were aware that he was impelled by a strong, almost abnormal sexual drive. It was a tendency he never tried to combat. He would discuss it openly and admit it had nothing to do with love.

He could not work unless he had a woman to sleep with every night. Particularly on lecture tours—he was the world's worst speaker—this was a necessity. He was a fairly old man by that time. His lecture managers in America will still tell the most hair-raising and amusing stories of what they had to do to keep H. G. Wells, with his urges, satisfied.

But he was genial to those whom he liked. His choosing Elsa to play in three of his short films was a great break for her. We shall never know just what Charles thought of seeing Elsa and Wells together on the studio lot—Wells homely and fat, with wonderful manners and an overwhelming egotism, which he shared with many other creative persons.

Wells did not call himself an author, a novelist or philosopher, but as a higher title than all these he called himself a "publicist." He was convinced that journalism on a high plane had more influence than any other kind of writing. Certainly he was an influence on Charles and Elsa—both in a personal and professional sense.

For Wells to go to see Elsa and Charles in *Payment Deferred* was a tribute naturally noted by all the newspapers. It boosted the play and its performers.

Charles was still indifferent as to how he dressed, although his looks had improved considerably. However, a new person now entered his life—a tailor. Sir Gerald du Maurier had recommended him. Once Charles discovered him, he went about telling everyone who cared to listen about this wonderful fellow. "He's a real artist and such an amusing chap—he always thinks in terms of clothes. Translates everything into them. I was rehearsing this gangster role in *On the Spot*. I went to him and said, 'I'm going to play a gangster. A tough bootlegger, vain, mad about women and with oodles of dough.'

" 'Right, Mr. Laughton. Lounge jacket, with a distinct waist; pink silk shirt, large pearl pin, coat sleeves too short and too tight.' "

In describing such an incident, Charles did a wonderful little skit in which he acted the tailor with a light, lively touch.

"And when I went to him to say that I was going to be the city clerk in *Payment Deferred,* he at once said, 'I understand—his collar's got the gore at the back of the neck and his trousers had better be a bit tight in the bend of the knee. That will be it.' "

Since then, tailors have always been respectfully treated in Laughton productions.

Payment Deferred lasted three months at the St. James. Morbid and gruesome as it was, it could not expect a long run. Still, the reviews had been so enthusiastic, the audiences so excited, that Gilbert Miller decided to transplant the entire cast and show to New York, to open on September 30, 1931.

There was not much time for Laughton to pack and make final arrangements. The play closed late in the summer, and the Laughtons had to scurry, completing arrangements for the building of a new cottage to replace "the Hut," giving up their London apartment and getting ready for the first trip to America.

Neither of them dreamed that the trip to New York would lead to a Hollywood contract. Charles never gave the possibility a thought. He had never had much contact with the movies, with the exception of the time he visited Elsa out in Rye when she was doing the lead in the H. G. Wells films. Once out there, more for fun and as a joke, Charles used some of his leisure time playing a police constable in one film and a sinister rajah in another film. The silent picture *Piccadilly* has a very small bit in which Charles portrayed an old gourmet protesting about a plate of food during a cabaret scene. In *Frankie and Johnny,* he and Elsa sang a duet. All this was less than a full day's work. It surely was nothing to constitute film experience.

Their ocean voyage was not exactly a pleasure. Charles never was a good sailor.

No visitor to American shores can fail to be impressed by the Statue of Liberty, by Broadway, Fifth Avenue and Central Park. The giant city of New York, utterly unlike any other in the world and lacking the charms of Paris or Vienna, Florence or Rome—casts its own kind of spell. The Laughtons found it strange, bewildering, confusing—it was too hectic and too new.

They opened on Broadway with *Payment Deferred.*

When late after midnight the first reviews appeared, they could tell beyond a doubt that they had taken the American citadel by storm. Not a single morning newspaper failed to give the play the highest praise. The evening papers were even more enthusiastic. John Mason Brown, the high-strung, ebullient, thoroughbred Kentuckian, who had become America's leading theatrical critic, went overboard in praise in his *New York Post* review:

"It included one performance of such brilliance and finish that the evening becomes something which no one interested in acting can afford to overlook. I refer, of course, to Charles Laughton's Mr. Marble."

No one in America had heard of Charles Laughton before, but after October 1, 1931, American theatergoers and fans were no longer surprised when John Mason Brown continued:

"Mr. Laughton's face is one of the most expressive masks that I have ever seen in the theater. . . . His hands and feet and his whole body are ever the willing and expressive instruments of the things he has to say. . . . He does not say the lines, he thinks them. They can be seen gathering like clouds in the eyes. . . . He can be cross with peppery violence, carnal with a grossness that is repellent, merry with the expansiveness of Falstaff, cruel with a hideousness that is sickening and afraid with a whimpering terror that is almost unendurable."

Mr. Brown ended with a statement he has seldom made before or since: "He is the most remarkable character New York has been privileged to see in years."

What more could any actor ask for? Elsa's performance was also superlative and most difficult, but Laughton overshadowed the entire cast.

A wonderful Broadway career seemed in store for Charles. Nothing like this had happened for years. The illustrated magazines ran his pictures with such captions as: "A mechanician in activity. Every twitch of the fore-

head, every wrinkle of the eyebrow is well calculated."
It was a total success. Few of the critics and admirers
realized that the exhausting role of this realistic murderer was sometimes too much for the actor's own good
and peace. His nerves were upset. He was close to a
breakdown.

He needed plenty of rest and sleep. The day after the
Broadway première, when Charles had just got up after
his "first-night" vigil, the telephone rang. Hollywood
was on the phone. The New York offices of the studios
had seen the reviews and had had scouts at the opening.
Now the first motion-picture offer had come. Charles
turned it down. More telephone calls followed. He was
made more and better offers; the salary ascended—$1,000,
$1,500, $2,000, $2,500 a week.

The Hollywood offers were all long-term affairs. But
none of them offered him a choice of roles. Any decision as to the type of character he was to portray was
up to the studio. Charles wanted to have a chance at
something else besides the morbid and sadistic murderers
he had been playing.

"It was not easy to decline such wonderful offers. We
were not monied people and we found America full of
tempting things to buy. We were now taxed by both
countries, which cut deeply into our income."

Charles would go to see the movie people, only to
report to Elsa that New York motion-picture studios
seemed not to understand him at all. They could not
see why any man would turn down such offers. "Why
should it matter to me what I played—gangster, murderer, villain—so long as I played it well?"

"This is the way we do things," they tried to explain.
"We settle the parts you are to get." His British stubbornness and his artistic conscience were so new and
shocking to some of the executives that they only shook
their heads. The movie executives were not annoyed.
They were rather puzzled and at a loss. They were not

Evidently Gregory Peck does not scare easily as he gazes at Charles in *The Paradine Case.*

A lustful beast looks down on beauty. Laughton, Rita Hayworth and Stewart Granger in *Salomé.*

"Good Lord, Charles, neither you nor I are faded lilies." Ethel Barrymore and Charles Laughton became fast friends in *The Paradine Case*.

Reveling in a pleasant role. Laughton as Tony in *They Knew What They Wanted*. Costarring is the lovely Carole Lombard.

used to people who said "no" to offers as good as the
ones they were making.

The New York offices of the Hollywood studios were
all located around West 44th Street. They were in huge
buildings, and all had story departments, projection
rooms, film and research libraries. The New York executives of the magic lantern industry were highly paid
employees.

Knowing they were not in the center of the industry
at Hollywood, they were under constant pressure to produce more and to be doubly as efficient as their Coast
boss.

They tried to sell Hollywood to Laughton by talk of
its glamour and the alluring future that might be in
store for him. Laughton appreciated the situation thoroughly. They were after him.

But Laughton could not be had easily. Above all, he
wanted to be the one to decide in which roles he would
play.

One of the film moguls seemed disgusted with
Laughton. "You remind me of the man with the message," he said.

"What message?" Laughton asked.

"We once bought a book from some hot-brain. A
grand story. We paid him $50,000. He had never seen
so much long green in all his life. And what do you think
this young louse did? He comes busting into my office
after the picture was released and cries on my shoulder:
'You have destroyed my novel. I can't recognize it any
more. Everything is gone, the entire message is lost.' "

Everyone looked at the mogul for the rest of the
story. The "yes men" around the huge table smiled in
expectation.

"What did I say?" asked the executive. "I told the
young man that we had paid him princely for his tale
and not to slam the door when he left. If he had a message he should take it to Western Union."

Everyone laughed but Laughton. He never thought that sort of joke funny, for he himself always had a message and was not willing to compromise.

Finally the meeting broke up and they shook hands. But Laughton still refused to accept the industry's terms that would force him to play any role they picked for him.

He left West 44th Street with a vague repulsion, feeling that his personality was still more important than glittering schemes he could not quite understand.

Charles was holding out. He signed no movie contract. He could afford to keep the studios dangling, especially since Jed Harris had given him his second role on Broadway, the revival of his English success *Alibi*. The play, however, did not go too well. Its action was a little slow for American taste. Elsa had left in the meantime, to return to England, and Charles was determined to follow as soon as *Alibi* closed.

Charles was now being haunted by American newspapermen anxious for an interview. But he took all this fuss lightly; it was to his mind no more than he deserved for his performance on Broadway. He was not particularly impressed by the enormous motion-picture offers which he had turned down. As a matter of fact, he struck people as perfectly sure of his talent. He seemed to be in the driver's seat. Hollywood was after him; purely unconsciously and with no deliberation about it, he was adopting the best tactics to achieve success in Hollywood.

"Why haven't you ever done a movie?" he was asked by the interviewers.

"I have never been what you call a glamour boy," he said.

Hollywood studios didn't know what to make of this nonchalance. It was unique. The less interested he was in Hollywood, the more they ran after him.

"What is the secret of your acting?" another journalist asked him.

Charles shrugged. He really did not know himself. He

thought it over, running his fingers through his hair in one of his typical gestures. His answer was: "Perhaps the actor should stimulate the audience to use its imagination. When I play a drunk scene, a criminal, I try to underplay and let the audience sense the turmoil the man I portray is in."

He was strictly a character actor during those New York days, minding his own business and standing up for what he thought were his rights. He was still a British actor believing in the tradition of the classic theater; of course, he never read a statement made by one of the Hollywood "big shots" who was asked to comment on the matter: "I don't go in for this art form stuff. I'm ready when they want me and I'll take a drop of Scotch when they don't." It was Humphrey Bogart who said that. He had never seen Charles Laughton nor heard his name before.

There was a great deal of excitement, but when it boiled down it was all only honor and glory—no film contract had been signed. Laughton still refused to compromise. He was rather sorry about it—they really ought to see it his way, he felt.

"You can't start at the top in America. We are a democracy," said one of the executives at their final conference. "We know what the American market wants. Listen to us and you won't be sorry. Accept our terms and we will make you famous overnight."

Laughton was bewildered by the agents' idea that he was just flesh that some flesh peddlers were putting on the market. He did not accept their terms.

Laughton was certainly confused by all this, but a second man inside him had warned him, and warned him wisely, too. New York was good enough for him. Hollywood could come later, if ever. After all, he could always return to the London theater. He was well liked there. Why worry?

Charles was now a Broadway star. Broadway's limelight was frightening, too. How long could an actor stay on top there? Every actor had heard stories of the fate of erstwhile Broadway idols. A star on Broadway had less security than the proprietor of a corner newsstand. American actors who had put in a lifetime entertaining millions on Broadway were often depressed and tense from the constant struggle involved in gaining and regaining Broadway success and popularity. Laughton instinctively felt that Broadway was a wild fairyland where the law of the jungle still prevailed. Its most lucky sons often discovered that Olympus is a lonely place.

To take an example, "first night" on Broadway was very different from the premières Laughton had gone through in London. It seemed that New Yorkers had strange tribal customs. Bad manners seemed the equivalent of sophistication. Dowagers and debutantes flocked into the theaters in the same spirit that they filled the exclusive and expensive shops—to spend money, to kill an evening. The steady, true friends of the theater who made up the bulk of London audiences were missing. "Peanut heaven" was not quite the same as "the gallery" in London.

While New York fell in love with the new actor Charles Laughton, Charles felt terribly homesick for London. The motion-picture negotiations would have to be continued at a later time. Charles booked his return ticket. Nothing had been settled with Hollywood. The ship he was on steamed out of New York Harbor—it passed the three-mile international zone, but New York's silhouette was still in sight when a wire reached him.

Jesse Lasky of Paramount was willing to compromise and to give Charles the kind of contract he had asked for. But there was no way of returning, for he was out on the ocean on his way home; even Hollywood would have to wait. "I couldn't very well swim back," he told Elsa laughingly on arrival.

They rushed out to Surrey to see the "new Hut," a

brand-new, four-room modern cottage. The bathroom was still rather primitive, utilizing stored rain water, for they could not afford an artesian well. At least they had a telephone. It came in handy, with Hollywood calling from the other side of the ocean. The final offer from Paramount was two films a year for three years. "This seemed fair and would leave me enough time to do anything else I wanted to do, so I accepted."

The first film they wanted him to consider was *The Devil and the Deep*. Benn Levy, whom Charles had always known both as writer and friend, had worked on the script.

Before Charles gave his final signature to the contract, he cabled Levy asking what his part was like. Promptly by cable the answer came back: "Even if I played in it, it would steal your picture."

Charles had been in England only two days when, on a Saturday midnight, he accepted the Hollywood offer. Elsa, who at first was not prepared to go, was to leave after all. They packed in six hours and rushed to catch the eight-o'clock Sunday boat train at Waterloo Station.

It was Sunday and they had been out in the country. "The banks were closed. We had no money for the boat tickets nor for the trip to Hollywood. We had no stateroom reservation. It was all a terrible rush, but when we reached the boat a solution was found. With the Paramount contract as security, the shipping line would not press the question of money. We could get the whole ocean voyage on credit."

The Laughtons left England in a gay mood, a little drunk from the craziness of it all, the madness of all this rushing and the trip into the blue. As far as Charles and Elsa were concerned, they knew nothing of Hollywood, nothing of what the future would bring them on the Paramount lot. There they were off to that fabulous place, to the make-believe world of Greta Garbo, Charlie Chaplin, Walt Disney, and Cecil de Mille. What a strange whirl! If Paramount had sent its wire one hour earlier, he would never have left for England where he had spent just three days before dashing back across the ocean.

He knew nothing of what faced him. But he was determined to conquer Hollywood as he had conquered London and New York, and waste no time over the conquest either. "It was only five years since I had left the Royal Academy. Six years ago I had still been the cashier's clerk at Claridge's, after being promoted from the kitchen to the front desk."

The seas were rough. Charles was seasick again. "I couldn't even whistle 'California, Here I Come'— because I had never heard the tune."

Chapter 6

THE LAUGHTONS arrived in Hollywood only to discover that no one had ever heard of them. Charles's great success in *Payment Deferred* had never, apparently, reached the West Coast. It took Paramount Studios almost four weeks to become aware of the British actor or take cognizance of their own commitments to him.

Charles went to the hotel and said to Elsa, "They are mad. They pay me a fortune and have no work for me. They don't even know who I am. They are funny people."

"As long as they pay, let's enjoy Hollywood and see what's to see here," replied Elsa. Secretly she felt that if Hollywood had never heard of Charles, it surely had never heard of her. It would be quite difficult for her to find a movie role.

"Why worry," smiled Charles, "let's go out and conquer Hollywood."

As Elsa commented, "Charles was a nobody and I was the wife of a nobody." Still Paramount paid the steep salary to the obscure Englishman whom somebody had signed up for them. It always took Paramount quite awhile to catch up. Meanwhile Charles was to consider himself on the waiting list. "We had our fun anyway," he said. "I loved to discover Hollywood on my own."

This interval was actually most advantageous to the Laughtons. It gave Charles and Elsa a chance to get their bearings in Hollywood, to familiarize themselves with this absolutely unique community.

First they stayed at a residential hotel, The Garden of Allah, located in the heart of Hollywood, whose facilities included private bungalow apartments and a swimming pool. Later on they moved into a house which they rented on a short-term lease. Charles had no idea how long he would stay in Hollywood and what Paramount intended to do with him.

Charles loved the new setting, the gardens, the year-round sunshine. It was exciting to live far from London fogs among small white houses surrounded by palms and orange and avocado trees. "I can pick my own orange for breakfast in the garden," he wrote to his family in England.

Charles accepted the luxury and the "paradise-like" atmosphere of Hollywood. Elsa, coming from a socialist and vegetarian home, felt almost out of place. She could not get used to the waste and the splendor of Hollywood.

Charles only laughed when she angrily told about a luncheon party to which she had gone. "They had table napkins of double-sided yellow satin damask about twelve inches square. They were almost as thick as they were large."

"And why not?" asked Charles.

"You have given up your own past fast," answered Elsa, and both laughed. If they were to live in a town that looked like a studio setting where all the façades gleamed like cake icing, they might as well eat of this strange cake.

But Elsa still thought it was wrong to wipe one's mouth with satin when half the world was starving.

She seemed restless. She had nothing to do. She started to explore Hollywood with a Leica. At home Charles tried to keep her amused with a cat he had bought and had christened Nero.

For his part, Charles was gradually getting acquainted with Paramount—its executives, its legal departments and its producers, directors and story editors. He too was exploring this town of "dream factories" as he was taken through the Universal City, Burbank, Westwood, Hollywood and Culver City studios.

From story conferences and studio discussions he tried to absorb as much as possible in the little time that was available. He had to orient himself in this strange world, among these strange people.

He would go home every night, totally exhausted. Laughton had never seen so much in such a short time. "These film studios are towns in themselves, I love their gardens and all the flowers. It is only irrigated desert, after all," he said.

Laughton and Elsa were delighted when they saw in the flower beds of studio gardens signs reading "Let me grow" or "Don't step on me."

The setting, with the high mountains in the background, convinced them they were in a place which most people in England would say came closest to paradise.

The town itself fascinated them. Neither Charles nor Elsa had ever before seen huge supermarkets where every kind of fruit and vegetable could be found, from strawberries to oranges, peaches to mangoes. Most of these fruits could be had all year round, too. For days they ate nothing but fruit, as Elsa disliked American food at that time. She admitted she never did get used to Coca-Cola or chewing gum.

They were rather lonely those first weeks, forgotten by the studios and forgotten by the world. No actor likes to be forgotten, so they visited some English friends, Benn Levy and James Whale. The latter had been Elsa's stage manager for *Riverside Nights*.

Exploring Hollywood on her own, Elsa returned home to tell Charles of the thousands of new cosmetics they sold in drugstores and the strange way they sold beautifying gadgets and remedies to the women. "I'm afraid I'll use some of them, too, soon."

"Go ahead," Charles encouraged her. Then he told of *his* newest discovery: American slang.

"I never heard a language like it. They pulled my leg today at the studio and really well."

"They had a lot to pull."

"Oh, come on, Elsa, you don't understand the American lingo either, do you?"

"No, it's Greek to me when I hear it."

"Where do you hear the slang?"

"At the beauty parlor."

"Well," said Charles, "I learned *my* first lesson of American slang today."

So he told what had happened.

Hollywood lingo was like a new language. All that he knew of American speech he had learned from the record of President Wilson—and Woodrow Wilson had never used the words which now rattled down at him from every quarter. Complete strangers in the studio would address him as honey, sweetie, baby, fella, darling, lover, sugar. "I was repeatedly asked how my 'bride' was." How could anyone coming from the Royal Drama Academy know that in the movie colony a wife of even ten years' standing is called a bride—not, of course, that many Hollywood wives last that long.

He was completely bewildered by the artificial atmosphere of superenthusiasm which pervaded the place. Everywhere he went he encountered the stereotyped big handclasp and public-relations smile. He could not understand that, not knowing that in Hollywood enthusiasm is mandatory. Relax it for a moment and failure, disaster and layoff loomed ahead for you.

In his usual blunt way, Charles asked embarrassing questions of people no one else dared to embarrass. On the Paramount lot he repeatedly wanted to know when he was to begin working. No one knew. The transocean

telephone calls had been on the theme of "Hurry, hurry."
Now it seemed they had all the time in the world before
casting him and preparing him for his first role in
Hollywood.

With the usual "enthusiastic" tone and great big smile,
they gave him the customary advice. "Don't worry, your
time will come. Take it easy. How do you like America?"
And off they were, to another project!

Hollywood studios pinned their artificial enthusiasm
on like a medal; Charles told Elsa how they wore their
optimism on their sleeves. But no one would commit
himself to anything. To Charles it was very strange. As
far as he could observe, this state of mind extended from
the business managers to the agents, from the press agents
to the actors' mistresses, from the waiters in the com-
missary to the script writers. Some even had part-time
mistresses.

It was a considerable shock to Charles to discover that
box-office receipts were the only thing that counted in
Hollywood. Films were the province of the directors and
producers; the actors had nothing to say.

People talked of nothing but movies, and everything
about movies was discussed in the open. There was no
privacy, no discretion and no mercy. All one ever heard
were remarks about "incompetent" directors, "dud"
script writers, "stupid" critics, "idiotic" audiences, low
and high budget pictures.

Charles kept his eyes and ears wide open. He never
uttered a word of criticism. This was a challenge to him.
If this was Hollywood, he was ready to conquer even it
as soon as he was let loose on it. But when would that be?

After his studio tours and friendly discussions with
fellow actors who were waiting for scenes to be shot, he
had the feeling they all suffered from delusions of
grandeur. But sometimes the faulty reasoning came
through. A picture that cost half a million dollars could
gross five or six million dollars if it had mass appeal.

Everybody was always running—everyone always had an appointment. It always sounded so important, as if they all had an appointment with destiny. But when they came to their appointment, they had to wait for hours. The executives were still in conferences, in the cutting rooms, looking at previews or at film strips.

"They certainly have the world's best-looking secretaries," said Charles to Elsa one day.

"If you get as colossal as they are," answered Elsa, "you can have everything you want. Soon you will have a lawyer, too, a masseur and a special agent, and maybe a beautiful secretary."

"I think I will," he said, with a secret thought on his mind.

Everyone told him he had to have an agent. Laughton didn't like agents in general. In addition, he did not know whether he could trust any of the agents in such a strange and new environment. He was aware of how little he knew the ropes. If Broadway operated by the laws of the jungle, Hollywood must be much worse. Were agents honest? Would they have his interests at heart? They were all smiling and smooth. This mechanical pals-with-the-world attitude aroused his deepest suspicions. Even the agents back in England didn't act like that.

Laughton had learned that some studio people hired personnel directors, actors, technicians, publicity men with the understanding that a ten-per-cent kickback of a year's salary would go to the man who helped in the hiring. No wonder he had to be careful with agents.

Public relations seemed to mean so much in America, especially in Hollywood. Paramount had not yet moved a finger to put him to work, but their public-relations experts and hucksters besieged his house. They took pictures of him—front, profile, from above, from below, and even upside down. They treated Elsa as though she were a piece of furniture, calling her in to pose only in one or two publicity pictures.

A strange and crazy world.

Producers and directors making one hundred and two hundred thousand dollars a year and often spending twice that amount on houses, butlers, swimming pools, horses, women and gambling.

Gin rummy at a dollar a point.

All Charles wanted to do was to act.

"Take it easy. Don't we pay you anyway?" was the standard studio answer.

This policy left Charles free to prepare himself for Hollywood as he had prepared himself for all the situations of his life. He studied, absorbed, learned, picked up information, collected insights, did research and generally kept his ears open.

He shared his findings every night with Elsa, who felt quite lonely. It did not take him long to discover that Hollywood's standard formula for artistic success was derived from the world's greatest, best and unsurpassed best seller—the Bible. What Hollywood extracted from the Bible may sound blasphemous, but the Bible always has been, still is and will remain the one and only infallible prescription for the celluloid town: God, Sex and Action.

At first Charles was amazed at how well-read the producers, directors and story editors were. They seemed to know everything from Shakespeare to Dickens, from Wilde to Bernard Shaw. It was disillusioning to find out that professional readers made synopses of all the famous works. Everyone read the synopses and knew the contents of literary works secondhand.

Charles was amazed, but not critical. It was somewhat the same with Hollywood architecture, which imitated a hundred exotic styles but was like no other on earth. Charles found a name for it—"late marzipan." He found many things besides the architecture terribly strange, but he never uttered one word of criticism of Hollywood. As a matter of fact, he has never done so.

"These technical men amaze me. Nothing is too great or too complicated for them," he said to Elsa. "They are good businessmen, expert merchants, but they are imaginative too."

Coming from the conservative school of British acting, that was a remarkable but honest statement. Charles realized that he was far from grasping everything as yet. But he was willing to plunge into its midst, to take full responsibility for his presence in this metropolis of a new art. For he clung to his conviction that the film was an art. Even if the other actors did not think so, he, at least, was going to bring art into the film world.

That he promised himself to do, but Elsa was rather doubtful and seemed to evaluate Hollywood's glamour much more realistically. She realized the star system was carried to extreme. She said to him during one lonely night, "Garbo has only to pluck her eyebrows and millions of eyebrows are plucked. Katharine Hepburn has only to accent her slashlike mouth and the Cupid's bow disappears overnight." Elsa still seemed unhappy.

The two had serious discussions about the American motion-picture industry. Slowly Elsa convinced Charles that King Hollywood had a sort of split personality. One part of his ego was the fabulous producer, the imaginative dreamer, the reckless spender, the pioneer and the man who, at heart, liked to reach out for art. The second half of this split personality was married to the world markets from San Francisco to Timbuktu, to the distributor, and movie owners, to the hard-boiled sellers and buyers, the shopkeepers, the controllers of real estate and the wizards of accounting systems, finance and banks.

"It is not art. It is the largest commercial enterprise you have ever seen," said Elsa—and Charles knew she was all too right.

His self-education went on. He learned that a film audience does not want to strain its eyes or ears, that overacting is fatal, that every scene in a screenplay, every gesture, every shade of expression, every word must be functional.

Naturally everyone who had got anywhere in Hollywood told him that violence was always good box office. Another bit of wisdom passed on to him was that actors had learned "to take the money and damn the art." Laughton listened poker-faced. Not by the faintest shade of expression did he betray what he himself thought in regard to these facts of life in Hollywood. He knew he would never compromise when it came to his own art. He never did.

He also noticed that many movie stars made plenty of money but did not know how to handle it. He would manage things differently. With Elsa's help he would use his money for greater and more important things to come.

Laughton noticed something else. Side by side with enthusiasm and the public-relations craze was the drive for fame. Everyone in the motion-picture industry wanted fame, more fame and nothing but fame, not realizing that all small talents and medium-sized talents burn out eventually, sometimes very soon.

Many of those fame hunters camouflaged their vanity with aristocratic exclusiveness. Others went in for pretentious Hollywood parties in their mansion-like homes. But all were hungry to be noticed, no matter how.

The world noticed those people all the time. The fame hunters were constantly in the press. Scandals surrounding the great actors, their marriages and multiple divorces, the "extra" girls trying to get into the news with blackmail and sex, the enormous lawsuits, alimony scandals, perverted love, comedians arrested for reckless driving, big names involved in gambling, famous actors caught in using dope—all this was daily news in Hollywood.

Laughton learned of all these complaints and threats and dangers. Actors went to jail for shooting agents out of jealousy; embittered Thespians accused competitors of being Communists, and real Communists infiltrated the industry.

Charles also recognized why so many of the talented in Hollywood had lost their perspective. They really believed they were powerful and great and important and at the center of the world. But in fact they were not. There was New York, still the literary center of America, and there was Broadway. Many successful Hollywood actors dreamed of returning to the theater—Katharine Hepburn, Tallulah Bankhead, Henry Fonda and the Barrymores, for instance.

England was most generous to the Hollywood films. Laughton knew that the future audiences of his own Hollywood pictures would be large outside the United States, as well as the rest of the world. Paramount knew it too.

Charles and Elsa saw many Hollywood pictures and studied the acting technique. They reached this conclusion—American musicals can hardly be topped, but most other pictures were shot almost like Westerns. Even a classic would be approached with the oversimplified spectacle of a Western picture pattern: the big chase, the good man almost losing, the bad man finally destroyed in the last second. There was much fighting, shouting and suspense. Then, only the budget would decide if it was to be a colossal "A" picture or merely a colossal "B" picture or an almost colossal "C" picture.

Those fame hunters were all gamblers at heart. Many worked for a few weeks only and had enormous dreams the rest of the year.

Normal home life existed in the movie colony with many, but there were just as many who had lost perspective of what family, love and marriage really were. They

Elsa Lanchester in the stage version of **Payment Deferred,** a role given to Maureen O'Hara for the films.

Merle Oberon and Laughton are fitted for costumes for *I, Claudius.* With them is Director Von Sternberg.

even acted when not before the camera. Some had had
four or more wives or husbands and precocious children.
A very talented child actor told Laughton the story of his
twelve-year-old friend.

"Tommy's mother, Mr. Laughton, was married four
times; now she has married a new star, Mr. X. Tommy
came to me today and asked me what Mr. X is like and I
said to him, 'Oh, Mr. X is wonderful as a father. You are
lucky. I had him last time.' "

There were tears in Laughton's eye as he hugged the
boy and kissed him on his forehead.

Was this all a necessary part of the mad hunt for fame?
Was he, Charles Laughton, one of those fame hunters?
His mind went back to what he had learned in school
under Komisarjevsky. It was worth remembering that the
great in history and the great in the theater had their own
philosophy of fame. That philosophy was that one must
not pursue fame but rather fly from it—then and only
then would the Goddess Fame and Success come after you.

A man who took this Olympian point of view could be
very lonely in this high-geared town where fame was
coined like counterfeit money.

Meanwhile Charles, although very well paid, was still
waiting. But Paramount's machinery was slowly beginning to move. Laughton got his screen test. He was
superb. Now he was given a free run of the orbit of the
technicians. He watched wardrobe tests, make-up tests,
and learned that a ten-second strip of a film scene might
involve a dozen retakes before it was right.

He decided that his own technique would have to be
modified.

"The screen has the advantage of pantomime," he said,
"which can be done more effectively and in the interesting
use of close-up. I've always had a particular fear of
overacting."

Paramount officials knew exactly what they were doing.
They considered the Laughton contract a most valuable

property and wanted to give their expensive protégé time to adapt his acting technique from the stage to the film. They generously threw open all doors to him: he had access to the production end as well as to script and directors' conferences and meetings.

Charles, as temperamental as any actor alive, discovered that the temper of the Hollywood studio is even more uncertain than April weather. Time and again directors and actors started with huge enthusiasm. It was unbelievable how easily that could be exhausted. From this Charles could deduce that there was something more important than enthusiasm—patience.

The studio world had its own madness, charm and absurd customs. Charles daily discovered something new.

The time he had gone out to Rye to watch Elsa working in the H. G. Wells films he had not encountered the whole pharmacy of pills waiting for everyone working on the set. Few movie-goers realize that no Hollywood film would ever be shot if it were not for the counter full of pills—green, blue, pink and lavender, pills of every color, size and shape. Benzedrine tablets to keep you awake, dexedrine pills to give you pep, vitamin pills to keep you strong, cold pills to help against the sniffles, emperin, codeine-aspirin pills to offset fatigue and headaches, histamines and antihistamines, iodine against an oncoming cold, and naturally the sleeping pills that enable you to sleep after all the tensions of the day. For everyone has to be "rested" when he goes back next morning at seven or eight to start the next shooting day with another benzedrine tablet.

Strange as the whole process of American motion-picture production was to Laughton, the invisible factor in the whole thing—the American audiences for whom the picture was geared—was even stranger. As far as the audience went, both he and Elsa were mystified, and to a certain extent have remained so throughout their careers.

At a cinema hall in Britain "God Save the Queen" is

still played after each performance. In America, the sale
of popcorn, candies, soft drinks and hot dogs accounts
for a substantial part of the income of the show exhibitors.
Most American movie houses smell of popcorn. (Charles
has always had an overdeveloped sensitivity toward
smells.) The rustling of popcorn bags, the munching of
many jaws, the teen-agers accompanying the music with
the rattling of candy wrappers and the sipping of Coca-
Cola, were thunder to his ears. These habits of the average
audience are hard to get used to for someone not born
in Uncle Sam's country.

When the Laughtons went to Hollywood, they were
English through and through and made no pretense
about it. Far from resenting this, Hollywood approved.
But if people thought that Laughton was going to be
snobbish about American picturemaking, they had a
surprise coming. In spite of his British stage background,
he nevertheless came out strong for Hollywood. "The
American film is a valid art form," he said.

He outlined his ideas on Hollywood in an early interview with Quentin Reynolds:

"It seems the custom for stage people who come to
pictures, to decry Hollywood. It is all tinsel and make-
believe, they say. There is no art but the theater—and
then they complacently draw large checks. Such people
give me a large pain. I worked on the stage for a long
time, and before that I studied and was trained for the
stage by competent teachers. I have worked in pictures,
too, so I think that I can say without conceit that I am
qualified to talk of both. I'll tell you this, for every bit
of fine direction you see on the stage you see twenty bits
of fine direction in Hollywood. . . . What I am trying to
say is that Hollywood and pictures are on the whole right.
Producers in the main are intelligent. Directors are not
the posturing poseurs that some think them. The actresses
in the pictures—the topnotchers—are not merely a lot of
cute-looking girls."

*   *   *   *   *

Then came a great surprise. The Paramount Studios were still not ready to shoot *The Devil and the Deep*. Therefore Universal Studios asked whether they might "borrow" Charles for one of their pictures, written by another Englishman, J. B. Priestley. It would be only a small part in *The Old Dark House*, but it was just the role for Laughton.

Charles's first reaction was that anything was better than waiting. Both Paramount and Charles felt that a little film practice would do him good—Paramount would have a more experienced and camera-trained actor for *The Devil and the Deep*.

The Old Dark House was a horror picture featuring Boris Karloff as a mad servant, while Laughton portrayed a rather jolly and friendly Yorkshire businessman. The British script in a British setting attracted several British actors, such as Eva Moore, Ernest Thesiger and Brember Wills, but also included Melvyn Douglas and Gloria Stuart. Melvyn Douglas, a veteran actor of both Hollywood and Broadway, has told me, "Laughton was magnificent—we all admired his great talent."

Laughton had not taken long to learn the differences between acting for the stage and for the films. He had been watching movie-making for weeks and had come to the conclusion that if he controlled his gestures and kept from overacting, he would do all right.

The director was very much pleased. The close-ups turned out excellently. Charles's performance was believable and natural throughout.

The Paramount people saw the preview. They, too, thought that their protégé had acquitted himself well. Now, they said, everything was set for *The Devil and the Deep*.

Even the explosive Tallulah Bankhead who met Laughton in an overcrowded restaurant on the Hollywood strip remarked, throaty and alluring, "Da—h—ling

— hear you're to be in *MY picture.*" Charles has never forgotten this wisecrack.

"In this gem," Tallulah Bankhead has reported, "I was the wife of Charles Laughton, playing fast and loose with Gary Cooper in a submarine. Laughton, Cooper and I were supposed to be some hundred fathoms down throughout the action and illusion.

"*The Devil and the Deep* didn't cheer me up. I grew morose," the inimitable Tallulah concluded. Why? This she never discloses. But we do know that Charles stole the show completely. Without intending to, he overshadowed both Tallulah Bankhead and the popular Gary Cooper, whom Laughton liked so much.

When Laughton played, hard-boiled stagehands stopped what they were doing, watched and applauded. This sort of thing didn't usually happen in Hollywood. "A new Emil Jannings," said those who watched him.

His final death scene was so magnificent and so real that even Elsa, watching him, thought he had actually entered into the mood of the suicide. The water closed over his head while the camera continued to shoot, conveying the point that the submarine commander Laughton was floating dead under water. Both Elsa and the watching fireman believed that Charles was carrying realism too far and that he might really not come up again. The fireman jumped into the ocean to rescue Laughton, only to find him swimming calmly under water. As it turned out, this scene had to be taken ten times before it was finished—and all at night. The whole cast felt the strain. The suicidal atmosphere made Tallulah even more morose. An oxygen tank was waiting, just in case of a mishap. It did not serve to lighten the mood any. A mobile dressing room was on hand for Laughton's use. Here two changes of clothing were alternately pressed, ironed and dried between water scenes. To warm him up between underwater bouts, Charles had to drink plenty of whisky. As a result of all this, Laughton looked fifteen years older on the screen. His comment when this underwater stint was finally finished was, "I'm tired and I always was a stinking sailor."

Shooting time for the suicidal water scene ran to exactly twenty-three hours.

Charles and Tallulah did their scenes together in a workmanlike spirit, but the fellow actor Charles became really good friends with Gary Cooper.

At their first meeting, Gary remarked to Charles, "London is the grandest city in the world because it is the one place on earth where one can walk down Piccadilly in a bowler hat and not feel silly."

So it was established right off that both loved London. The words were music to Charles's ears—he was going through a spell of homesickness and any kind words about London helped.

"I was thinking myself in a part that this boy Gary Cooper can do in a flash," said Laughton. "Cooper was lighting a cigarette in front of the camera and looking up at a woman's face. I knew in a flash then that he'd got something I would never have. I went across the set and asked him to tell me how he did it. He looked shy and bewildered and said I ought to know better than he did: I was from the stage and he was just a ham movie actor."

Quite convincingly Laughton elaborated on his Gary Cooper praise. "We act in opposite ways. His is presentational acting; mine is representational. I get a part from the outside. He gets at it from the inside, from his own clear way of looking at life. His is the right way, if you can do it. I could learn to do it," he continued, "but it would take me a year to do what he can do instinctively, and I haven't the time . . ."

Naturally, such an attitude cemented friendship more easily and better than any Dale Carnegie could have prescribed.

Nevertheless, *The Devil and the Deep* was no box-office success, and Tallulah recalls in her memoirs:

"*The Devil and the Deep* never surfaced. And no wonder. Too many people were involved. No one had the authority to fuse conflicting elements. Cameraman, star and director worked at cross-purposes. They reminded me of humorist Stephen Leacock's knight who jumped on his horse and rode off in all directions.

"I was victimized by the mechanics of the whole business."

When the picture was finally released, *The New York Times* criticized it for "unimaginative direction," but had good words for the actors. "Miss Bankhead is at her best in this film, Gary Cooper gives a sympathetic and rigorous interpretation . . . but Mr. Laughton's forceful and resilient portrait is the *outstanding histrionic contribution.*"

Naturally, everyone noticed Charles's British accent. It was rather an incongruity, since it was ostensibly an American submarine that the story centered around. Still, it wasn't hard to transpose the whole thing to the British Navy.

The *Los Angeles Times,* the most widely read newspaper in Hollywood, ran its review of the film under this headline:

NEWCOMER STEALS SHOW

"Laughton . . . he's superb," was the verdict.

Charles did not suspect that *The Devil and the Deep* would be a flop. But this still lay in the future. Meanwhile, Charles, who had put in some very hard work, was given a week's vacation before embarking on his second picture. He needed the rest. He wanted to get some new perspective on it all. Hollywood was proving to be a great strain, both mentally and physically. He was still suffering from homesickness. Elsa would be leaving for England soon for her own engagements there.

He had been invited for a weekend visit to a ranch near Lake Toluca. Its narrow winding waters edged by lawns and drooping willows reminded him of England—especially of the stretch of the Thames near Marblehead. On the spur of the moment he decided he would take the next train to New York and go home to England. He even sent for his agent to break the news gently. A stormy scene followed. There were angry words and even tears. It took some fancy persuading, coaxing and reasoning to make Laughton stay and fulfill his Hollywood contract and commitments.

Laughton hasn't much British stoicism when it comes to certain things. His love for pure beauty is so great that he will walk miles to find the first crocus. When he visited the University of North Carolina to do a reading there, he was so touched by the Chapel Hill flower gardens with their masses of daffodils and narcissuses that he broke into tears. His Southern hosts did not know what to say or do.

In this he reminds me of the late pianist, Arthur Schnabel, the great interpreter of Beethoven. The first time Schnabel heard Negro spirituals he broke into tears. It was the purest music, the purest and simplest expression of melody he had ever heard.

Charles Laughton shares some of the qualities of the great figures of the theater—Edwin Booth, Sir Gerald du Maurier, Edmund Kean and the great Barrymore. All were untamed, unpredictable, with a touch of the vagabond prince in their characters.

For such natures it is not easy to become assimilated into Hollywood's movie colony. In the case of Laughton, his British background made it all the harder for him to get used to Hollywood's unique community, its superficiality, its excitement, its glamour, its pitilessness and all its astounding people and exotic habits.

Paramount asked Charles to take an important part in a picture intended for global distribution on a mammoth scale. It was to be a giant spectacle, another picture of the sort the great Cecil B. de Mille was famous for: *The Sign of the Cross*. That was what Laughton had been waiting for, a real big picture and a chance to work under De Mille, who to him was never "run of de mille." The script dealt with a vestal virgin of the highest Roman family who embraces Christianity and dies as a martyr.

Plans were no sooner announced than the battle was on—the battle for parts. Everyone wanted to be in this picture which offered great rewards. Besides the Hollywood recipe of God, Sex and Action, there were to be hordes of raging lions and thousands of half-naked Christians thrown into the amphitheater. In short, a superproduction.

The part of Nero was destined for Charles. Instead of being suitably grateful, he began having arguments with De Mille, the script writers and the directors. From these discussions it became obvious that Charles knew more about Rome and Romans, Nero and ancient history than all the script writers put together. He saw in the role of the debauched emperor Nero all sorts of potentialities, both dramatic and personal. Here was his chance really to put himself across in a remarkable role. But he had his own ideas about Nero's part, and he would not give an inch.

De Mille was and is an extraordinary man. He is the force behind a mass movement not surpassed in this century—not even by such men as D. W. Griffith, Reinhardt, Kazan, Zukor or Mamoulian. He has an eye for every detail and a dynamic feeling for huge effects. No one knows as well as he what the screen audience wants. It is a revelation to see him work. He runs around the set in riding pants, in a constant ferment of excitement, bubbling over with energy. His grand gestures and patriarchal attitudes are part and parcel of his character.

To Laughton, De Mille was a fabulous creature. Here

was a man who believed a picture had to start with an earthquake, develop fast and firmly and end with an atomic blast.

Laughton told Elsa he had never seen a man with so much energy, so many ideas and such an enormous capacity for work.

Given such a man, a clash with Charles Laughton was almost inevitable. Laughton put on his calmest demeanor and refused to be drawn into the razzle-dazzle and circus atmosphere produced by De Mille.

Laughton's picture of Nero has no parallel in history. He did not discuss the part with De Mille, but played Nero as a funny creature, an imbecile, a moron whose name must be entered in history's black books as a monstrous disgrace. De Mille was taken by surprise. He could not see Laughton's point at all. There was nothing about it in the script—where did the man ever get this idea?

"Nero was one of the wickedest men who ever lived. He was a menace to the world. Look how he treated the Christians," he lectured Laughton. Charles went on playing Nero as a colossal fool. He knew just what he was doing. He had put in long weeks of study and thinking about the part.

De Mille was not in the least satisfied with Laughton.

After the preview of the picture, De Mille called Charles Laughton. His worst suspicions had been confirmed. "Well, they were all laughing at you. You sure spoiled everything."

"But I wanted them to laugh at me."

In the cast with Charles was Elissa Landi. She had landed the leading female part after the customary intrigues—in the course of which it looked as though the coveted role might fall to Sylvia Sidney, the latest pet of Paramount's Benjamin Schulberg. In the end, the powers-that-be decided in favor of Elissa Landi, whose type, while less "toothsome," was considered more classic. Laughton himself maintained a serene impartiality in this affair. Among his costars were Fredric March, who was to become a lifelong friend, Claudette Colbert and Ian Keith. The incredible De Mille had assembled a distinguished cast for his modern "bread and circuses."

As always when he took on a part, Laughton made it his business to find out the less obvious things about the character he was to play. A curious fact about Nero, and one which tickled Charles greatly, was that he was a passionate actor. As Laughton explained it, "Nero used to give what amounted to command performances. Only the command was all on his side. He used to command audiences to come and watch him perform. And when they were in the theater, he would have all the doors and entrances locked so they couldn't leave until he was finished. Actors ever since have envied him that."

Among the added attractions of the picture were the lions, including De Mille's favorite, Rudolph. Charles wasn't sure what he thought of all these wild beasts tearing around the set. He asked one of the stagehands what would happen if the lions should get out of hand. And he learned that Hollywood lions are not considered dangerous.

"The insurance companies see to it that they don't come too close to the actors," the stagehand told him. "Besides, we can always chloroform them."

A greater attraction than the lions was Mae West, who swaggered onto the lot to be photographed with her head in the mouth of the lion, Rudolph. That was the kind of trick shot De Mille loved.

"Haaaaaaalo, Charlie," she hailed Laughton. "What I couldn't tell that lion about halitosis."

Adolph Zukor had a proprietary interest in diamond-studded Mae West, who was then enjoying her heyday. The publicity releases called her the one woman who was "hitting the high spots of lusty entertainment." Zukor seconded these words: "When I look at those busts I know what lusty really means."

There was much talk about Mae West around town, and Charles got all the low-down on that bizarre personality who wore a diamond tiara as matter-of-factly as a hair net. For himself, he knew his success had to be won in a harder, more "intellectual" way. "You've got to use your brain a lot more in pictures than on the stage," he said, "because you don't depend upon your instinct so much. It's more technical, acting in pictures. You rely a great deal on direction—De Mille was marvelous to work with."

Laughton was pretty marvelous too, otherwise De Mille would never have stood for his strong-mindedness and obstinacy. The figure of Nero was a very significant one at that time, for dangerous dictators were cropping up all over the world—Mussolini was solidly entrenched in Italy, Hitler was grabbing power in Germany, and Stalin was consolidating his position within Russia.

More than twenty years later De Mille did his famous *Quo Vadis* picture again. For the part of Nero he took Peter Ustinov (of *The Love of Four Colonels* fame). The entire picture centered around the funniest man Rome ever gave birth to, the imbecilic "poet" Nero, who read imperial poetry while Rome burned. De Mille had taken over Laughton's old idea of Nero.

Charles has consistently offended many people in the theater and the film world by presenting "his one and only version" of a play, and not theirs. No one was prepared for such originality from a raw beginner. It seemed a mad way to behave. Many great names looked upon him, for years, as an upstart. Who the devil was this fat fellow who took such a high-and-mighty attitude?

They were soon to find out.

The De Mille picture was a success. This was not surprising, as all De Mille spectacles, from the silent

Quo Vadis to the latest technicolor production of it, have broken box-office records. De Mille did *The Ten Commandments,* and all kinds of anecdotes relating to it circulated around the lot. There were plenty of the long waiting periods when Charles was apt to get impatient. The others told him to take it easy—De Mille was always either having fits because things didn't go fast enough or feeling that he had oceans of time for preparation and detail work. "You should have been with us during *The Ten Commandments,*" one of the stagehands told Charles. "Then you could see Moses, Aaron and De Mille waiting for hours to see God."

When Charles's part in the picture was finally over and he was shaking hands with the great De Mille, he thanked the director for a great experience. "C.B.," he said, "I'd love to play *you* as a character in a film."

It was evidently not the wrong thing to say. De Mille laughed heartily, as though he were rather looking forward to Laughton's carrying out that threat.

Chapter 7

I NEED A LIVING audience," he declared. "Hollywood is a lotus-eating country. It begins to get you when you become too familiar with it. . . . You lose your tautness. An actor's life is not an easy one. The rewards can be large, but they can stop coming after a relatively short period."

An actor who ceases to please the fickle fancy of the public is soon forgotten. Any economic or political disruption hits him hard—he cannot switch to some other field and so finds himself completely helpless and confused.

When the great depression hit the United States, Hollywood straightway became the capital of the unemployed. "Wall Street had laid an egg," and the consequences reached farther than anyone could have imagined. Millions were affected—losing jobs, homes and everything that had spelled security—as the richest country on earth faced its greatest crisis. Twenty-five thousand actors were unemployed, and actors' organizations protested strongly against the twelve thousand foreign actors working in the United States. Film attendance had dropped forty per cent. That meant sharp curtailments all up and down the line in the movie industry. Actors were lining up for free dinners in Holly-

wood or on Broadway. Writers, actors, directors were
selling apples on the street. The future looked pretty dim.

"I was personally protected by my long-term contract,"
Laughton said, "but I saw what was going on in the
country and was bewildered."

During those days of economic crisis Elsa and Charles
grew very, very close. It had taken them a long while to
see the miracles and wonders of America and her generosity and carefree ways. It was not easy to adjust to life
on another planet, and Hollywood seemed just that
to them.

Now the two saw depression and starvation. Both were
European and knew poverty better than the average
American. But still it was a heartbreaking spectacle. The
ghosts of capitalism, communism and socialism were
performing their *danse macabre*. Laughton was shaken
deeply and tried to help some of the unemployed actors
he knew. Elsa had no work.

Paramount Studios had seemingly weathered the storm
miraculously. In the midst of wholesale bankruptcy and
depression, they made more than fifteen million dollars.
In 1930 their profits totaled eighteen millions. But in
1932, Paramount suddenly discovered that it had lost
sixteen million dollars. Naturally, everyone in Paramount
was having the jitters. De Mille was highly conscious of
the need to produce profits. *The Sign of the Cross* had
to be a smashing success. The team, De Mille, Laughton,
Colbert, Landi and the rest put everything they had into
the picture.

Their efforts paid off. The film was a success. Said the
New York Daily News: "For acting, first honors go to
Charles Laughton."

Naturally Charles was very happy about all the reviews.
The critics were unanimous in acclaiming his performance; he had thousands of enthusiastic American fans.
The box-office response was gratifying. The question was,
would it last?

All Charles knew was that he would go on working, acting, creating roles just as he had in the past, without compromise.

He had put in a year of terrific work. He needed a rest badly—Hollywood acting methods took a lot out of him. "I had had only short respites in the form of weekends at Palm Springs."

The Palm Springs denizens of the Hollywood movie colony still treasure amusing stories about Charles Laughton dating back to that time. Once photographers caught him. They promptly asked him to pose just as he was, in swimming trunks, with Johnny (Tarzan) Weissmuller. "Nero" refused. "To get a good shot," he said, "you would have to take his body and my brain."

Charles sometimes gave the impression of being very coy. Since his "Nero" was played in sandals and toga, it meant that his toenails had to be painted red. The pedicurist had embellished the five toes of his right foot with red polish when she was called away; she never showed up again that day. Charles went out for his usual Palm Springs weekend, but when friends asked him to go swimming with them, he had to decline. He wouldn't appear with five red and five plain toenails—for in spite of all his efforts he had not been able to get the polish off.

All these incidents, of course, stemmed from his terrible self-consciousness about his looks. Many a Laughton eccentricity can be traced back to that. It underlies many of his likes and prejudices. For example, there is his deep and lasting devotion to one of the screen's greatest and most beautiful actresses, Marlene Dietrich. The foundation of this feeling was laid on an occasion far in the past. Meeting Charles on a studio lot in Denham, Marlene said, "I would rather act a love scene with Charles Laughton than with any other actor in the world."

The Dietrich bon mot made headlines. What was more

important, Charles was so flattered and happy that he almost danced for joy.

Marlene's attitude toward Laughton was very different from that of a certain movie star who was not quite so charitable. She had been cast opposite Charles in a picture. Before it was to be shot she looked at Laughton and noticed he was not quite so tall as she. "Now I suppose I'll get a cold again," she grumbled. "I'll have to play without shoes, I'm taller than you are."

To which Charles smilingly retorted:

"Just wait until we start. I'll cut you down to size."

Agnes Moorehead, who played opposite Laughton and Charles Boyer in Shaw's *Don Juan in Hell,* ended the discussion on an actor's charm, and on handsome or homely lovers once and for all with the words: "Say what you like, Charles is a big bear with a big pink plush heart."

Charles was not costarring with Marlene Dietrich; he had just completed his stint with De Mille's lions, Christians and barbarians and afterward let himself be lent to Metro-Goldwyn-Mayer, where Irving Thalberg had decided to do the film version of *Payment Deferred.*

Elsa had hoped for a part in *Payment Deferred,* the same part she had played on the stage in London and New York. But Thalberg had already engaged Maureen O'Sullivan. It was too late. Elsa had real difficulties getting her start in Hollywood.

"Don't worry, you will make it. Just sit it out until the great crisis is over," said Laughton. He also suggested that Elsa try to be more chic. "American women all look glamorous even if they are grandmothers," he said. He advised her to keep up with the Hollywood styles. "Too bad that Thalberg can't help," he said.

Payment Deferred did not have the expected success. In New York it ran for only two days instead of the hoped-for week—in spite of the picture's undoubted power and one of the most realistic murder scenes in screen history, where Charles was shown putting cyanide of potassium into his nephew's glass.

The plain fact was that the economic depression had hit the movie houses. Even the most glowing reviews could not produce large audiences. The N.Y. *World-Telegram* praised the picture and called Charles's acting "splendid," but the box office did not read reviews.

By the middle of 1932 it was obvious that Hollywood could not do without Charles Laughton. The original contract idea of only two pictures a year with Paramount was thrown overboard. *Payment Deferred* had been made for Metro-Goldwyn-Mayer, *Old Dark House* for Universal; *The Sign of the Cross* was his second contracted picture for Paramount. The studio now suggested a third picture, based on a famous H. G. Wells novel, *The Island of Dr. Moreau.* Hollywood gave the picture the snappier title of *The Island of the Lost Souls.* It made the fifth picture Laughton had done in 1932.

This picture was intended as one more in the run of horror pictures designed to scare movie-goers at midnight shows. Dr. Moreau was a sinister professor who had holed up on an isolated island to experiment on animals until he found the super-formula which would turn animals into human beings and vice versa. A thoroughly nasty character, he did what he pleased with the poor creatures who fell into his power.

Having just finished Nero, Charles prepared to inject life into the cliché figure of the evil scientist.

It was a strange picture, both in its making and in its net effect. The cast included Bela Lugosi, Richard Arlen and Leila Hyams. They all embarked for Catalina Island, where the shooting was to be done. With them on the boat were two lions, a tiger, forty dogs, a cheetah and a puma. The Pacific was rough—both actors and animals got seasick. The wild animals raged and roared, and the tiger clawed one member of the company by reaching through the bars of its cage. The stench of the confined beasts was unbearable, as were the animals' shrieks, barks, cries and roars. What with the high seas and the wild beasts, no one could manage to eat a thing on the trip.

Laughton has never seen such horrors before. "I remember," he said, "each horror and monster had more hair than the one before. Hair was all over the place. I was dreaming of hair. I even thought I had hair in my food."

Laughton himself was not required to display hair and he was grateful for it.

The film's outdoor scenes and animal parts were shot in a matter of weeks. Charles was glad when that ordeal was over. He hired a seaplane to take him back to Hollywood—rather than return on the Noah's Ark of a boat. The animals had gotten on his nerves, as well as the part of Dr. Moreau. As always, Charles had made a study of real evil. The film, in fact, was so disturbing that it was banned in England. The British censors decided that, with all due respect to H. G. Wells, the theme of turning men into animals ran counter to the laws of nature.

By far the largest factor in the picture's total effect was Laughton's portrait of the sinister scientist. Deciding that his own face wouldn't do for the part, he designed a mask. This new face was based on an actual life model—Charles makes it a practice to lean on life whenever he can.

Charles's eyes had been bothering him for some time from the strain of the glaring lights of Hollywood sets. He went to see an eye specialist. The doctor in question wore square glasses and had an odd little beard and mustache. Charles no sooner set eyes on him than he thought, "There's my man." The respectable oculist became the model for the sinister Dr. Moreau.

Dick Arlen, who was of the cast on Catalina Island, once greeted Charles with the words, "How are you, Buster?" That started the fad of calling Charles, Buster. Charles took it with a laugh, and after a while got completely used to it.

Paramount had hired a double who was supposed to substitute for Charles in the scenes where a whip had to be cracked. "I, however, surprised everyone by being perfectly competent with a stock whip. There is quite a trick to cracking a whip so that no one gets hurt. I had mastered this difficult art—known mostly to circus members—in the course of preparing for *The Man with the Red Hair* in London. My coach had been a street entertainer from the sidewalks of London. What I had learned under London's Adelphi arches I now put to use in a most realistic and terrifying way on California's Catalina Island, temporarily renamed the island of lost souls."

Elsa Lanchester grew quite indignant over the banning of the picture in England. "If the British censors are saying that the picture is against the laws of nature," she countered tartly, "so is Mickey Mouse." But when it comes to censorship, many an artist has to learn to face it. Truth and art have to bow to convention.

The British market was cut off by the action of the censors, and since Hollywood has always depended on export profits the picture was another commercial failure. But even in America the rechristened H. G. Wells mystery thriller just did not catch on. The publicity office of the studio decided to do something to push it—it would be necessary to inject enormous quantities of "publicity adrenalin if it were to accumulate healthy grosses," to quote Arthur Mayer who was put in charge of this "noteworthy campaign."

It occurred to publicity expert Mayer that Laughton was still comparatively unknown in America. He therefore dreamed up a colossal nationwide contest to select a lovely young girl whom the sinister Dr. Moreau—

Laughton—would turn into a beast. The fortunate girl would receive a large prize and the title of "the panther woman of America."

This was a typical Hollywood notion. Charles, to whom such huckstering was completely foreign, shuddered at the whole thing and did not want to have any part of it. But the plan went along perfectly well without him. In fact, the Moreau Panther Woman Contest became a national sensation. Through the co-operation of the newspapers, each of the forty-eight states and Hawaii was combed for potential panther women. Later, each of the state winners competed for the crowning title of Panther Woman of America. In the end a Chicago girl won the contest. Charles, who had watched the men directing this "merely colossal" advertising campaign, said only, "The Panther Woman of America resembled a panther as much as Boris Karloff looks like a lamb."

When the day dawned for the final ceremonies in Chicago, where the prize was to be awarded and the all-important pictures taken, Paramount found that they could not locate a baby panther. They had to manage with a baby leopard, but the audience and movie fans were "not avid students of animal life. . . . No one was one whit the wiser."

Laughton carefully stayed out of the whole business, though he was the original Dr. Moreau. The campaign produced thousands of newspaper columns, radio interviews and picture-magazine publicity, but promotion boss Arthur Mayer was frank and experienced enough to warn Laughton, Paramount and the movie-goers that "no promotion campaign, regardless of its fanfare and its acceptance by the fans, is a substitute for old-fashioned word-of-mouth audience approval."

The picture proved to be a resounding dud. Everyone concerned was disappointed and worried. As for Laughton, the picture left a lasting mark on him. "I was never able to enjoy a zoo again. The very smell of caged animals reminded me of the Dr. Moreau picture, and made me sick."

Charles, who hadn't wanted to sign movie contracts for fear of being tied down, who was going to restrict himself to two pictures a year so that he would be able to play the classics on the stage, seemed to have turned a mental somersault. He now signed up for another picture—his sixth within his first Hollywood year.

When he decided to do that, he realized that the chief thing about it was that it gave him a chance to act under Ernst Lubitsch's direction. The picture was *If I Had a Million,* and Charles's part in it was very small. The shooting took only two days. But as Charles said, "To work with Lubitsch was worth my whole trip to America." The picture was made up of eight episodes in which eight different people unexpectedly receive a million dollars each. Charles was one of the eight "millionaires" picked at random from the telephone book.

For fear of more censorship troubles in England, Lubitsch shot two versions of some of the Laughton scenes. At one point Laughton had to give his boss the raspberry. He did it with such consummate artistry that it became something almost shocking. "My God, Charlie," Lubitsch exclaimed, "what shall we do? The English censor won't pass a raspberry." So they did a retake in which Charles conveyed the same mood in a more delicate fashion.

If I Had a Million had an enormous cast of stars, including Gary Cooper, Wynne Gibson, George Raft, Richard Bennett, Jack Oakie, W. C. Fields, among others. Everyone was eager to work under Lubitsch. Actually the picture was a kind of anthology of film scenes—eighteen authors, seven directors and fifteen stars were involved. "I played a wretched clerk who gets a million-dollar present and runs up flight after flight of stairs until I get to the top floor of the office building where the vice presidents and finally the great president of the company are to be seen." Here Charles performs that hilarious raspberry act.

Lubitsch was the one director in Hollywood who had his own complete staff, mostly Germans, which worked with him on every picture he made. Short, swarthy and scowling, with wildly rolling eyes, Lubitsch was the sort of man who seemed in motion even if he was sitting down. He had directed Mary Pickford, Emil Jannings and Greta Garbo. His technique was like no one else's—his whole approach to movie-making was unique. As a German, he was a fanatic for exactness. He never shot any scene without having every detail first worked out on paper. He insisted on the entire cast's assembling and going through a careful rehearsal. He personally would go through the rehearsals along with the actors, taking each part in turn. Once the shooting was under way, he had to sit back, but his face reflected every emotion of the actors.

He was one of Hollywood's really great figures, the man who had once been a bit actor under Max Reinhardt in Berlin. He and Laughton worked together in perfect harmony. Both of them conceived the clerk in the same way, as a man who had been entirely reduced to his functions as bookkeeper—a white-collar slave, more an adding machine than a man. It was a difficult role to put across, but Laughton did it. The reviews again referred to him as a great actor, but the film as a whole received a tepid response.

Elsa and Charles were quite concerned by the failure of the pictures. Elsa still had not found any steady acting job and she had rather good offers from London. Besides, there were film opportunities in England, too, at least for Elsa. Charles was never a good letter writer, but he promised to send cables, and the two parted.

When Thalberg started shooting *Payment Deferred* without her, Elsa Lanchester left for London, where she was famous in her own right and where she could be assured of a large, loyal audience. Attending the première of *The Sign of the Cross* in London, she met Alexander Korda. He asked her to come and talk business in his Grosvenor Street offices. The project he had in mind was to get Elsa and Charles into a picture he wanted to direct in Britain.

But this project had to wait until Charles went back to England, which he finally did after finishing his sixth picture. Everyone had heard of Charles's phenomenal success in America—by it he had become transformed into a famous Hollywood star who had to be treated accordingly.

Charles was very happy to go home to England. He planned to go out to their country place for a long rest— that is, for a few weeks. He was too active and keyed up to want more vacation than that. What he really wanted to do was to play the classics. He had done so little really serious acting that he was rather fed up with movie work for the time being.

Shortly before embarkation Laughton found that he was actually afraid of how he would fit into England again. Had he already eaten too much of the Hollywood lotus? He was very nervous on the boat, unable to relax or get a good night's sleep. He impressed the other passengers as erratic and tense. A reporter commented on his habit of "sitting with his legs under him, Buddha-like, on the edge of a sofa."

"I hate to face the press in England," he told a New York interviewer before he departed. "They are likely to resent outside popular acclaim. I'm frightened they will say I've gone Hollywood."

But Charles was wrong. He got a royal welcome in England, from the press down to the man on the street. Everyone had seen him in the pictures; even the porters at the dock and the taxi drivers knew who he was. Their smiles and greetings convinced him he had made good in America. He was a famous man now. "This fame allows one absolutely no private vices," he remarked.

How did he like Hollywood, everyone wanted to know, from reporters to his brothers and parents, uncles and night club entertainers.

"They are just grand people. I always had such fun on the lot, enjoyed every minute, found them all so jolly, such a lot of good stories and wisecracks going around, that I used to laugh until I was tired out, and that meant a wonderful night's rest. I never slept better than out there."

He was willing to admit that he had liked Hollywood. It had presented a great challenge to him, a challenge he'd met by voluntarily taking on six instead of the stipulated two pictures.

Publicity chief Arthur Mayer could not have promoted Hollywood better than Charles did on his home-coming.

But how had he liked the blondes?

Charles hesitated for a second. "Oh, the blondes," he said urbanely. "They are numerous, a collection of indistinguishable females."

The reporters noticed that he had arrived in London with very little luggage. He must have left most of his belongings in Hollywood—did that mean he was planning to return?

"Oh, not for a long time to come."

What were his plans?

"A vacation—perhaps the Old Vic."

"The Old Vic, really?"

"Why not?"

No one answered that question, but it was understood that nowhere in England would he be paid the twenty-five hundred dollars a week that Hollywood could afford.

Along with his one suitcase and small bag, Charles carried four unfinished cactus walking sticks.

"And what are those for, Mr. Laughton?" the reporters asked.

"They're a present for a chap who collects them. Just a small token of my great admiration for him."

"Might we ask for whom?"

"The greatest actor of us all."

This put the reporters on the spot. Who was the greatest living actor in England?

Laughton relieved their curiosity. "Gerald du Maurier," he said. "I thought you'd be able to guess it."

What did he think of British pictures, the reporters wanted to know.

"England's motion-picture production will not begin to rival those from the mills of Hollywood for more than ten years."

That was his final dictum to the press. Neither he nor the reporters knew how soon Charles's prognosis was to be reversed. For, while it might be argued that it would take ten years before J. Arthur Rank put Britain's motion-picture industry on the global map, it was only a matter of months before Alexander Korda, working in England, produced Laughton's greatest and still unsurpassed picture, *The Private Life of Henry VIII*.

Chapter 8

LAUGHTON'S RETURN to his homeland was triumphant. The London press accorded him a warm reception. He was heavily applauded for his declaration of loyalty to the London stage—Hollywood, he said, was only incidental to his stage career.

Laughton felt ready to tackle the classics, which in England meant Shakespeare and George Bernard Shaw. He was only thirty two; he felt it was important to prove he could play Shakespeare as well as the abnormal characters, the deep-dyed villains and unscrupulous gangsters he had occupied himself with hitherto (not that villainy was absent from Shakespearean dramas). But Charles was aware of the problems posed by Shakespearean language. There was much he would have to learn.

He hoped that after a well-deserved rest and a short vacation in Paris he would be ready to try his luck at the Old Vic. He had made enough money in Hollywood to manage with a curtailed income for a while. The main thing was to play Shakespeare.

It was a sort of restlessness which forced Charles to attempt Shakespearean roles at the height of his success. It is one of the peculiarities of genius that it drives its possessor to accomplish more and still more, never to rest on one's laurels, never to waste unexplored creative

111

abilities. This inner drive was nothing new. All great actors have been ridden by it—from Edwin Forrest, Edmund Kean, Edwin Booth, Joseph Jefferson, John Drew to John Barrymore. An actor likes to surprise his audience with some new and unexpected portrayal. Each role has to be greater and more brilliant than the one before—that is the surest way to preserve and add to his reputation and keep his place in the sun.

Laughton's agent, however, had different plans.

Charles had been in London only a week when his agent took him to see Alexander Korda. Korda was not yet Sir Alexander. He was known as an excellent director, but an inexperienced producer who was eager to go into movie-making in Britain.

Korda and Charles became friends immediately. Korda had been following Laughton's career in Hollywood with intense interest. He would love to make a British picture with Laughton in the title role. Would Charles consider a thing like that?

But all plans were still vague and indefinite, particularly the financial end of them. Conditions were such that a British film project seemed far in the distance. Laughton was not sure that anything would ever come of Korda's dreams. Charles determined to go on with his Shakespeare plans.

But when he went across to Paris for a weekend, he ran into Korda again. They had dinner together and Korda developed his idea.

"Charles, people have been after me to do a picture about Henry VIII. That would be just the thing for you."

Charles pricked up his ears. As a matter of fact, he had thought of Henry VIII himself—that little-played drama of Shakespeare's, that is. But Korda was going to work with a modern script. The film, besides being a lavish costume picture full of historical color, would present a new psychological portrait of that great eccentric monarch. Korda was interested in developing the

theory that the Bluebeard of kings was a deeply mis-
understood man. True, Henry had got rid of six wives;
but what had they done to him first that drove him to
extreme measures?

Here was Laughton's chance to do Henry VIII,
stripped of the glamour of being one of the monsters
of history. Did the idea appeal to him at all? Would he
care to play the wife-butcher with a new twist? Right
there at the dinner all fundamental decisions were made.
Charles was excited. As he saw it, the project promised
fun and challenge and a tremendous opportunity.

The project was to be organized along highly unorthodox lines—it was to be a co-operative, without salaries,
everyone to share in the profits and losses. Elsa would
play one of the six wives, Anne of Cleves. Korda's
brother would do the cutting, and friends were to be
recruited for subsidiary roles and jobs. The idea was to
keep costs down as much as possible.

Elsa had believed in the Korda production from the
very first. She was fascinated by the co-operative idea.
But she knew Charles wanted to think it over, to talk
with agents and to get legal advice.

It was not easy to save money in Hollywood. "I worked
hard for it—remember the hairy horrors," Laughton remarked to his wife. He did not want to lose what he had
saved in a film venture that might turn out to be a
stillborn child.

"You don't have to invest *all* the money," said Elsa.

The part of Henry VIII was the perfect role for
Laughton and he knew it. The co-operative idea meant
pioneering. It also meant to be young and daring. "That
is what I like," Laughton said.

After a long night's discussion—and the long tension
of indecision—the production fever took hold of both
Elsa and Charles.

Finally Charles picked up the phone and called Alexander Korda.

"Count me in. Elsa and you have sold me."

The Korda-Laughton team, in spite of tremendous differences and clashes of character, was the most creative and artistic production partnership the British film industry had ever seen.

The two men started hunting a cast as soon as they got back to London. They approached such top-flight stars as Robert Donat, Binnie Barnes, Merle Oberon and John Loder, and told them about the co-operative production idea.

The actors were hesitant and dubious at first, but finally they agreed to go into it. The general reaction was that if Korda and Laughton were crazy, they might as well be, too.

So began the filming of *The Private Life of Henry VIII*, with a scenario by the Hungarian, Lajos Biró. It was literally produced on a shoestring. The grandiose settings were mostly constructed out of canvas and pasteboard and decorated by young artists whom Laughton knew in London. "We were all young people and almost like a family group," said Charles later.

The whole technical staff, with very few exceptions, was Continental. The cameramen and stage designers came from the seven corners of Europe. There was some grumbling from certain quarters about a Hungarian's having been called in to treat British history, but Korda waved the criticism away. "Why not?" he demanded. "An outsider often makes the best job of a national film. He gets a fresh slant on things."

The sets looked so flimsy and so frail that Laughton often wondered whether the scenery would hold out for the duration of the shooting. "We were often apprehensive that while we were saying our lines the sets would collapse and smother us," Charles later recalled cheerfully.

The entire picture was shot in only five weeks at the amazingly low cost of fifty thousand dollars, but every-

one concerned had put in many months preparing the
actual shooting, polishing the screen play and creating
the beautiful dècor. Laughton was the moving force
behind the whole splendid teamwork. Everyone on the
set was caught up in his enthusiasm. He improvised,
revolutionized, added, cut, overacted, shouted, cried,
laughed and always gave the best that was in him. For
Laughton, the actual reading of the script was the least
part of it. In the back of his mind there was a living
model, a conception of character built up from a thousand little details.

He had put in weeks of advance work. For example,
he studied Tudor architecture in the belief that the arts
of the period would provide insights into the mind of
a man living in the Tudor period. He spent many days
in the famous Hampton Court Palace, with its spirited
decorations, great halls and pillars. Hampton Court was
the king's favorite residence, and Laughton endeavored
to steep himself in the atmosphere of the palace. He ate,
drank and slept Tudor history, and walked in those historic halls until he was almost convinced he was Henry
VIII. He embarked on a study of the king's love letters
and came to the conclusion that the monarch was not
just a scoundrel and a brute, but a man of many moods,
many unrequited hopes, wishes, loves and desires. Even
Henry's most infamous action—the execution of his wife
in order that he might marry his mistress—Laughton
found to have some basis in the king's concept of honor.

That was Laughton's typical way of preparing himself
for a role. He will spend months and, if necessary, years,
investigating the background of his character from every
angle. Added to this work is the continuous, unconscious
preparation that goes on within himself. Like so many
other great actors, he never reads a book or a play merely
to know what is in it. He absorbs it into himself, swal-
lows and digests it until it becomes a part of him. Every
actor has to get this outside nourishment if his subcon-

scious is to remain fertile. He has to renew himself constantly. The great actor is, in his way, an explorer of old and new frontiers. Life in all its manifestations interests him, even while he stands outside and above it. A great actor such as Laughton has the characteristic feature of a split personality—for the simple reason that he must play actor and spectator at the same time. Living in a make-believe world, the great actor never loses his sense of reality. This is one of the secrets of Laughton's long and unbroken success.

His finished portrait of Henry VIII was a masterpiece of boldness and complexity. Here was a king long dead— all that was left of him was history. But Laughton resurrected him as a living, breathing human being. As Laughton himself said, "I wanted to make him a true-life presentation, a man with livable and lovable qualities, for such he must have had to have achieved such tremendous popularity as he enjoyed. He was a fine linguist and accomplished musician; he composed two complete Masses. It has been my effort to show him as the man he was rather than as the despot he has been painted."

Charles went to look at Holbein's famous picture of Henry VIII at least a hundred times, searching to find out what lay behind the impenetrable, watchful, lusty, genial and kingly mask. That was how he looked—it was all there in the Holbein picture. But what was this man like who had ruled over England and Ireland, who had declared that "the law of every man's conscience be but a private court, yet it is the highest and supreme court of justice."

Laughton never worked so hard as he did on that picture. It was the role which "stretches everything you have and then asks for more," he said. There was, first of all, the problem of reconstructing the king physically. Some months before actual shooting, while the technical end of the picture was being prepared, Charles decided

As emperor in *I, Claudius,* Laughton was a little man with a stutter and a lame leg.

Laughton and the late Carole Lombard examine a small set for *They Knew What They Wanted.*

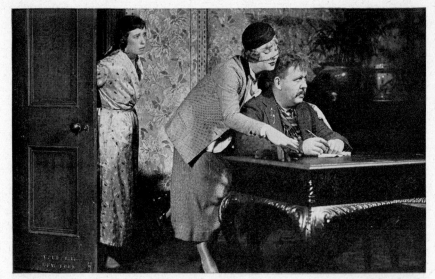

As Murder Marble, in **Payment Deferred,** Laughton plays the part so well deaf-mutes would understand him.

Having a twirl. As Ruggles, in **Ruggles of Red Gap,** Laughton gets into the swing of Americanism.

it was high time to start growing a beard. The beard was only an odd-looking tuft when Charles turned up at London's most prominent court tailors and asked the managers when their firm had been founded. It was an odd question and sounded all the more so coming from that strange character; but with British politeness they answered to the best of their ability.

Laughton had something definite in mind. He knew that tradition was very powerful in England and he reasoned that some of the royal tailoring firms in London must have been in business as far back as the sixteenth century, and consequently entrusted with the task of clothing the Tudor king.

His hunch was right. Three London firms traced their origins back to Henry VIII. The original sketches for the king's uniforms and dress were no longer in existence, but certain copies were. The firms produced the sketches out of their files.

That was a major stroke of luck. With the Holbein painting and the new-found sketches Charles could be outfitted as Henry VIII down to his hand-embroidered shirts and monogrammed handkerchiefs. The coats of gold brocade and the jewels without which the costumes would not have been complete were lent to the actor by Messrs. Simmons, one of the firms of tailors. The king's armor was easy to copy, as the original suit was on exhibit in the Tower of London—all two hundred and thirty-five pieces of it, weighing ninety-four pounds and standing six feet three inches.

Having solved the problem of costumes, having steeped himself in historic sites and having read everything there was to be read on the social and political history of the time, Charles still had the most difficult task of all—to create a psychological portrait that would be both convincing and original.

As in the case of Nero, Charles was not content with the standard picture of the cruel tyrant. Honesty demanded a deeper analysis of the man who had established Britain's firm supremacy of the seas, a great statesman and a great ruler, a man who loved women and destroyed them—who was perhaps a moral monster but who had succeeded in being a very popular and powerful king.

Laughton solved the enigma by playing his Henry VIII as a man split into many men. As a lover he had written daily love letters to Anne Boleyn, whose execution he was later to witness, drumming his fingers against the window glass. With his wedding slated for the day after the execution, he reminisced over his happiness with the late queen.

In Laughton's viewpoint, the king was not a man with two souls in his breast, but dozens of souls. A man, humble and arrogant, infantile and extraordinary, full of paradoxes, tired of women and still mad about them. He who dared to break with the Pope went to confession daily during the days of the London plague. But the greatest scene in the picture was the one in which the fifty-one-year-old king enters a wrestling match in order to impress his new, young and sexy wife, Catherine Howard, with the fact that he is still in the prime of life. The king actually wins his victory over England's finest wrestler—he proves his strength only to collapse afterward. Weak and sick, he hides away from his new wife. His great fear is that she will see him "old and defeated." Actually, she takes advantage of his absence to go to the arms of her former lover.

The wrestling match scene was marvelous. Laughton had taken lessons from a professional wrestler just so that he could handle that one scene. But in the scene that followed he really surpassed himself. It was the greatest bit of acting he had ever done, because Laughton could enter into it fully. He knew what it was like to fear rejection on physical grounds—he had gone through many such experiences in his younger days. In fact, if Laughton

was so superb in this picture, it was because in many a
scene he played himself.

He had much to contribute at story and production
conferences. He gave Korda points he had picked up in
Hollywood—particularly from Cecil de Mille, the master
of spectacle and mob scenes. De Mille, of course, had
a Hollywood budget to work with, but certain of his
tricks could be duplicated less expensively. *The Private
Life of Henry VIII* employed many of the illusions of
De Mille extravaganzas. Where the effect of splendor
and royal luxury was desired, Laughton warned, the producers had to be prepared to throw economy to the
winds. The scene picturing the household of King
Henry VIII at dinner was played by 150 men in a dining hall seventy feet long by forty feet wide. The walls
were twenty-four feet high and were hung with Holbein
tapestries. The servingmen and carvers passed in continuous processions along the tables which were laden
with hundreds of chickens and capons. Meat pies three
feet in diameter, and loaves of bread four feet long,
weighing fifteen pounds each, helped to give the proper
Tudor atmosphere.

The eating habits of the king have been immortalized
by Laughton in the unforgettably hilarious scene where
he eats capon after capon, throwing the bones over his
shoulders. This scene was based on sound research. As
Laughton put it: "The real Henry ate so dirtily that
they had to hold a cloth in front of his face. He was
a dirty-mouthed monster, but a great statesman for all
that."

But this was only one of a succession of memorable
scenes. The picture had everything—drama, color, thrills,
excitement, terrific love scenes and wild orgies. The
funniest scene in it took place in the canopied royal bed,
depicting the wedding night of Henry VIII and Anne
of Cleves. For character creation Elsa Lanchester's performance was equal to that of her husband's. She pre-

sents Anne of Cleves as an utterly green young woman, so wholesome, so naive, that Henry, old libertine that he was, did not know what to do with her. She had arrived from Germany that same day—the marriage having been arranged on the advice of Henry's diplomats, who had pointed out the advantages of an alliance with Germany in case of future trouble with France. So Henry went through with the marriage, never bargaining with what actually happened. Elsa Lanchester did a consummate job of portraying a placid German girl who had never been told the facts of life and who still believed in the stork.

The king had never known anyone quite so stupid, so hopelessly innocent, so idiotically funny and so entirely without sex appeal. Here was a fine mess. What should he do with this new wife? Behead her as he had done the others?

The truth of the matter was that Anne of Cleves was not half so innocent as she seemed. She was in love with another man and had to extricate herself from the marriage with Henry before the king sent her to the gallows, and above all, before the wedding night was over.

As Anne seemed to know nothing about sex and love, Henry finally asked, "What can you do?"

"I can play cards," says Anne, seating herself demurely on the edge of the bed. She is in her nightgown and Henry is in his dressing gown and nightcap. He sends for cards, claiming that he is the best card player in England. Giggling furiously, Anne starts playing. The astonishing thing is that she wins and keeps on winning.

The scene ends with a gentleman's agreement. Henry still does not know what to do with this impossible girl.

"You can't chop off my head," she says coquettishly. "Not my head—because all of Europe will call you a wife butcher and there will be political trouble."

Henry's face lights up—has he heard aright? Is there

a way out after all? Can this stupid German girl know
the score, after all?

"Why don't you divorce me and behave like a civilized
gentleman?"

Elsa pronounces these words in a high-pitched voice,
with a wonderful German accent which must have taken
weeks to acquire. She sits back to watch her own husband, as Henry VIII, smirking with relief. For the
moment, Henry is the happiest man in England. Anne
can have everything she wants if she will agree to a
divorce and spare him the necessity of getting rid of her
by more drastic means.

As always in the realm of art, Laughton was unpredictable. He was a surprise to everyone, even to Elsa
Lanchester. He acted like a tornado let loose and yet
with superb control. He gave the character of Henry
wit, grandeur and veiled pathos.

Of his acting he himself said, "It is by far the best
I've ever done. The film has smart dialogue, and the
method of telling a story is new. It is as if someone ran
a penny camera along the sexual life of a man. Still, I
like to shade my characterization on the side of repres-
sion, at least until the climactic moments arrive."

What Charles liked most about the picture was that
it concentrated squarely on a man. Too many movies,
he felt, depended for their drama upon anything else
but human character. Here was a lusty and ever-inter-
esting film about a single person. And the part of Henry,
with its rich gamut of emotion, was ideal for Charles.

His genius shone out in that picture like a beacon
light. His acting was so great and so free from exaggeration that it defied imitation. The role seemed to offer
wonderful opportunities for artistic exhibitionism, but
the fact was that Charles had already developed beyond
this. He was less interested in himself as an actor than

in the art itself. Quite unwittingly, he was establishing himself as the first man of the stage.

This did not mean that he was easy to work with. Alexander Korda had a terrible time with Laughton. He turned out to be a perfectionist, demanding rehearsals and still more rehearsals, insisting on getting every detail completely right—when Korda was trying to keep expenses down. Korda's final comment was: "What he needs is not a director but a midwife. He has a feverish will for being superlatively good, a wonderful sincerity."

Charles always has been a real perfectionist. Like Oscar Wilde, he could say, "I've worked very hard all morning," and when asked, "At what, Charlie?" he could answer with the utmost gravity, "I wrote a comma into the script."

"And what did you do in the afternoon?"

"I took the comma out again."

Finally Charles was willing to let well enough alone, and the picture was finished. With some trepidations it was loosed upon an unsuspecting world. "We were fairly satisfied with it," Laughton said later, "but never for a moment did we think it would be the great financial success that it was. We would have sold it to the first bidder."

Only there were no bidders.

The morning after the London trade première found Korda in a deluge of wild, enthusiastic and genuine praise. The film seemed to have made a hit. Charles, however, was not present—he had gone back to Hollywood. There was no sense waiting around for the picture to be released, he thought. Besides, the trade preview had little or no bearing on the ultimate success of a picture.

It was many months later when the official opening took place in Paris. Both Laughtons made a point of attending—this was the crucial event.

With them in the audience were a British princess and

Maurice Chevalier. The princess and Charles were deep in an interesting conversation when the latter, deferentially and with his most charming smile, whispered to the royal guest, "Do you know, I don't know how to address you properly."

The princess whispered back with as charming a smile, "Don't tell anyone that I told you—you ought to be calling me 'Ma'am.'"

Maurice Chevalier gave an after-theater party for Charles and a few close friends, including a well-known American newspaperman. He had picked one of Paris' most elegant restaurants for the occasion—had ordered the dinner in advance—the choicest hors d'oeuvres, frogs' legs, fish and a variety of wines. Charles was very happy—he was enjoying the little party to the hilt when the American journalist, with her somewhat raw sense of humor, called out to the waiter, "Garçon, what about some ketchup?"

Happy, proud, exhausted and renewed, Charles immediately set out for London. He had postponed getting to the classics long enough.

Meanwhile, Paramount was distributing *Henry VIII* in America. They spent a fortune on promoting the picture. Catch lines for the picture appeared everywhere, handbills and posters were distributed, and the advertising department of Paramount outdid itself. The film was advertised as a supercolossal portrait of "a forgiving soul, always ready to bury the hatchet—in his wife's neck."

"Laughton," some ads read, "never raised his hand to a woman—he just chopped off their heads."

"Every woman got it in the neck eventually."

"Every woman was merely an ax-dent in his life."

Wrestling contests were held all over America in the style of Henry VIII. Eating contests were staged in imitation of Charles in his famous bone-throwing scene. The restaurants in one large town where the film was being shown displayed posters, such as:

How To Eat à la Charles Laughton

1. Tear bird to shreds with your hands.
2. Pound with fists to flatten bird.
3. Devour as fast as possible.
4. Throw bones over left shoulder.
5. Finish meal with a few choice burps.

Newspapers, radio commentators, interviewers and columnists quoted from the picture *ad nauseam*. They concentrated on the idea of Henry VIII as a Bluebeard— a rakehell who had disposed of six wives and knew everything there was to be known about love and marriage.

"If you want to be happy, marry a stupid woman," was a characteristic quotation.

The film swept the world. It was shown in Nazi Germany, where its humorous treatment of a despot was disliked by the powers that be. Charles attended the London première with his full harem of wives—all six queens were present in the flesh, underlining the fact that Laughton had played with the most beautiful women an actor could desire. The crowning success of all was that America bestowed the Motion Picture Academy Award of Merit on Charles Laughton for his superb performance. He was hailed as the outstanding actor of the year 1933—Katharine Hepburn sharing the honors as the year's outstanding actress.

A thousand people witnessed the ceremonies at Hollywood's Ambassador Hotel.

Charles was in London when the award was announced. It was some months before he could be on the scene and offer his brief comment:

"I never thought it would be given to an English actor in an English picture. But there shouldn't be any barriers between the English and the American stage, and

I think this gesture will help to impress that on the people. . . . That was a sporting gesture."

Looking over the audience, his eye fell on Walt Disney. With typical unconventionality he suggested that Disney should have got the award instead of himself. "There's your great man. Great because he is simple and unaffected. . . . He is already a greater storyteller than Hans Christian Andersen, and there is no telling to what heights he will still rise."

Disney was somewhat nonplused but was quick to return the compliment. "Charlie, no one of us knows what heights you'll reach after this award."

The prediction came true. *Henry VIII* was a high point in Laughton's career, but by no means the only high point. And twenty years later he returned once more to his pet creation—representing Henry VIII in *Young Bess,* shown during the coronation festivities of the *second* Queen Elizabeth.

Chapter 9

ᴬLTHOUGH I HAVE, so to speak, slept with the classics at my bedside, I haven't had a classical education. I asked myself how I intend to face myself in later years if I never accepted the opportunity to obtain something of a classical education. I realized that I was getting older and that if I didn't realize the desire soon I would in a short time be set in the money-making class and the ambition would disappear."

London was amazed by Laughton's determination. In spite of his enormous success as Henry VIII, and the fabulous motion-picture offers that flowed from that success, he turned his back on those temptations and joined the stock company of the Old Vic—The Sadler's Wells Company, home of England's classic repertoire. For eight consecutive months he appeared in Shakespearean and other classical plays, sometimes in the leading roles, but as often in minor parts. His salary was one hundred dollars a week, which was not even a twentieth of what Hollywood had paid him. He put in an average of fourteen hours a day studying, preparing and rehearsing his roles—and was immensely happy doing it.

All his life Laughton had cherished the idea that the greatest thing an actor could do was to play Shakespeare. Not that he did not have certain misgivings as to his own competence.

He had joined the Old Vic Company in an almost religious spirit. This was his way of laying an offering on the altar of drama.

Other motives entered into his desire. He must have felt the move would improve him and uplift him as an actor—perhaps purify his actor's soul.

What else did Shakespeare represent, besides personal salvation from commercialism, to Laughton? Shakespeare was the supreme master of the English language. The Shakespearean texts were the great proving grounds of an actor's ability. And that was the rub. For Laughton's great respect for classical drama and all his hard work did not help—he was simply not cut out for a Shakespearean actor. He himself will nowadays confess, when he is in a humble mood, that Shakespeare was the one defeat in his life. But this was not at first apparent.

"I went to the Old Vic," he explained at the time, "to learn to speak." People thought it strange that an actor who had won the coveted Academy Award should feel that his speech needed improvement. But Charles meant more than the mere speaking of lines. He was haunted by the feeling that he had not yet given his best. "As we English say, I've just muddled along, clowning a lot and playing with roles." There must be a more profound approach to acting, he thought.

Fame had come to him, it was true, but he was out for the higher glories. He wanted to study and work, not cash in on an easy Hollywood success. That's what he had gone back to England for, instead of lolling in Hollywood.

Elsa had found a flat for them on Jermyn Street. Together they enjoyed walks through St. James's Park and over Westminster Bridge. Both felt suddenly as young as students, excited by the experimental venture into which they had thrown themselves.

For the Old Vic's Shakespearean productions were not the old-fashioned, cumbersome affairs Londoners had been accustomed to. A spirit of modernity was in the air. "The group at the Old Vic was scrapping old conventions in favor of something more vital. We tried to go back to the Elizabethan open stage, without any curtain drops. This is the sort of stage the plays were written for originally. Why not use it now? There is a chance to build up excitement that you don't have when an intermission takes place."

All his life Laughton has been an iconoclast regarding theater tradition, so that kind of experimentation was familiar to him. Here was his chance to do Shakespeare under the very conditions for which the plays had been written. He discovered, however, that "real" Shakespeare demanded a kind of acting different from anything he had ever done. New techniques had to be discovered, new approaches tried.

"I found that those monologues should not be kept down as part of the play. They were much more effective if I stepped right down as near the audience as possible and addressed those rhetorical questions—that, after all, is what those monologues really are—directly to the audience."

Laughton became a Shakespeare expert within a few months. He had arrived at some theories which he passed on to his fellow actors at many a midnight session at his flat. "On the stage everything must be projected through the voice," he told them. "The voice is the important thing. The closer you get to the audience, the more effect will the voice have."

There was a good reason why Laughton put so much stress on this idea. His main task was to rediscover the power of his voice, for the motion picture focused attention on the visual end of acting rather than on the spoken word. Charles was having a tough time making the readjustment back to the stage and to a living audience after two years of working exclusively for the camera—which is nothing more than a giant eye.

The Old Vic was a repertory company, and Laughton was in a new play every month. He was Henry VIII in Shakespeare's play of that name, was Angelo in *Measure for Measure,* Prospero in *The Tempest,* Canon Chasuble in *The Importance of Being Earnest,* Tattle in *Love for Love.* Finally, like a dream come true, he made his appearance as Macbeth.

This is where the tragic flaw of Charles Laughton's art became apparent for all to see. From the time he had been a boy, Charles's dream of glory had been to act in *Macbeth.* But he could not do it—he could not carry it off convincingly.

He would have given his right arm to have been able to speak Shakespearean lines with the grace and power of John Gielgud or the easiness of Laurence Olivier. As it was, he bollixed up role after role. His fellow actors watched what was happening and shook their heads. He had done much more and had explored wider fields and won far greater success than the rest of them—Ursula Jeans, Flora Robson, Athene Seyler, Marius Goring. He had had the kind of recognition every actor must hope for. But when it came to Shakespeare, he couldn't get to first base. No one seemed able to help him, not even the great producer Tyrone Guthrie.

After playing Macbeth at the Old Vic, Charles said of himself, "I stank it up." Flora Robson, who had played Lady Macbeth, analyzed it this way: "He had the intensity needed for Shakespeare, but no feeling for the poetry. He just rolled it out like a steam roller."

From his try at Macbeth, Laughton learned his lesson. The great Shakespearean roles were not for him. He had dreamed of doing King Lear—every great actor in history had had a try at it. But the eternal tragic element eluded Laughton—he was essentially a child of his time. He put everything he had into the part, but the effect was somehow wrong. He could be bold and forceful, but he lacked delicacy.

For a while Charles nursed the illusion that the trouble lay in not having enough time to prepare his role. The role of Macbeth had already driven Charles to the verge of exhaustion. "If I have to do Macbeth six times a week, I'll be ready for the hospital," he said. He was beginning to realize that there was something about the concept of tragic character which was beyond his scope. Up to that time he had conceived of tragedy as the plight of an unfortunate fellow in bad circumstances. His great trick —his way of giving three dimensions to a character—had been to project the commonplace, comic side of a figure. He had used that trick with great success in dealing with Henry VIII, Nero and his London stage roles. But this typically Laughtonesque trick would not apply to the tragic heroes of Shakespeare. When playing Shakespeare, even the greatest actor has to play Shakespeare and not his own highly individualistic variations. In tackling Macbeth, Laughton, for the first time in his career, was in a position where he could not play Laughton.

The reviewers were not pleased with him. "An unhealthy portrait," was the verdict on his Macbeth. He had made his Macbeth a soft, flabby man, a weakling tied to his wife's apron strings. He had overacted the big scenes. The resulting portrayal might have been interesting, but it was not true to Shakespeare, as Charles knew better than anyone else. The only newspaper that had a good word to say for the Laughton performance was the *London Observer*. While not lauding him as a great interpreter of Shakespeare, it stated: "Laughton communicated what Shakespeare originally craved—something to make the senses giddy."

Charles did his best to compensate for the deep-seated weakness by giving a heavy emotional charge to his performance. But nobody was fooled. A lesser actor could have gotten away with it, but not Laughton. London expected first-class acting from Laughton. He drew full houses anyway—people had heard about his strange

Shakespeare performances and came out of curiosity—
but this was not Charles's idea of success. He did not give
up. He kept at it, hoping that he could break through to
the real thing. The miracle never happened. Shakespeare
was and has remained Laughton's major stumbling block.

He did get something out of those eight months of
playing Shakespeare—and that was a command of spoken
English. One might say that it bore fruit when, later on,
he gave his masterful reading of the Gettysburg Address.
But as far as Shakespearean poetry went, he had to give
it up for good. The man who in the eyes of the public
would make the ideal Shakespearean actor shuns it as
if it were a plague. He has a positive terror of it. "I
wouldn't tackle Shakespeare without a metronome," he
will say.

Over the years Laughton has evolved some very definite
ideas about the right way to recite Shakespearean lines,
ideas which would probably shock most lovers of the
Bard.

"The verse of Shakespeare has always made nonsense
to me unless one follows strictly his iambic pentameter—
de-dum, de-dum, de-dum, de-dum, de-dum; but the whole
thing is bound up in wanting to communicate something
you like to others and have them like it too. I knew that
some people might be angry with me for saying this. . . .
I know a particular friend of mine who would be disappointed in me. Her name is Margaret Pendergast
McClean. She is a speech teacher and she coaches
Shakespeare classes on voice control. I know that we have
to have standard speech on the professional stage; in great
centers like New York and Chicago you couldn't put on
plays with all the actors speaking in the several accents
of their home towns. Still I would like to hear *Julius
Caesar* in Iowa in the strong speech of the Middle West.
And *Julius Caesar* in Oregon in the speech of the Far
West, and *Julius Caesar* in New Orleans in the soft and
lovely speech of the South. This would not do if your

interest is strictly in ancient Rome, but I think *Julius Caesar* is more about man as a political animal in the town in which it is being played in that year and at that moment. I hope Mrs. McClean will understand this and will know that we are not ungrateful for what she has so effectively and patiently taught us."

As late as 1950 Laughton still remembered the trouble he had had with Shakespeare. "Not all Shakespeare suits me," he said. "I would warn beginners away from his sonnets, even as I imagine young violinists are urged not to break their hearts on a Beethoven sonata."

His personal failure as a Shakespearean actor has not prevented him from continuing to idolize Shakespeare and from being most critical of Shakespeare productions by others. He was indignant when he saw the Max Reinhardt Hollywood production of *A Midsummer Night's Dream* which threw in a wolflike pack of dogs. "This may have fitted Reinhardt settings, but did not fit the Shakespearean text," Laughton felt.

Thanks to his bout at the Old Vic, Laughton's voice developed amazingly. It was a revelation to hear him speak. His perfect diction, his control of tone, his power to convey tragic and elemental depths—were all new. For eight months he had struggled with rhythm and alliteration—with the greatest poetry of the English language. For Laughton, no experience has ever been wasted, and it may be said that that period in his life was one of the most rewarding of all. He remembers it with very happy feelings. "The young people loved it. It was as exciting as a four-alarm fire," he said. In time his own difficulties took on a comic guise. "I was not so hot—there was some spitting from the critics but no coughing from the stalls."

After one season at the Old Vic, it was time to think of heading west again. Charles had his American contract to fulfil. It would not seem that his recent training would come in handy in Hollywood. The typical American

A quiet day at home before filming *The Beachcomber.* "If Charles puts his hand in mine I do not have to act."

Laughton's part in *The Beachcomber* brought out romantic tendencies.

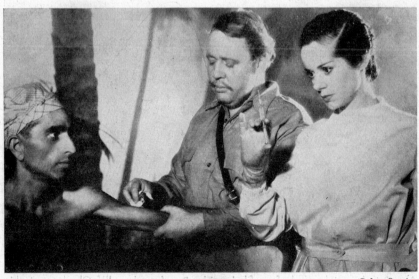

A lovable cad and a missionary lady aid victims of a typhus epidemic.
Laughton and Elsa Lanchester in *The Beachcomber.*

Culver Service

Even with this expression he won the lady over.

Penguin Photos

Smiles—his and hers.

In spite of De Mille's objections, Laughton's Nero in **The Sign of the Cross** was that of a colossal fool.

movie actor had never bothered much with voice training, and the language of the average motion picture
seldom rose above the level of Mickey Spillane, the fan
magazines and the confession magazines. Even on the
general scene, in the fields of politics, education, etc., the
standard of speech was low. It was an open secret on
Broadway that the poorer the actor's speech, the more
money he stood to make.

America had no "classic" drama tradition. Those who
tried to foster some such thing in the theater were
written off as "high-brows." The new type of serious
American play was folksy, colloquial and called for plain
speaking and plain acting. As for the actor on radio or
television, he would do better to study current slang than
Shakespearean poetry.

Before leaving London for Hollywood, Laughton had
another experience which was to be crucial to his further
development. It so happened that Stefan Zweig was in
London. Hollywood had just bought Zweig's best seller,
Marie Antoinette, and Laughton had advance word that
he was being considered for the role of the French king.
It was only natural that author and actor should meet.
The two had many interests in common. Laughton could
describe how he had gone about reconstructing the
character of Henry VIII. His researches had touched on
Mary Stuart, whose biography Zweig was then writing.
Then there was the whole fascinating subject of the
relationship between Louis XVI and Marie Antoinette.

Stefan Zweig was living at Portland Place, not far from
Edgar Wallace's old residence. Newcomer to London as
he was, his home had already attracted some of the
greatest figures of contemporary music and literature.
Bruno Walter and Arturo Toscanini were faithful visitors
—Zweig knew them from early days, as he had written
biographies of them both. John Drinkwater was a visitor
and H. G. Wells. It seemed that Zweig had something to
contribute to such diverse personalities as Austen

Chamberlain, Lady Astor or Dr. Rudolf Bing, who later was to become director of the Metropolitan Opera. As for Laughton, he felt at home with Zweig from the first minute. That writer had a special interest in actors—he had once written a penetrating study of Vienna's greatest character actor, Joseph Kainz. In many ways Laughton reminded him of that genius of the stage.

Zweig was deeply shaken by developments in Germany and Central Europe since Hitler had come to power. The horrors of Nazism were on his mind constantly. Through the conversations with Zweig, Charles was, for the first time, brought face to face with the reality of the Nazi regime, its terror, its brutality, its smashing of culture. A recent incident in which Zweig had been personally involved brought it all home. Zweig had written a libretto for a new opera by Richard Strauss, *The Silent Woman*. Strauss's position in the new Germany had been quite secure—Hitler had personally always liked Strauss's music and had therefore appointed him head of the Nazi Music Chamber.

However, a few days before the première of *The Silent Woman*, the Nazis discovered that Strauss was going to present an opera based on the libretto of the Jew Stefan Zweig and the half-Jew Hugo von Hofmannsthal. This was a real crisis. Strauss was called before Hitler, who said he would make an exception just once and let him put on the Zweig-Strauss opera in Dresden. But after the second performance, Goebbels and the Nazi Party raised such a howl that the opera had to be discontinued. As a result of all this, Strauss was fired from the presidency of the Music Chamber. His letters of indignation at the state of things in Germany had been intercepted and turned over to the Gestapo.

Laughton was horrified. He thought there must be some effective way of protesting such barbarous cultural censorship. "Isn't there some way for you to fight back?" he asked. Zweig answered him quietly: "Not I. It's up to those whose books were not burned in Germany to do the protesting."

The discussion turned to Louis XVI. Charles felt that the French monarch was "not a very pleasant character to play; an interesting characterization, though." He was looking forward to doing it, but was sorry that the Hollywood film moguls did not see fit to bring Stefan Zweig to Hollywood to help with the film script. Perhaps if Laughton had had his way and the great writer had been called to Hollywood, things would have turned out differently and Zweig would not have committed suicide, as he was to do a few years later in Brazil.

Zweig's final comment on Laughton was: "Laughton *ist klug wie der Tag* ("Laughton is clever as the Day"). This great actor can make figures out of the past live before our eyes. No piece of writing can ever quite do as much." But Zweig was wrong.

They said good-by, Laughton never suspecting that he would not see the great Austrian writer again. When, during the war, news of Zweig's suicide reached Laughton in Hollywood, he was deeply depressed. There was something the matter with a world in which men like Zweig could not survive.

Zweig's death always seemed to Laughton as if Goliath had won against David. When Goliath Hitler finally vanished from the earth, Laughton knew David had won the final battle. He began to read the Bible story of young David in English, Spanish, and French. His audiences loved these readings, which put Laughton squarely on the side of David in a world full of would-be Goliaths.

Chapter 10

THE *Berengaria* sailed for New York with Charles and Elsa on it. They had boarded the swift luxury liner at the very last minute. They were expected at the Hollywood studio within a week. Charles seemed physically exhausted. The last days in London had been maddening, with evening performances still going on, farewell parties, packing, seeing agents and commuting weekends between the country cottage in Surrey and London. The Laughtons hoped to snatch a bit of a rest on the *Berengaria*. After all, Charles had played seven Shakespearean roles within eight months. That was something of a feat.

In spite of his physical tiredness, Charles felt mentally newborn as an actor. The spell with the Sadler's Wells Company had been an emotional holiday for him. It was personal progress even if it had not been a public triumph. The reviews certainly had not been anything to boast about—one critic had gone so far as to call him a complete flop. But Charles was returning to America spiritually refreshed, inspired, his art enriched with a new vitality, subtlety and significance. He felt he had reached maturity.

During the long night hours—Charles always slept badly on board ship—he felt the hard waves pounding monotonously against the *Berengaria* and he evaluated these eight months. When all was said and done, he

136

decided, they had been the most important months in his life.

Still a young man, Laughton knew he had some important accomplishments behind him. But he also knew that Hollywood success was about as substantial as a soap bubble. It was neither secure nor final. Every new picture was a new start.

The Barretts of Wimpole Street was to be his first film on his return. He had been away more than a year. What would Hollywood be like this time? Economic logic dictated that he go back to Hollywood every so often, but he did not welcome the prospect—especially now, when he was constantly on the verge of seasickness. In the long hours when he lay stretched out in his cabin, he fixed on the policy he would adopt toward Hollywood. He would conserve his emotions and vitality and not let himself get excited about anything or anybody. Because Hollywood is the most excitable city on the globe, obsessed by a sense of its own importance and determined to impress every one of the then two hundred and fifty thousand movie-colony employees—whether stars, set designers, camera-men or producers—with a sense of their own individual littleness compared with the city's supreme might.

The first-class passengers on the *Berengaria* soon heard about the famous personality in their midst. Soon every-one was staring or pointing Laughton out to others. The many on board who had seen him in the movies or on the stage felt they had a special claim on his attention. Charles's and Elsa's hopes of being left alone and allowed to rest almost immediately came to nothing.

The newspapermen also caught scent of them. It turned out that there were reporters from six nations on board, hunting for stories. There was the usual swarm of auto-graph seekers, too, and the more forward passengers had questions they wanted to ask Charles. One reporter collared Charles in the lounge and asked when his ambition to go on the stage had really begun. Laughton could not answer that one because he honestly could not remember. All he knew was that he had never wanted to be anything but an actor. "You have got to remember," he said, looking around at the luxurious surroundings, the rich, pampered first-class passengers, "that I was brought up in a country pub and that all my people were hotelkeepers. I'm just stepping into the world of culture."

The other passengers were, of course, thrilled to be traveling with such celebrities as the famous Mr. Laughton and his wife. In casual conversation Laughton tried to make them understand that the life of a star is far from being all glory and enjoyment. What did they know of the secret fears of an actor, of the tensions and emotions before, during and after a film production? Movie-making was a crazy business. He doubted whether any of the fortunate folk on board appreciated this. Just to give them an idea, he described what Claudette Colbert, that wonderfully warm and gentle actress, had gone through during the shooting of *The Sign of the Cross*.

Miss Colbert was plainly scared during the climactic scenes of the picture. The entire cast had been terrified. After controlling her nervousness as long as possible, she had given up and burst out with: "Gosh, here's the corner where we turn to face the cameras. I hope my nose doesn't itch—or the mascara doesn't melt into my eye—or that darned leopard behind me doesn't make a move. Why in heaven's name does Mr. De Mille have to bring in the zoo on scenes like this. If the leopard moves even a little, I know I'm going to scream."

Charles re-enacted this little scene and got a laugh for it. But it wasn't so funny when it really happened, as well he knew. To contend with such worries and bother-ations every day was something like hard work. And all that was in addition to the deeper fears and anxieties faced by every actor.

No actor returns to Hollywood with calm emotions

before a new picture. "It's a goofy place," Charles told
the ship reporters, "but I like it. It's the perfect
mummers' home. If you weren't a little bit mad you
wouldn't go there."

With good reason he thought much of De Mille during
the voyage. The great director had taught him so much
in the past. Now his mind kept reverting to something
De Mille had once said, "The only formula for a good
motion picture is a good and true drama, and cold people
never make a warm picture."

What did that mean for Charles's own future? He knew
that there was some sort of almost magic current running
between himself and his audience. He, for his part, was
immensely suggestible; at the same time he exerted a
curious attraction upon his audience. But in those hours
of re-evaluation he realized he would have to put his foot
down to prevent the studios from typing him as the
eternal monster. He would also have to have the strength
to reject temptations, particularly the temptation of the
almighty dollar, which was America's most blatant lure.
Thus and only thus would he be able to assert himself
as an actor in the mad mill of make-believe which was
Hollywood.

No more rude savages for him, no matter how high the
offers. "I don't care what kind of parts I'll play," he told
the shipboard reporters, "so long as they are varied. I
would rather be called a versatile ham than a one-part
actor."

The reporters seemed to be merciless in their curiosity.
"Why aren't you a Shakespearean actor?" they asked.
Why? He had asked himself that question many a time
during the painful hours of self-analysis. Why? It was
obvious—he could only play his ideas about a Shakespeare
character; he never entered into the character's actual
being. His worst trouble was his satirical view of human
nature. It was nothing he could assume or set aside. Satire
was an essential part of his equipment as an actor. He had

always given a satiric twist to his interpretations of monsters—so much so that critics had compared him to Charlie Chaplin.

Charles Laughton did not give that notion much thought. On the whole he did not pay much attention to what critics had to say about his art, although he always made a point of co-operating with the press. At that time and since he has acted on the assumption that, on the whole, newspapermen were people of intelligence. But there were glaring exceptions.

He took the opportunity to speak his mind on this subject to the ship reporters. He said he would be perfectly glad to work along with them if it weren't for certain unpleasant incidents where members of the fourth estate had overstepped their privileges. Occasionally notices which definitely riled him appeared in fan magazines. As an example he quoted a piece by a well-known woman journalist. While he wasn't one for keeping clippings, this one had stuck in his memory. It began:

"Charles Laughton, homely to the point of repulsiveness, sprawled on his couch in the Metro-Goldwyn-Mayer dressing room and stroked the legs of the golden statuette awarded him by the Motion Picture Academy."

"I'm not sensitive about my appearance," he told the newspapermen, "but this was a kind of shock. And stroking the golden legs—my God, what in the world was the woman thinking of?"

But the lecture on professional ethics was not necessary. The American press gave Charles a wonderful welcome, as did the Hollywood studios.

The Laughtons remained in New York only one day and flew to Hollywood via Chicago. They used a short stop in Chicago to see Thornton Wilder, whom Charles had admired for years, ever since meeting him at a dinner at Arnold Bennett's. Wilder is one of America's foremost intellects, thrice winner of the Pulitzer Prize. He is known all over the world for his novel *The Bridge of San Luis Rey*. The famous bridge, by the way, was one entirely of his own invention, though visitors to Peru have been so persistent in their inquiries—"And where is the Bridge of San Luis Rey?"—that guides have had to dream one up to please them.

Wilder speaks English, French, German, Italian and Spanish fluently. He has lived in Yucatan and Rome, Hong Kong and Connecticut. He was friend and disciple of George Bernard Shaw and Gertrude Stein, a watcher at the sickbed of Sigmund Freud and an occasional inter- preter for Ortega y Gasset. He has taken walking trips down the Rhone with boxing champion Gene Tunney. Wilder's circle of acquaintances is wide and varied. Among his friends are actors and professors, prize fighters and Chicago gunmen, waitresses and erstwhile members of Alcoholics Anonymous. Laughton became one of Wilder's real friends.

That genial gentleman, full of vitality and energy, has contributed enormously to the American theater. Theatrical director Garson Kanin said of him: "When- ever I'm asked what college I've attended, I'm tempted to say: Thornton Wilder."

The plane stop in Chicago was only for thirty minutes. By careful prearrangement, Wilder met the Laughtons at the airport. He wasted not a moment, and immediately started to exposit the difference between the European and the American mind. He felt it necessary to set Charles Laughton clear on this point, for Charles must have grown up in the belief that the European mind with its tradition and training had a greater claim to culture than the American. Said Wilder:

"From the point of view of the European, an American is nomad in relation to place, disattached in relation to time, lonely in relation to society, and insubmissive to circumstance, destiny or God. It is difficult to be an

American, because there is as yet no code, grammar, decalogue by which to orient oneself. Americans are still engaged in inventing what it is to be an American. . . .

"Americans could count and enjoyed counting. They have lived under a sense of boundlessness. And every year a greater throng of new faces poured into their harbors, paused, and streamed westward. And each one was one. To this day, in American thinking, a crowd . . . is not a homogeneous mass . . . but is one and one and one.

"Every human being who has existed can be felt by us to be existing now. All time is present for a single time. Every American has this sense, for the American is the first planetary mind."

Laughton would lend a respectful ear to anything Thornton Wilder said. For Wilder's memory and erudition, when it comes to the theater, was boundless. He could tell Charles which *Othello* production had been shown in Berlin in 1927, in Glasgow in 1929. Wilder is an expert on Shakespearean plays. Still, this matter of a "planetary mind"—wasn't that going a bit too far? Laughton and he were in the midst of a lively discussion when the loud-speaker announced the departure of the plane. There was no time to settle the matter just then. Laughton and Elsa hurried up the steps, waving good-by to a good friend who promised to visit them in California.

The Laughtons found things in Hollywood in their usual state of confusion. They had no sooner settled at the good old Garden of Allah when Charles was in conference with Irving Thalberg, who was about to produce *The Barretts of Wimpole Street*.

It turned out that Thalberg was by no means enthusiastic about casting Charles as the father in this tender, simple story dealing with the beginning of the love affair of poets Robert Browning and Elizabeth Barrett. It wasn't that Thalberg had anything against Charles—quite the contrary. He felt that the part of Papa Barrett was too small for an actor of Charles's caliber. Also that Charles might lose popularity by stamping himself in the public eye as the wicked head of the Barrett family. And Thalberg, if anyone, should have known that, for he was considered one of the canniest brains in the business— besides being famous for his taste in all matters of movie-making.

Laughton, however, insisted on taking the role at his own peril. He came forth with the disconcerting idea that there were great comic possibilities in Mr. Barrett. This certainly seemed farfetched, for on the face of it Mr. Barrett was a strait-laced Puritan who ruled his family with an iron hand, driving one daughter into semi-invalidism and another into outright hysteria. The whole set of characters, in fact, were case histories that seemed made to order for Dr. Freud.

Charles won his point and joined the cast. Norma Shearer, Thalberg's beautiful wife, was to play the bed-ridden poetess, and Fredric March the poet. It was imperative that Charles grow a beard, and above all, lose fifty pounds. A genial stoutness would not do for Mr. Barrett. Elsa, who was hard at work in *David Copperfield*, hired a top-notch dietician for Charles. Bread, cake and potatoes were stricken from his diet. For months he lived on fruit, yeast and halibut liver oil. Charles felt much better for losing weight. He went at it wholeheartedly, sticking to his diet and undergoing massages. Following the example of other film people, he hired a special trainer to help him with his reducing, and went in for punch ball and boxing in a big way. Once the filming began, it was sometimes a strain for Charles to watch Norma Shearer having her daily breakfast on the set and satisfying her hearty appetite with Canadian bacon, marmalade and toast, while he had to be satisfied with orange juice.

The results of the diet amply justified the sacrifice. Fifty pounds lighter, Charles looked like a very proper

Victorian, with muttonchop whiskers and gray hair. He played the part with all the stern straight-facedness the script called for, but he also gave it something that he had given to his Henry VIII—so much so that his Mr. Barrett brought down the house. The laughter was the audience's triumph at the impending defeat of a thoroughgoing villain.

For again it was the role of a villain. But this time it was a villain with a cause, a scoundrel who epitomized a whole morality, a great psychological study.

Certain lines of the stage play, when spoken by Laughton as Mr. Barrett, took on such an appalling significance regarding the attitude of the father toward his sickly daughter that they had to be eliminated. Thalberg was afraid that the expurgations, although necessary if the picture were to pass the censors, would take the guts out of the story. But Laughton reassured him. "They cannot censor the gleam in the eye," he said. The finished movie proved Laughton to be right. He succeeded very well in getting the point across without disturbing the censors.

Alva Johnston, one of America's greatest publicists, reviewed the picture and recalled that Laughton was given to unregulated merriment as well as to emotional carnivals. He was no doubt thinking of a very expensive outburst of private mirth during the filming of *The Barretts of Wimpole Street,* when Charles singlehanded stopped the shooting. The scene, as far as anyone else could see, was a perfectly serious one. Laughton had just taken up the Bible and was on the point of making his younger daughter swear on the Holy Book never to see her lover again. A highly dramatic bit, and everything was going well when Charles, for no reason that anyone could see, broke into laughter. He roared so infectiously that everyone on the set joined in. Charles laughed even more heartily. Norma Shearer and Maureen O'Sullivan were laughing so hard that their make-up was ruined. Their faces had to be retouched before the scene could be started again. As Mr. Barrett once more started to extort the oath, Laughton started laughing again. Now even the cameramen caught the bug. The technicians were next. Finally everyone on the set was laughing as he had not laughed in a long time. Time after time they all sobered up and started the scene again—only to have Laughton collapse in a fit of giggles. To lose a full day of production on the set cost the studio thousands of dollars.

When Laughton finally got a grip on himself, he explained what had been the matter. Every time he picked up the Bible he found it irresistibly funny. He would start thinking of his own youth—the terrible times he had had trying to memorize Bible verses—the torments he had suffered when he accused himself of being a sinner. It seemed too good to be true that he had shaken all that off. He was having a fine revenge on the doctrine of hell-fire and damnation.

But thanks to his youth in which he had experienced savage Victorian piety in action, Laughton did a superb job of Mr. Barrett. He poured the heartiest malice into the great praying sequence in *The Barretts of Wimpole Street*. When asked how he did it, he had a ready reply. "I have an uncle in England," he said. "I copied him. He was both a magnificent prayer and a magnificent disciplinarian."

Charles was now under personal contract to Irving Thalberg. Thalberg exercised considerable influence over him, even to the point of being able to change the actor's mind on one matter. Laughton had been fairly set on commuting for several years between London and Hollywood, accepting stage contracts in England and film productions in America. But Thalberg's genius and great directing made Laughton decide to stay and work with him. Thalberg had also been helpful to Elsa Lanchester in establishing her in Hollywood. She broke into the motion-picture industry with a fairly attractive contract from Metro-Goldwyn-Mayer.

Norma Shearer and Irving Thalberg were considered Hollywood's ideal couple. Their Santa Monica house, with its two swimming pools, one fresh water and the other salt water, was one of Hollywood's finest. It was the scene of many small, intimate parties. Only the cream of film aristocracy attended—Jeannette MacDonald, Nelson Eddy, Jean Harlow and Greta Garbo. Charlie Chaplin and Douglas Fairbanks, Sr., were also frequent guests of the house. Fairbanks had just finished Alexander Korda's *The Private Life of Don Juan,* and Greta Garbo her *Anna Karenina.* Those were great actors and great days. And the Laughtons fitted into the group.

Charles Laughton has remarked that as far as he knows there is nothing shy about Greta Garbo. He has never known her to be other than kind and natural. The Garbo he knows has a perfectly normal attitude toward people. Vulgar newspaper publicity, when it pictures her as running away from people, misrepresents her completely.

Thalberg, Laughton and Garbo used to discuss the frenzied mobs who hurled themselves at the Swedish actress. Of them Greta Garbo said: "I have often seen the huge mob fascinated by my face. Everywhere and always it seemed to me the same crowd, the same tamed monster from which the incense of thousands upon thousands of cigarettes drifted toward my face."

Hence her attempts to shield herself from the public eye, to live her life in privacy. She couldn't stand the idolatry, the curiosity, the greedy possessiveness of the movie fans. One night at the Thalberg house she remarked, "I'm a woman who is unfaithful to a million men." For a great movie star is in a peculiar position, figuring as she does in the erotic life of countless males. She inspires dangerous emotion particularly when, as in America, people are not content to worship the celluloid image, but will go to any lengths to see the actress in real life.

This tolerant goddess, as Alistair Cooke has called Garbo, felt no particular triumph over the fact that her beauty had made conquests over millions. Actually the matter quite depressed her. Trying to put her feeling into words, she said, "I destroyed myself, I sacrificed myself to the image of beauty which alone could satisfy each and every one of those limitless frustrated desires."

Laughton had long admired Garbo's greatness, and Garbo, as it turned out when they met, felt the same way about Laughton. The respect was mutual. At the Thalbergs, where she felt herself among friends—smiling, laughing, relaxed, her lovely face innocent of make-up, she charmed Laughton all over again. People were always at their best at the Thalberg parties. The tact of the hostess, Norma Shearer, the wonderful food and the high level of the talk made each evening enchanting.

Charlie Chaplin was invited specifically to meet Laughton. Thalberg had been teasing Chaplin with the warning that he had a formidable rival—Laughton nowadays could get as many laughs from an audience as Chaplin. Chaplin refused to become alarmed. "I'm used to tough competition," he said. "Don't you know what happened to me not so long ago?"

"What was it?" everyone wanted to know.

"I happened to be passing a Hollywood movie house. There were some stills of Douglas Fairbanks at the entrance, and I stopped to look at them. I noticed another fellow hanging around—a rather decent-looking chap who seemed to be watching me, so I asked him—had he seen the show.

" 'Sure,' he replied.

" 'Any good?' I asked.

" 'Why, this Fairbanks boy is the best in the business. He's a scream. Never laughed so much at anyone in all my life.'

" 'Would you say he was as good as Charlie Chaplin?'
I asked wistfully.

" 'As good as Chaplin!' he said with superb scorn.
'Why, Fairbanks has got that Chaplin guy looking like
a gloom. They're just not in the same class. Fairbanks is
funny. I don't care what anyone else says, but it happens
I feel pretty strongly about that.'

"I had had about enough," Chaplin continued with
magnificent aplomb, while Thalberg and the whole
party listened with excitement. "I didn't know whether
I ought to laugh or get mad. So I up and told this
cheeky stranger, 'It happens that I'm Charlie Chaplin.'

" 'I know you are,' said the stranger cheerfully. 'I'm
Douglas Fairbanks.' "

Charles Laughton's admiration and respect for
Chaplin have only increased with the years. He felt
pretty grim when the political storm was raised over
Chaplin and it was made difficult for the greatest
comedian of the century to return to Hollywood. But this
lay far in the future.

For the present, Thalberg invited the stars and a group
of discriminating people to a private preview of *The
Barretts of Wimpole Street* in his own projection room
at Santa Monica. The enthusiasm was enormous. On the
strength of the advance reaction, one million dollars was
allotted to advertising the film. Everywhere it met with
a uniform reception. The reviews were loud in their
praises of Thalberg's direction. And the box-office
receipts were all that might be expected.

The acting of the whole cast was acclaimed, and
as usual Laughton had distinguished himself. Una
O'Connor wrote of him, "He is humble as all great artists
are. He acts the way a skilled novelist writes, intuitively
and with precision. To Charles Laughton a part is to be
studied and blended and woven into a perfect fabric.
Perfection is his ideal, and striving for it his recompense."
Which was unusual praise for a mere film actor.

Beset by witches. Rehearsing a scene from **Macbeth**.

Ahead of himself! Laughton pulls a neat trick in **The Canterville Ghost**.

Alexander Korda supervises a scene from *Henry VIII.*

Elsa, as Anne of Cleves in *Henry VIII,* gambled with her real and stage husband in the hope of saving her head.

The Barretts of Wimpole Street was one of the master-pieces of the motion pictures. It was, alas, one of the last pictures Thalberg did. He was to die a few years later, at the age of thirty-seven.

At the Thalbergs Charles had met the two foremost singing stars of Hollywood, Jeannette MacDonald and Nelson Eddy. The two teams became extremely friendly. The Laughtons took an instant liking to Jeannette MacDonald, this—as Elsa described her—"completely unaffected, natural person who really seems to enjoy being a success."

Jeannette MacDonald, in addition to her naturally beautiful voice, had a rich background in operatic study. Tall and stunning, with Titian red hair, she was a striking figure wherever she went. She was one of Hollywood's most brilliant hostesses, famous for serving delicious and unusual European foods. The bond between the households was cemented the more firmly when she gave the Laughtons a cat named Marie Antoinette, the second cat they had acquired in Hollywood.

Nelson Eddy, star of *The Chocolate Soldier* and costar with Jeannette MacDonald in many a sparkling operetta, also became a fast friend of the Laughtons. They would always remember a Christmas they spent with him and his mother in their pleasant home. It was a California Christmas, without snow; outside, the sun shone on the smooth surface of the swimming pool. But inside the house the Eddys did their best to make it a real Noel with a decorated Christmas tree, turkey and plum pudding, and old-style hospitality. A good part of the day at the Eddy home was spent playing with recording machines. Nelson Eddy was a wizard with these gadgets and he had the Laughtons do readings and songs for his collection. They also listened to some of their host's recordings. Nelson Eddy is still one of America's popular vocalists. His wonderful baritone, his keen blue eyes and his sturdy athletic figure have endeared him to millions of movie-goers.

He is an ex-newspaperman and extremely proud of his Scandinavian ancestry. In those days he never went anywhere without being accompanied by his singing coach, Dr. Edouard Lippe. That Christmas Day he confessed to the Laughtons that the high point of his life was when he sang with Lauritz Melchior in *Lohengrin* at the Metropolitan.

Eddy's unforced gaiety and buoyancy made itself felt in the atmosphere of his home. The Laughtons deeply appreciated a bit of the Christmas spirit in Hollywood— where they still felt themselves strange.

Charles at heart is not what is called a social person. By and large he doesn't like drinking and getting "high" with a lot of people. Most amusements bore him. When people start singing at parties, he grows silent. That does not mean he doesn't love to give parties and to entertain lavishly. His parties nowadays are famous and sometimes last until five in the morning. He can be as convivial as the next fellow if he is with people he likes.

One morning when Charles woke up, he was in pain, with a feeling of general tension. It seemed that a major operation was indicated. Charles, to whom Hollywood was still a new city, did not know what hospital or doctor to choose. In his bewilderment he told Josef von Sternberg of his troubles. His difficulties were immediately over. Sternberg took complete charge of everything. He made arrangements to obtain the best surgeon, the best hospital, the best nurses. Within a few hours everything had been settled.

In spite of the pain and unpleasantness of the illness, the spell in the hospital seemed heaven-sent. It was the first long rest the actor had taken since he had begun his ambitious career. He assiduously cultivated the whims of an invalid, watched over the virtue of his three nurses, and after several weeks discovered other Hollywood actors in the same hospital.

Being ill and confined to bed brought Laughton in contact with the American radio, which he had hardly sampled before. He seemed to enjoy the programs, in spite of the bothersome commercials, and listened to everything from plays, boxing and wrestling matches to the pulpit thumping of evangelists.

The hospital brought out another side of his character. He had been a rabid hater of fans, though he was less plagued by this tribe than other stars—the fellow who plays "monsters and villains" doesn't get much fan mail. He had had only the most fleeting contact with his film audience and detested the autograph seekers' glittering eyes and their impertinent curiosity. Now he had a chance to meet his own public in the hospital. The other patients had all seen his pictures. His antagonism toward fans was completely cured by the following incident:

In the hospital was an elderly man whose wife was suffering from an undiagnosed illness. The two men often met each other in the corridor, and one day Laughton went along with the elderly gentleman to visit the sick woman, who was under narcotics most of the time. She smiled when her husband introduced Charles Laughton as the man who had played Henry VIII.

After the visit he was told that that smile was the first that had crossed the face of the sick woman in eight weeks. It made a very deep and lasting impression on Laughton —his eyes would fill with tears when he described the incident. Although it did not make him condone the frenzy of the fans, it taught Laughton what his art meant to millions in the world. Henceforth he would have to discriminate among fans, everyday movie-goers and genuine admirers of his art.

Many fellow actors came to visit him in the hospital— among them Josef von Sternberg, to whom Laughton was forever indebted for his help.

It was on one of those hospital visits that Laughton heard from Sternberg (the *von* was strictly phony) the true story of the one and only Maria Magdalene von Losch—better known to the world as the fabulous Marlene Dietrich.

Laughton wanted to know all about it.

It seemed that Sternberg had gone to Germany to produce Emil Jannings' first talking picture. One evening he dropped into a typical German dance hall. Marlene was among the girls there. He heard her speaking one line: *"Dreimal Hoch für den Herrn, der das grosse Los gewonnen hat"* (Three cheers for the gentleman who has just won the grand prize).

Joe Sternberg was stunned by her beautiful enunciation, her tragic air, the quality of her voice, her face, her pent-up emotion, and naturally her long and beautiful legs. He hired her on the spot to play opposite the great Emil Jannings in *The Blue Angel*.

Laughton listened to the story breathlessly. He had a vivid memory of the picture—Jannings as the newly awakened, love-mad professor, and the tantalizing Marlene in Sternberg's production, whom in the end the professor strangles with the piercing cry of cock-a-doodle-doo. That had been her first overwhelming success. Later Sternberg directed Marlene in *Morocco, Dishonored, Shanghai Express, Blonde Venus, Scarlet Empress* and *The Devil Is a Woman*.

Both Sternberg and Dietrich were under contract to Paramount. This studio had had an awkward situation to face when Mrs. Reza von Sternberg sued Marlene for five hundred thousand dollars for alienation of her husband's love and an additional hundred thousand dollars for libel.

All this gossip made an interesting afternoon for the sick Laughton. Sternberg brought his friend up to date on the complications of his personal life. Laughton was a tolerant and intelligent listener. Life had not been all

roses for the man who had discovered Dietrich, but
Laughton assured him that it had not been a mistake.
"Marlene Dietrich will always remain the greatest actress
Hollywood ever had," he asserted.

Twenty years later Laughton, who by this time was
earning 400,000 dollars a year, finally fulfilled an old
dream of his. He had signed a contract with Marlene
Dietrich for fifteen weeks with options on one of
Laughton's own theatrical productions. Marlene was now
a grandmother but looked as young and beautiful as ever,
and seemed at the peak of her career.

When Laughton met Marlene, they laughed heartily
about their early comments about each other. They still
had never played together. It was understanding and
admiration from the first moment. "You cannot trust
your brain, but you can trust your heart," said Marlene. Laughton only nodded and seemed happy. So did
Marlene.

"You look happy and content," said Laughton to her.

"Of course," Marlene replied, "discontented women
are not loved for long."

But all this happened twenty years later.

At last Charles was fit to begin work on *Ruggles of Red
Gap*. Here was a role in which he was not playing either
a human monster, a villain or a maniac. The film was
based on Harry Leon Wilson's classic story of an English
butler who is thrown in with American cowboys. It was
a hilarious tale. A full-blooded but wife-ridden ranch
owner from the "Wild West," in the course of a trip to
Europe, wins Ruggles, the perfect manservant, in a poker
game. The year is 1908. The new master brings the man
home, but does not dare to tell his fellow cattlemen who
he really is. For the time being he passes Ruggles off as a
British colonel, while Ruggles gradually gets wise to the
precepts of democracy. In this film Charles Laughton
paid as great a tribute to his adopted country as any
foreign-born person can. His adventures in the fantastic

pioneering Western community were wittily handled and ended on a note of love with the best recital of the Gettysburg Address ever heard since it was delivered by Abraham Lincoln.

Leo McCarey directed the picture. He found this comedy of two countries a difficult job, because of the English jokes that had to be put across to the American public and the American Western jokes to the English. Above all, there was the problem of conveying the spirit of the Wild West as it was at the turn of the century. Exaggeration was necessary; at the same time it had to be made clear that this was a period piece. The average Englishman has some grotesque notions about what the Wild West is like. Charles himself commented on this: "Although *Ruggles of Red Gap* takes place during the robust 1900's, many English and colonial filmgoers will take it as a true picture of current life in the West of the United States. When I first came to California I rather expected to see stagecoaches and scalp-collecting redskins as soon as I crossed the Rocky Mountains."

This refreshing excursion into the Wild West was soon followed by a foray into more distant history. The Stefan Zweig movie was still pending. Charles was all ready to play Louis XVI, but Norma Shearer, who was to be Marie Antoinette, was expecting another baby and the film was indefinitely postponed. Still, France would also be the background for his next film, Victor Hugo's *Les Misérables*. Elsa Lanchester said: "I think Charles gave one of his best performances as Javert." He once again played with Fredric March, whose performance as Dr. Jekyll and Mr. Hyde had established his world fame. Fredric March was Jean Valjean, the escaped convict, and Charles was the police inspector Javert who dogged Valjean's footsteps and would not be cheated of his prey.

In the film Laughton, Javert, the fanatic agent of the law, reveals his own unhappy background in the famous court speech: "It's all quite true—my mother was a

gypsy . . . my father died on the gallows . . . I myself was
born . . . in prison. . . . [Here Laughton sobbed with
bitter recollections.] There are only two kinds of people
in society—those who attack it—and those who guard it.
I knew nothing; I had to teach myself everything. I've
studied, I've worked, I've slaved. My record is my Bible
. . . I would never fail in my duty to the law. It's my
whole life."

Laughton's policeman's costume was a marvel of
design. Long pointed shoes gave him larger and greater
steps; the tight uniform and the peaked helmet gave him
an uncanny appearance. He was the very essence of the
heartless detective.

Though Elsa thought this was one of the best performances Charles had ever given, some critics mentioned that
Laughton overplayed his lines. He actually overdid the
"beast" in the policeman. His acting came close to
buffoonery, which was not the right interpretation of
this villain of the classics. But his general acting was so
superb that the audience really did not care if, in parts,
it was overacted.

Laughton's many admirers have long ceased to remind
him of some less successful portrayals, and to them he
seems so great when at his best that he transcends his
minor overacting failures. But some of the movie critics
watch those failures with cold and fishy eyes.

It was a difficult film to do—with not a few grueling
sequences. Javert not only ends his life by jumping into
the river, but has long scenes in the Paris sewers—where
the climax of the chase takes place.

Charles had to wade through a make-believe sewer
where mud and slush and slime were only too real. It
was one more "watery experience," as he said, the second
since *The Devil and the Deep.*

The famous chase and sewer scenes took so much out
of Charles that the studio provided an especially comfortable suite at the United Artists lot, consisting of dress-

ing room, sitting room, bathroom and kitchen—a fully equipped apartment in green, chromium and white. The make-up table held an array of strange accessories, from grease paint to false hair, false eyelashes and nose putty. But it was always open house in the Laughton dressing room. Charles had a great time playing in the Victor Hugo classic, the success of which was to be greater in Europe than in the United States.

Now came the third watery experience in Laughton's film career. He was again working under Irving Thalberg. The *Mutiny on the Bounty* became one of the greatest triumphs in the history of the film capital. The action took place in the seas around Tahiti and then on the island itself. But in actuality the scenes were shot on Catalina Island. Sending the stars as far as Tahiti was expensive business, so the director resorted to many trick and "process" shots. When Clark Gable spoke to some of the native girls, for instance—he was on Catalina Island and the actual girl was in Tahiti.

The two ships in the film were tiny, extremely faithful replicas of the original ships. While the stars remained in California, fifty technicians and minor actors made the four-thousand-mile voyage to the South Seas. They were fully equipped with wooden legs, costumes and four electric generators to produce the stupendous waves. The background shots of the picture were taken in forty native Tahitian villages. Twenty-five hundred natives were employed, but the five hundred canoes and all the spears and bows and arrows were brought from Hollywood.

In providing the equipment Thalberg showed more realism and common sense than his later colleagues who went to the Belgian Congo to arrange the screening of *King Solomon's Mines*. There they found themselves in an embarrassing situation when they discovered that the

Watusi tribesmen were quite up to date—were running around in sport shirts and tennis shoes and using pomade on their hair like many a movie actor! It was necessary to cable Hollywood to have a few hundred wigs of authentic African hair styles flown to the Congo for embarrassingly civilized natives.

The staff working on *Mutiny on the Bounty* wanted to adhere as closely as possible to the facts of the true story. It took Hollywood some ten months to round up the original logbook of Captain Bligh—the precious document being finally found in Sydney, Australia.

The flogging scenes were re-created from the logbook. The very breadfruit trees mentioned had to be located also. Laughton, with his mania for historical accuracy, visited Gieves, the tailor in London who is cited in the diary of Captain Bligh. The logbook contained a note that Captain Bligh's uniform was especially water-resistant.

Laughton had tracked down sketches for Henry VIII, so it was with complete sang-froid that he went to the tailor on Bond Street and said to the first clerk he saw: "I believe you made up a uniform for one Captain Bligh. I should like to have duplicates made to my measure."

"Captain Bligh, sir?"

Laughton nodded.

"And what year would that be?" the clerk wanted to know.

"1789," Laughton replied.

Not in the least ruffled, the clerk replied, "I'll see, sir."

"And do you know," said Laughton later, "the clerk was back in a few minutes with the complete record of the transaction with Captain Bligh, his measurements, the price, the nature of the material, and so on. I had the duplicates made and wore them in the picture."

The shooting of *Mutiny on the Bounty* was a tremendous enterprise, with the screening in Tahiti and California at the same time. Rough seas in Tahiti and on the California coast brought losses of equipment and damages up to fifty thousand dollars. One cameraman was thrown overboard.

Elsa Lanchester was in London when that accident took place. London newspapers phoned her and asked, "Can you tell us what has happened to your husband?"

Elsa had heard nothing about the accident.

But the newspaper people were able to enlighten her. There were rumors that the *Bounty* had sunk and several people had drowned.

Elsa was terrified, until Charles's cable arrived informing her that he was safe.

Charles has described the filming of this gigantic historical sea drama: "Most of the time we had to stand on the deck of the vessel, and the only seats were guns, anchors, chain cables and suchlike restful things. Before I took the part of Captain Bligh I considered myself to be one of the world's worst sailors, but after rolling around in a small wooden ship for seven weeks, I think I could stand anything now."

It was a strange life they lived at a specially built village on Catalina which served as headquarters for 600 people. In California and Tahiti exactly 652,228 feet of film were shot—and only 12,000 feet were utilized. Three thousand costumes and 600 uniforms were used in the film. A typical day's schedule was as follows:

6:30 A.M.	Awakening.	
7:00 A.M.	Shaving and putting on uniforms.	
8:00 A.M.	Breakfast.	
9:00 A.M.	Finishing up first scene.	
10:00 A.M.	First quarrel between Laughton and Clark Gable.	
11:00 A.M.	Laughton threatens Gable with flogging.	
12:00 M.	Cut and jail break—"jail break" in movie slang means lunch time.	

A typical scene: The launch from the mainland draws up alongside the *Bounty*. Prop men, electricians, the whole cast lean over the sides of their ship and hoist up the cans and buckets of steaming food. Waitresses and chefs are helped aboard the *Bounty*. An informal lunch is served, the sun-broiled mutineers lining up for chow as docilely as the rest.

Another scene: The ship's peg-legged surgeon has just died. Clark Gable accuses Laughton of causing the man's death. Laughton orders Gable to be put in irons.

Here they broke off the scene. The picture, like so many others, was shot in disconnected bits. The drama of the great mutiny was to come much later.

Another scene: Gable leaps at Laughton for a friendly tussle. Laughton breaks free, does a few steps of soft-shoe dance and begins to recite—Shakespeare.

6:00 P.M.   Clark Gable and Charles Laughton don evening dress and leave by speedboat for the St. Catherine Hotel on Catalina.

In this picture Laughton was again depicting an unlovable character who puts his whole crew on half rations, orders brutal floggings and in general carries on in such a way as to earn the hatred of the audience. Tall, handsome Clark Gable, on the other hand, was a shining hero. In a mischievous mood Gable would describe a fit of location blues Laughton once had. He was found out on a pier in the moonlight, watching a fisherman in the bay and muttering, "I wish I were that man."

Laughton admitted to having the blues. The picture was a strain on him. "When I have a part like Captain Bligh or Father Barrett, I hate the man's guts so much that I always overact. Parts like that make me physically sick," he said.

But Laughton did not overact this time. The trio, Laughton, Gable and Franchot Tone, made a masterpiece under the Thalberg-Frank Lloyd guidance.

In addition to its compelling drama, the film had good dialogue. Laughton has always appreciated John Galsworthy's dictum: "Good dialogue is character marshaled so as continually to stimulate interest or excitement."

The film was a success. The New York critics called Laughton the outstanding actor for the year 1936, and Mark van Doren, one of America's most discriminating critics, gave Laughton the highest praise he had so far received: "Charles Laughton's performance as Captain Bligh in the *Mutiny on the Bounty* fixes him in my mind at any rate as by far the best of living actors."

But Charles felt that the effectiveness of the film was not due only to him. Each actor had given the best that was in him—especially Clark Gable, whom Laughton considers one of Hollywood's most dynamic figures. "Gable dramatizes himself. He makes you feel full of pep. You see Clark Gable and you say, I'll go out and have half a dozen dates."

By rough estimate, some two thousand stories have been written on Clark Gable. Ex-factory worker, ex-oiler and lumberjack, Gable for years has been the idol of female movie-goers. Though Clark has a good share of self-assurance, he has never slipped over into conceit or swagger. Even in real life he has a quality that draws everyone to him, a kind of personal magnetism which means very much in Hollywood, where the whole city is engaged in trading on charm and physical attraction. Gable represents an ideal American type. Most men wish they were as sound and calm, good-looking, virile, brave and resolute—and certainly many women wish their own husbands would be more like Gable.

In those days Joan Crawford, one of the great ladies of the movies, used to be seen with Clark Gable. She was on Catalina Island at the time of the historic shooting of the *Bounty*. As Miss Crawford always admired Laughton, I recently wrote to her asking whether she remembered those days at all. Indeed she did, she said, and went on:

"I doubt if Mr. Laughton has any foes. I know he used to frighten me—as he does a great many people in our industry, merely because of his great talent.

"You know, I discovered a very interesting thing. He was on location making *Mutiny on the Bounty* and I was on location at Catalina at the same time. I discovered that Charles Laughton has the most charming, divine sense of humor in the world. You know, actresses and actors really show their true colors on location. There are at times hardships to endure or put up with or adjust yourself to. It's according to your personality how you react. This is a man who adjusted himself calmly, serenely, and happily. Sometimes it was the food that wasn't too good; sometimes sleeping conditions that were not too comfortable; or the hot sun. He's rather a pixie, too. He has a sense of humor that's a combination of an adult's and a small child's. I only hope that one day I'll be able to work with this great talent. I hope one day to work with him on Shakespearean plays.

"I could write a book about my admiration, respect and fondness for Charles Laughton. Just the recalling of it was such a happy few moments to spend."

Joan Crawford discovered Laughton's great sense of humor during the days of waiting and rain when bad tempers flared up on Catalina. He imitated everyone from Joan Crawford to the producer, the other actors, even Clark Gable and the cook. When they were served tasteless food, he started them all laughing when he made up the fanciest names for the most terrible dishes.

Yes, Laughton was good to have around on rainy days.

The story of *Mutiny on the Bounty,* however, is rounded off by another great and gracious lady. The beautiful replica of the ship which was the studio's working model had come into the possession of this woman's husband. The year was 1945 and the lady was packing the contents of her late husband's study. Her attention was caught by the ship model. "What ship is this?" she asked.

One of the servants identified it. "The *Bounty* from Charles Laughton's film *Mutiny on the Bounty*. A gift to the President."

"Oh, yes, I remember," Mrs. Roosevelt answered.

"We had dinner with some of the cast. They came from Hollywood and ran off the film for us at a special showing. We'd better put it with the rest of the collection. The *Bounty* is beautiful, isn't she? We better keep her because Mr. Laughton and I are often on the same lecture circuit and he might ask me about it.

"Have you ever seen him in the movies?" Mrs. Roosevelt asked the servant.

"Yes, ma'am. He's that fat, funny man with the English accent."

And so the *Bounty* finally dropped anchor at Hyde Park in the Roosevelt Museum.

Chapter 11

THEN TRAGEDY struck, after Charles had joined Elsa in Europe. Charles was on a train going from Geneva to Rome, where he was to play in *I, Claudius,* with Alexander Korda. Irving Thalberg had just died. The news hit Charles hard. The two men had been close both as creative artists and friends. Laughton remembered the long walks along the Santa Monica beach with Thalberg, when they discussed new films, new roles and plans for the future. All those ambitions were wiped out. Thalberg's death left Laughton professionally a free man, without a single contractual commitment to bind him. Depressed as he was by his friend's sudden death, he was glad of the respite. He wanted some time by himself—to come to terms with the experience of grief, to think what he could best do with the limited time any man had at his disposal.

It was then that he told the reporters, "Thalberg is dead. I've forgotten about my past. I've not kept a single photograph or clipping referring to what I've done. Let's talk about the future."

Fate came knocking at his door with one of the most daring assignments ever to come the way of an English-speaking actor. Charles was invited to go to Paris to act at the famous Comédie Française. He was to play the part of Sganarelle in the second act of Molière's *Le Méde-*

cin Malgré Lui at a gala midnight performance for the benefit of the children of the late Jacques Guilheue.

Laughton was the first English actor ever to appear at the Comédie Française in its three-hundred-year history. The idea of inviting him originated with Maurice Chevalier.

Chevalier was a phenomenon in himself. Earlier in life he had been a carpenter, had painted dolls in a doll factory, manufactured nails and tried his luck as an acrobat. He began singing at the Casino des Tourelles for three francs a day (then sixty cents), rose with meteoric speed to become the dancing partner of La Mistinguette at the Folies Bergères. In the thirties he became France's best-loved song-and-dance man, something like Fred Astaire.

The French theater was at the peak of its brilliance in the thirties. The atmosphere was singularly favorable to its flowering. The French had not only a love for the theater in the usual sense, but a sophisticated interest in all the arts. There were enough people of cultivated sensibilities to support a mighty upsurge of painting, music, theater, opera and ballet.

The French drama and theater lived "at the height of its time"—contemporary with the work of Valéry and Maritain, Bergson and Joyce, the painting of Picasso, the music of Stravinsky, Milhaud and Richard Strauss. It had benefited from the Russian and Swedish ballet and from the *avant-garde* experiments of all Europe. In its turn it was a vital influence upon many young English-speaking artists. T. S. Eliot, William Butler Yeats, Gertrude Stein, Virgil Thomson, Thornton Wilder and E. E. Cummings—all found inspiration and liberation in the Parisian theater.

Eugene O'Neill was living peacefully outside of Paris and working on his *Mourning Becomes Electra;* his wicked little Bugatti racer was often seen parked outside the Comédie Française.

Penguin Photo

Wife both on and off the stage. Laughton and Lanchester in **Henry VIII.**

Penguin Photo

Young Bess again gave Laughton the role of Henry VIII, with none of the vim and vigor lost.

In private life, Laughton views tenderly his award for acting in **The Private Life of Henry VIII.**

The late O'Neill was a lifelong admirer of Laughton. The two were as different as two men can be. Laughton always was ambitious; O'Neill never cared for success. Laughton played tragedies, but seldom lived them. O'Neill's own life was often more tragic than his plays. The suicide of a son, the estrangement from his daughter after she married Charles Chaplin, his long tortures from Parkinson's disease made him a lonely man in his last years. Laughton, on the other hand, shared life with more and more people as he grew older.

O'Neill was already a titan in the theater when Laughton played at the Comédie Française.

Now Laughton was summoned to this highest citadel. His traveling companion was Alice Gachet, his former teacher at the Royal Academy in London. She was still popular at the Academy, discovering and developing many more famous actors, such as John Gielgud, Robert Harris and Celia Johnson.

Laughton had five days in which to prepare his part. His grounding in French back in the long-lost days of Scarborough stood him in good stead. He turned up for all the rehearsals and did a little extra cramming at night, reading the lines with one or two members of the cast. For the official rehearsals turned out to be more confusing than anything else. The French actors had played Molière for years and so hardly bothered to go through their roles. They would point out this or that, walk on the stage to indicate where they would stand, dance around, gesticulating and gossiping among themselves. Charles had worked in the chaotic conditions of Hollywood, but he had never been through anything quite like the situation at the Comédie.

Important benefit shows at the Comédie Française started at midnight. It was 2:00 A.M. before the curtain lifted for the second act. Why had he ever let himself in for this, Charles must have thought. For the situation grew more uncanny by the minute. He was doing his best to be funny—the lines were humorous—the play was certainly a rip-roaring comedy. Yet try as he did, he could not draw a single laugh. The audience sat in stony silence and listened.

There were things about the tradition of the Comédie Française that Laughton did not know. A French actor thundering forth the Alexandrines of Corneille and Racine pauses for applause only at certain fixed and traditional points—usually only at the end of the more celebrated "great" passages. Everyone in the audience knew by heart the Molière lines that Charles was saying: The normal laughter and applause of an English-speaking audience were absent. Everyone was concentrating on appreciating the fine points. So the second act proceeded without a single interruption.

But at the end, furor broke loose. Laughton, as the first English-speaking actor to be invited to play Molière in French, had been completely original. He had given a new, robust interpretation to the time-worn Molière lines. At one point, for example, Charles had underlined the words, *Les ventricules de l'opoplate,* by slapping a girl's derrière. This bit of stage business has since been incorporated into the official version under the name of "La Tradition Laughton."

His performance was an unqualified success. Paul Vinson wrote in *Comédia,* "His diction was excellent." *L'Echo de Paris* said, "The interpretation of the great English actor was remarkable." Some French critics went so far as to say that Laughton was the greatest comedian since Constant Coquelin, the famous French actor of the late nineteenth century. Representatives of the English press were equally as hearty in their praise.

After the play Elsa and Alexander Korda went backstage to join the throng of photographers, actors, celebrities and well-wishers. Amid hundreds of bouquets, a champagne party was going on. The French critics were raving; Charles was complaining that he should have had at least another two weeks of rehearsal; Chevalier was congratulating Charles and himself for the bright idea of having invited Charles.

It was five in the morning when they left the theater and drove to the hotel for breakfast. On the spur of the moment, Korda and Laughton decided to drive to Holland. Before leaving for Paris, Charles had agreed to do something with Alexander Korda again. Korda had in mind a picture dealing with the life of Holland's greatest painter, Rembrandt.

Charles Laughton in a brown frieze coat, his head wrapped in a kind of turban of whitish cloth, his face marked with the deep wrinkles of a very old Dutchman, stood in a fish and vegetable market by the River Colne and ate raw herring.

The fish should have been cooked, but someone had forgotten to do it. Charles got a good grip on himself and started to chew, as the script demanded. After every take, shouting for whisky, water, disinfectant and tobacco, he would stagger down to the waterside to spit out what was left of the herring.

Sir Alexander Korda shook his head. As far as he was concerned, all that display was unnecessary. They could make a break and have the fish prepared. But Charles insisted they finish the scene.

With Charles's working methods, it would not have been surprising if he had gotten sick before they finished the Rembrandt picture. Korda offered a mild suggestion. "I think, Charles, that you would feel better if you left off eating that marzipan between whiles. Besides, you needn't bother with the head of the herring."

That scene took place at the Denham Studio where the old team of Laughton, Korda and Elsa Lanchester were back at work. Behind the setting of the Dutch market, parts of Glourie Castle could be seen. To the left a Spanish galleon was growing, while here and there

were relics of the passage of genuine Indian elephants—
which Robert Flaherty had used for his film *Elephant
Boy.*

The Denham Studio was crowded with celebrities.
Marlene Dietrich was on the lot; Richard Tauber was
practicing for his film *Land Without Music.* Paderewski
could be heard running through the *Moonlight Sonata.*
But Laughton was able to concentrate on the job in
hand. Concentration was necessary, for the preliminaries
to the filming of *Rembrandt* were as thorough and ex-
haustive as for *The Private Life of Henry VIII.* Charles
had a standing order with booksellers for every available
Rembrandt biography. He read Rembrandt's letters and
the letters of his contemporaries. He made a tour of the
museums and places hallowed by their connection with
the great painter. The Dutch government and the Dutch
art dealers were most co-operative. Mr. Schmidt-Degener,
the curator of the great Ryksmuseum, arranged a special
showing for Laughton of all Rembrandt originals available in Holland.

A prominent art dealer offered to lend six original
Rembrandts to be used in the picture. He even offered
to secure the use of the *Night Watch,* but Korda had
to decline this rare prize. High insurance costs made the
project unfeasible. Even without the *Night Watch,* one
million dollars' worth of art treasures were selected by
Laughton and Korda for use in the production.

Laughton as usual threw himself passionately into the
research. He had, besides, to grow a mustache for the
part; but this was a pleasure compared to the ordeal of
having it plucked in order to get the scraggly effect of the
Rembrandt whiskers. He spent hours studying the Rembrandt self-portraits and longer hours trying to print his
face with those signs of care, bitterness and genius which
the late self-portraits reveal. He tried to get to the heart
of the man. Later he said, "Rembrandt to me was one of

the most tragic figures in the world of art—a man to
whom recognition came too soon. He was a success at
twenty-one and an outcast professionally at thirty-five."

Laughton that day did not realize that his own success
and fame had come rather early in his life and that there
was a long career ahead.

Rembrandt had made a fortune painting the prophets
and princes of Biblical story. He had also been flooded
with commissions to paint the bigwigs and burghers of
Amsterdam. But as he grew older, an inner urge led him
to the markets and slums of the Dutch city, where he
took beggars and fishwives for his models. Then—fascinated by the oriental features and picturesque costumes
of the Amsterdam Jews, refugees from the Inquisition of
Spain and Portugal—Rembrandt moved into the ghetto
to be able to study those people at close quarters.

Laughton put in some of the same intensive study of
his great model. He looked so long at the Rembrandt
self-portraits that he managed to make one of his own
eyes smaller than the other, to match the physical peculi-
arity of the painter. Laughton even took up painting
and practiced holding the brush in the same way that
Rembrandt had done.

The Carl Zuckmayer screen play did justice to the
drama and tragedy of the artist's life. The movie accomplished what very few movies do—it brought its audience
closer not only to Rembrandt the man, but to Rembrandt
the artist.

As Laughton said of Rembrandt, "He loved the light,
but the times he painted it were as rare as the times he
was happy. He painted its reflection on men's faces and
in women's eyes."

The death of Saskia, the beloved wife of Rembrandt's
youth, was one of the greatest scenes ever to be shown
on the screen. Rembrandt's farewell to the dead Saskia
is still in Laughton's reading repertoire—the Zuckmayer

lines approach poetry when Rembrandt proclaims his great and eternal love for his dead wife: "Love one woman and you know the secret of all women."

Laughton followed Rembrandt's career from start to finish. He is first shown as the successful young artist living in the lap of luxury, wined and dined by all the foremost citizens. With the loss of his wife, he begins to slip from popularity. For the first time he encounters disfavor and misunderstanding. Alone and bitter, he finds some comfort in a liaison with his housekeeper, but he finds he cannot sympathize with her middle-class aspirations. He grows hard and reckless. More and more he lives for his art. He throws over the last vestiges of respectability, is completely indifferent to appearances, accepts humiliation and outward defeat. He is last seen in the slums of Amsterdam, an old man, ill and poor, living with a servant girl and painting the masterpieces of his old age.

Throughout the artist's life his inspiration came from the Hebrew poets. And when Laughton, as the aged Rembrandt, read: "While the sun, or the light, or the moon, or the stars be not darkened, nor the clouds return after the rain; . . ." or, "And it came to pass, when men began to multiply on the face of the earth, and daughters were born unto them. That the sons of God saw the daughters of men that they were fair; . . ." he went beyond acting and make-believe. The beauty of the words and the music of his voice restored the original glory to the texts.

Rembrandt-Laughton was a beggar when he painted his last great picture—a picture that was widely branded as blasphemous. The ragged old man replies to his critics with the moving passage from Ecclesiastes: "Wherefore I perceive there is nothing better but that a man should rejoice in his own works." For such passages, which he delivered with the greatest sincerity and eloquence,

Laughton was called, "The most eminent Scripture plugger in the world."

But the Rembrandt picture had been a most difficult film to produce. "It has been a terrible film for me and Alex," Laughton said at the end. "How we fought and suffered in the early weeks when we were still feeling our way. It had to be so simple, so serious, never a sign of acting."

With Charles Laughton in the cast was Elsa Lanchester as Saskia and Gertrude Lawrence as Geertke Dirx, the housekeeper. Miss Lawrence was tall, built on somewhat lanky lines; yet her bodily grace and her natural and infectious gaiety made her one of the best-loved figures on the Denham lot.

Charles Laughton remembers the gay times they had on the Denham lot. Miss Lawrence had a birthday while they were shooting the Rembrandt picture, and a little party was given. Laughton ordered a huge birthday cake with *Dirtie Gurks* written in frosting—a play on words, since Gertrude Lawrence's name in the picture was Geertke Dirx.

Everyone on the set loved Miss Lawrence. She had a huge fund of funny stories, but sometimes she became the subject of a funny story herself. One of those incidents which stage people love to repeat occurred during the Rembrandt filming. Gertrude Lawrence was scheduled to give her longest and most difficult speech when Korda ordered everyone off the set. The actress appeared. She stood there alone, waiting for the shooting. There was a dead silence, which is not unusual during the shooting of a picture. But not even the cameraman was there. Everyone had hidden. Gertrude Lawrence did not know what to make of it. She stood there for all of ten minutes and, finally deciding that this was some mix-up, strolled off to look for the rest of the cast. "I didn't know it was lunch time," she explained innocently.

Her face with its sparkling eyes, its upturned nose and mobile mouth always spread happiness and never betrayed any of her own sorrows. Sitting on the sidelines while waiting for her scenes in Rembrandt, she was never without her knitting. She had promised a pair of mittens to Bernard Shaw. This domestic side was one of her many appealing traits. Much of her attractiveness was a matter of magic personality. For, like many other great actresses, Gertrude Lawrence was, strictly speaking, never a stage beauty. Neither was Sarah Bernhardt. As far as the movies go, it cannot be said that there is a movie type, for almost every big star has had an out-of-the-way type of face. Some examples are Greer Garson, Katharine Hepburn, Bette Davis and Helen Hayes. Gertrude Lawrence herself was always making fun of her long nose.

A Londoner by birth, she was born in Kensington Oval, within the sound of Bow Bells. She spent most of her adult life in New York, where she was married to a prominent producer.

The death of Gertrude Lawrence from cancer in 1952, in the midst of her superb performances in *The King and I,* is one of the most poignant tragedies of the theatrical world. Books have and will be written about this great star of the British and American theater—she epitomized some of the greatest qualities an actress can have: warmth of heart, drive and authority, versatility and personal magnetism. Noel Coward said of her, "On the stage she is potentially capable of anything and everything. She can be gay, sad, witty, tragic and touching." He called her great kindness "insane generosity."

She was enormously gifted—a top-notch singer, comedienne, dancer and dramatic actress. Above all, she was a great human being.

Rembrandt received exceptional reviews—with honors showered on both Gertrude Lawrence and Charles Laughton. *The New York Times* wrote, "Mr. Laughton

becomes Rembrandt as nobody else in the world could—
of this we are firmly and unmistakably convinced."

Of Gertrude Lawrence's performance the *New Republic* said, "A fine example of divination and strong style."

There was, however, one question uppermost in the
minds of many of Charles Laughton's fans. Had he been
better as Rembrandt or as Henry VIII?

The world première of *Rembrandt* took place in Holland, with a full complement of British and Dutch diplomats present. The Laughtons dined at The Hague with
Sir Hubert and Lady Montgomery and then drove to the
theater, where they entered their box amid a storm of
applause. The house was dimmed, the lights went out,
and the film began. At Laughton's first appearance as
Rembrandt van Rijn, some cheerful soul spoke up in
the darkness, "Look, here comes Henry VIII." A great
laugh went up.

At the end of the movie, a dazzling spotlight picked
out the box where Elsa and Charles Laughton sat. The
actor received a tremendous ovation, and several page
boys ran up with an enormous laurel wreath, so heavy
that Laughton could not lift it by himself. For Elsa there
was a bouquet of Holland's most beautiful red carna-
tions. When they finally reached their hotel room, after
saying good-by to Korda, to Sir Hubert and Lady Montgomery, Elsa discovered that the note tucked into the
bouquet was for Gertrude Lawrence.

Once again they had launched a world-wide success.
Exhausted and happy, they could relax and remind each
other of the harassment they had gone through. There
was the time, for example, when Korda and Laughton
could not agree on a title for the picture. Korda had
asked Charles to submit a list of suggestions and Laughton, his frivolity getting the best of him, had turned in
the following: *Brush and Beauty, Rembrandt van Rin-*

Tin-Tin, The Twisted Tubes, Frame Up, Linseed Love, Moving Picture, Kanvas Kid, Charcoal Charlie and *Pop Go the Easels.*

Charles was glad to have the première behind him—the ballyhoo accompanying such occasions has always impressed him as a frightful bore. Pomp and circumstance, speeches, important personages and formality have never been Charles's own idea of fun.

The late Alexander Woollcott, discussing the phenomenon of first nights, seems to have expressed what Charles Laughton and dozens of other actors feel about the institution.

"Dramatic critics are honest," Woollcott said. "They're nice fellows. They write what they think. The trouble is, they don't know a damn thing about the theater. . . . But the critics are the only representatives of civilized, decent American life that you find in the first-night audiences that we have today. Where in the world can you get a gathering as dreary, as ruthless, as moronic as you do at a Broadway opening? First nights have lost their charm and flavor. I never go any more; I won't sit in that company. A première used to be a pleasant occasion; it has now become an unbearable one."

The première in Holland was perhaps one of the most gratifying and pleasurable in Charles's experience. But The Hague, which had been a happy spot for such an affair, was not to be so for long. Hitler's armies were to overrun the flower fields of Holland. For war clouds were gathering in ominous masses over France and Holland, Norway and Denmark, Poland and Germany, and over Laughton's native England.

Chapter 12

THE REMBRANDT picture on which so much labor and love had been lavished did not become a success. Perhaps it was a matter of unfortunate timing. Perhaps the subject dwindled to unimportance as the nations of Europe faced the critical problems of the thirties. People were too much worried about the menace of Hitler to sympathize with the personal tragedy of a lonely old man—even if his name was Rembrandt.

Carl Zuckmayer, who had written the screen story of the Rembrandt picture, was in trouble—his books were among those currently being burned in Germany. The dictators of Germany and Italy had not liked *The Private Life of Henry VIII.* They regarded with suspicion everything about it. What did Alexander Korda, a Hungarian, have in the back of his mind when he produced a picture about a dictator who was a mass of human weaknesses? What did this same Korda mean when he showed Rembrandt choosing to live with Jews in the ghetto? Hadn't Hitler proclaimed the Jews as inferior stock and introduced the Nuremberg laws? And what about this fat fellow, Charles Laughton, who had starred in both the Korda pictures? What was he trying to put over?

In the empires of the book burners there was no love lost either for Alexander Korda or Charles Laughton.

When Laughton left Hollywood in 1935, he had not

175

anticipated the dictatorship's power spreading so fast. Stefan Zweig had warned of the danger, but Charles never thought that Hitler could go unchecked indefinitely.

The Laughtons were planning a long stay in England. They hunted for a new apartment and finally rented a sumptuous flat in Gordon Square, Bloomsbury. Together they planned the necessary decoration. Walls were torn down and enormous windows added. They bought furniture, mostly pale-finished modern pieces of the most advanced design. But it was impossible to ignore the mood of the times—an oppressive sense of imminent disaster. The Hitler regime, which had driven Germany's greatest writers into exile, was now forcing out its most brilliant theatrical and film people.

Marlene Dietrich protested strongly against the Hitler tyranny in her native country. Henceforth she was to sever relations with German film-making. Ernst Lubitsch followed her example. Erich Pommer, one of Germany's outstanding producers, left Germany not to return as long as Hitler was in power. But the most telling example of all was when Elisabeth Bergner left Hitlerland and went to London with her producer husband, Paul Czinner.

The Goebbels propaganda machine waged unremitting war against Alexander Korda, which only strengthened Charles's ties of loyalty and friendship to Korda.

Long before Charlie Chaplin had done a parody of Hitler in *The Great Dictator,* Laughton had portrayed a ruler gone berserk in his Nero. Now he made another excursion into this field. He went to Italy to finish *I, Claudius,* the film based on the fascinating novel by Robert Graves. His friend Josef von Sternberg directed the picture, which was filmed at the Denham Studios and in Italy. It was a timely story dealing with assassinations and violent seizure of power in the Roman Empire.

Laughton threw himself into the role with zest. He played Claudius, the usurper who is later proclaimed a

god, as a little man with a stutter and a lame leg. Said
Laughton of the character, "They made Claudius an
emperor because they thought him insignificant, and
then found he was cold as hell."

After the *I, Claudius* picture was finished, Charles took
time out to enjoy London, the city which has been the
cradle and the Mecca for so many actors. He and Elsa
wanted to devote time to their friends. Their hospitality,
in fact, became a London byword; fellow actors, writers
and painters were sure of a welcome in Gordon Square.
London, in its turn, was glad to have them back in England. Department stores exhibited stills from *Henry VIII.*
Guards in the British Museum noticed that visitors per-
sistently stopped at Holbein's famous Henry VIII and
said, "Look, here's Charles Laughton."

Charles was now receiving more mail. Sometimes he
answered the letters with a witty note. Among the fan
letters he still has one from a titled lady who offered
to sell him a rarity, Henry VIII's wedding ring. Laughton answered, "Dear Madam: It's not quite a rarity.
Henry had so many wedding rings . . ."

Laughton had always gravitated toward London's
literary set. He now became good friends with one of
the most prominent and successful writers of the day—
Hugh Walpole, infallible best seller and popular lecturer, a tall, broad man with a jaw like that of a bulldog.
Walpole, usually the happiest of men, was at this time
consumed by a secret sorrow. Somerset Maugham had
lampooned him—portraying him as Alroy Kear in *Cakes
and Ale.* In the novel Walpole was presented as an opportunist and careerist sedulously cultivating his reputation
as a master of English literature. The resemblance was
unmistakable. Walpole felt that he had been brutally
ridiculed. He was deeply hurt and needed sympathy.

Charles was not quite so commiserating as he might
have been, for Maugham had done to Walpole what
Laughton had once done to Arnold Bennett—caricatured

a well-known man. All Laughton could do was to advise
Walpole to be philosophic about it. "It happens to everyone," he told the novelist.

Yes, London was wonderful. The Laughtons hoped
to be able to stay there permanently. They positively
luxuriated in their fine apartment, a perfect setting for
Elsa's striking flower arrangements. It was the scene of
many witty and brilliant evenings—as well as of earnest
talks with Alexander Korda, for it seemed as if Laughton
might team up with Korda on a more permanent basis.

Alexander Korda had founded London Films in 1932.
From the first, he had the gift of recruiting the best
actors for his projects, which were interesting, unconventional and bold. Korda knew that the seven pillars of
his company's success were Charles Laughton, Merle
Oberon, Vivien Leigh, Ralph Richardson, Deborah Kerr,
Sir Carol Reed and David Lean.

It would seem that every star who was made by Korda
has remained a friend and admirer of his. Often they
return to the fold years later and do another picture
under his great direction. Laughton, for his part, has
always remained grateful to Korda. They severed connections only because Laughton felt an urge sooner or
later to handle the production of movies or the stage
and not to limit himself to acting only. Laughton's praise
of Korda has always been unqualified. In this he rather
resembles actress Merle Oberon, who was married to
Korda in 1939. When she divorced Korda six years later,
she made it clear that she still held Korda in the highest esteem and gave him praise saying: "I'll always be
grateful to Alex, of course. We still are very great friends.
No one who has ever been closely associated with Alex
can ever be completely dissociated from him. He has such
great charm."

Charm is Korda's most conspicuous quality, but he is
also a man of enormous talent. He went to England in
1931 with a wide background in journalism and film-

making on the Continent. He is the star of any social gathering, and has an inexhaustible flow of good talk— everyone gravitates around this man who, in a heavy accent, talks motion pictures wittily and urbanely.

Success came to Korda perhaps because he was seeking more than money. When he first broached the idea of *The Private Life of Henry VIII,* he was frank enough to warn Laughton it was a gamble. People who knew the movie business all made a point of telling Korda that the subject was a dud. Audiences were more interested in the private life of the king's chambermaid, they said. Korda and Laughton chose to disregard the experts. They gave the audiences a great picture and proved that such a picture could be a success.

Of course the same theory did not hold when it came to the Rembrandt picture. There it was a case of unlucky timing. When Laughton finally made up his mind that the arrangement with Korda wasn't what he wanted, he nevertheless admitted, "It wasn't easy to leave the magnetic Korda charm." Charles had decided to return to the London stage. He had less qualms about leaving Korda than he might otherwise have had; it was clear to all that Korda was firmly established. He had just signed up Vivien Leigh for a five-year contract and was producing her first picture, *Fire Over England.* Financially, he was still on shaky grounds—in 1939 he was in debt to an insurance company for more than six million dollars. But his star was on the rise. He emerged from the war and postwar periods as one of the greatest motion-picture magnates in the world.

Both the Laughtons had been approached by the Daniel Mayer Company to play in *Peter Pan.* The Korda commitments had made such a move unfeasible. Now Charles was just in the mood to tackle such an assignment. He had long cherished the conviction that Captain Hook was one of the greatest comedy roles an actor could play. He had additional motives for wanting to play Captain Hook—motives that were personal and sentimental. The late Gerald du Maurier had won his greatest triumph in this unique role. Laughton, who for years had worshiped Du Maurier as one of the greatest actors of his time, saw this as a way to inherit the latter's glory. What fun it would be to imitate his mannerisms, and how he was going to love those priceless lines of the pirate king: "Spl—l—lit my infinitives" and "Oh, fame, fame, thou glittering bauble."

But while Charles gloated over Captain Hook—his mind already playing with the potentialities of the role, visualizing the laughter of the grownups and the shudders of the children, complications cropped up. The author of this highly sophisticated fable for children, Sir James Barrie, was a most difficult man. It was he who had the final word on any *Peter Pan* production. He took violent alarm at the idea of casting Charles Laughton in the role of Captain Hook.

When Charles heard that the author was bitterly opposed to him, he and Elsa decided to visit Barrie to learn what his objections were. The welcome they received was not the friendliest. The testy old man tried to embarrass them by saying in front of a butler, "I *thought* you would come to see me." He was certainly unfavorably disposed toward Laughton. "You'll terrify the children, Mr. Laughton," he said, "and after all, Captain Hook must not do that." Charles promised not to frighten the children. He would tone the part down, he would be as gentle as a lamb. Sir James still would not be convinced. He had a fixed idea about Charles—based on Captain Bligh, Nero and the various other monsters Laughton had played.

"Now you would make a *fine* Peter Pan," he said benevolently to Elsa. But he would not have Charles in the play. At that moment the telephone rang. Sir James went into the next room and talked for some ten minutes. When he came back, he said, "You should thank Elisa-

Culver Service

When Charles attended the preview of *The Hunchback of Notre Dame,* he was in agony and did not recognize himself.

No meaner or saltier sailor ever sailed the seven seas. Laughton, as Captain Bligh, in *Mutiny on the Bounty*.

In *Mutiny on the Bounty* Laughton's uniform was copied from that of Captain Bligh, dated 1789.

As Commander Sturm in *Devil and the Deep,* Laughton played his death scene so convincingly the cast feared he was dead!

Though Elsa portrays the "clicket" in *David Copperfield*, she wears her Peter Pan smile.

beth Bergner. She has just called to tell me that both of you would be perfect for Peter and Captain Hook. She assures me that it would be a great mistake if I did not let you do it." So it was only through the intercession of Miss Bergner that Laughton played Captain Hook.

The charming German actress was apparently one of the very few people who could sway James Barrie once his mind was made up. He was famous for being crotchety and stubborn. Norman Vincent Peale tells the story of an author who, in conversation with Sir James, mentioned that his finished book still lacked a proper title. "I wonder whether you can suggest something?" he asked Barrie.

"Any drums in your book?"

"No drums," said the author.

"Any trumpets?"

"No trumpets."

"I would call the book *No Drums, No Trumpets*," Sir James said triumphantly.

Sir James was on the scene to supervise every step of the production of his play. The Laughtons began to wonder why they had wanted to be in it in the first place. It was to be one of London's famous and indispensable Christmas pantomimes. The rehearsals were difficult. The rest of the cast consisted of children who had done the same play every Christmas season and knew their lines backward. Sir James's major complaint was that the children always did much better at rehearsals than at regular performances.

A difference of opinion arose as to how Elsa Lanchester was to dress. Elsa, a dancer, felt that the costume should be as simple as possible—it was a question of projecting Peter Pan by acting, not by fanciful clothes. But the old playwright had set ideas about his pet characters. Elsa finally bowed to the ailing Barrie.

The reviews were not bad, but they were certainly not overenthusiastic. Elsa's comment on her husband was that she wondered whether Charles would ever play Captain Hook again. He had not had the fun he had expected—on account of Barrie. He had toned the part down until there was no challenge to it. As an actor Charles needed the stimulus of a "big" part—he had guessed wrong on the possibilities inherent in Captain Hook.

If Irving Thalberg had lived, Charles would have become a Hollywood film producer as well as an actor, for the two men had dreamed of that possibility. But fate had dictated otherwise. Now Charles, independent, without a Hollywood contract and happy to be "unsigned," decided to go into British-American picturemaking together with Erich Pommer, who had been one of Germany's great producers before Hitler. They founded the Mayflower Pictures Corporation. The company harvested no great profits, but gave the world first-class movies. Their film property consisted of three shooting scripts: *Vessel of Wrath,* which was one of Somerset Maugham's short stories; *St. Martin's Lane,* an original screen play by Clemence Dane; and *Jamaica Inn,* adapted from the novel by Daphne du Maurier.

It was Charles Laughton's first real business venture, and he entered into it with almost childlike enthusiasm. It was jolly to be going to "the office" every day. He was now on the other side of the camera and in a position to leave a greater stamp on the picture than he could ever do as an actor.

Erich Pommer, his partner, was famous as one of the pioneers in the history of the motion picture. As far back as 1919 he made the first futuristic modern art picture ever produced, *The Cabinet of Dr. Caligari.* He was then head of UFA, the foremost German film company.

Caligari is still cherished today as one of the great milestones in the development of the movies. It was the forerunner of all the psychological thriller and horror

films. Through novel lighting effects and stylized back-
grounds, Pommer revolutionized film production and
made movie history. His was too original a mind ever
to fit readily into the Hollywood or even the European
movie world. He had been in movie-making since he was
eighteen, when he got his start with the French Gau-
mont Company. Later he produced *The Last Laugh* with
Emil Jannings, and *Passion* with Pola Negri. He introduced such stars as Lillian Harvey and Conrad Veidt. He
finally became production manager at Paramount and
revolutionized the film industry a second time by creating multi-language films—screen plays in which several
foreign languages are spoken. It was this man, with his
international outlook, who now became Laughton's
partner.

Maugham's *Vessel of Wrath* was the first picture on
the agenda. For American distribution the picture was
renamed *The Beachcomber*. Preparations took at least
six months. Erich Pommer and the Laughtons moved
to the south of France and set up headquarters at Ste.
Maxime. The two men then set about exploring the surrounding countryside for a location with the necessary
tropical background. They combed Antibes and Cannes,
Le Levandou and St. Tropez, where they stopped at
Somerset Maugham's villa to report progress. Maugham
was very pleased to see his story brought to life on the
screen. He extended his blessings to the whole company,
which included Elsa Lanchester and Tyrone Guthrie.

The story was novel and interesting. Ginger Ted, an
inveterate loafer and no-good, was to be reformed and
loved by Martha Jones, the missionary. The script was
sprightly and dramatic. Charles Laughton as Ginger Ted
played the beachcomber and remittance man who is the
public nuisance on a tiny island in the Dutch East Indies.
His drunken escapades and his dangerous charm make
him a prime source of irritation to the strait-laced missionary.

Erich Pommer and Laughton finally settled on two locations. One was near St. Tropez. The other was a large estate between Cannes and Nice, the Château Robert, formerly owned by a wealthy American who had established there one of the most beautiful mimosa gardens of the Côte d'Azur. It was now abandoned and going back to the wilds—with its lush, semitropical vegetation it could well double for the East Indies.

Though few married couples in the movies will do it, Elsa Lanchester has never objected to playing opposite her husband. At that time Elsa remarked, "Being married to Charles makes it easier to act two people in sympathy. If Charles puts his hand on mine, I do not have to act. There is a kind of 'natural naturalness' between us."

Most of the shooting was done under the midday sun in order to get the tropical shadow effects at which Pommer was a wizard. The protagonists, Ginger Ted and Martha Jones, had a tough assignment. According to the script, they had been tramping for many miles. They had to look the part. For the desired disheveled effect, their clothes were sloshed with water and they were sprinkled with ashes so that they looked sufficiently dusty. Of course the sun dried the wet clothes in no time. Every thirty minutes they had to be splashed again. Erich Pommer, with German exactness and conscientiousness, did some of the splashing and ash-sprinkling himself.

At the second location, near St. Tropez, the Mayflower Company had hired two boats. It seemed as if Laughton never would escape his ordeals by water. But then he was hardened to them by that time.

In one of the scenes Laughton had to carry the missionary lady from a broken-down boat to the beach. He was wading through the sea with his fair burden in his arms when he stepped on a rock, stumbled and dropped Elsa Lanchester into the water. The bystanders rushed to the rescue—was Elsa all right? She hadn't broken any bones or ruined her costume? Fortunately, the accident proved harmless. As a matter of fact, Elsa fell into the water eight times during the shooting, giving rise to the legend that Charles Laughton threw her off the Rock of Gibraltar.

The shooting in France had taken four weeks, but there was more to come. The Wonosombo or typhus epidemic with which the story ended still had to be filmed. Two studio settings were put together to make a tropical jungle. Artificial rain came down in bucketfuls to imitate a tropical storm. Extras of many nationalities, clothed in loincloths and brandishing spears, played the stricken natives. It was a hectic atmosphere not easily dispelled after shooting by the usual cold shower or the evening cocktail.

Finally, after numerous trials and tribulations, Martha Jones married Ginger Ted and the Laughtons could return to London. It was a pleasure to get back to their lovely apartment—which, however, soon began to house a collection of secondhand clothing to be used for Charles's next film. Lights burned late while Pommer and Laughton discussed *St. Martin's Lane* and *Jamaica Inn,* their forthcoming pictures.

Charles had greatly enjoyed his stint in *The Beachcomber.* For once he had not played a monster—merely a weak and lovable cad. In softer moments of self-indulgence he would admit, "I like romantic parts and romantic tendencies in characters very much." But his looks were against him. He was actually to wage a lifelong battle against the unwritten law that a stage or screen lover must be handsome. Everyone knows that in real life romantic heroes are not only plain, but often are downright homely. Fairy tales and folklore take this fact into account when they describe men like Bluebeard as ugly and irresistible. Still, the theater throughout its history has shied away from fat, homely lovers. By this convention Laughton is barred from Casanova, Adonis and Romeo roles. *The Beachcomber* was a particularly interesting episode in Laughton's career because it represented his challenge to this convention.

Commercially, *The Beachcomber* and the picture that followed it, *St. Martin's Lane,* were not very successful. Between finishing the one and starting on the other, the Laughtons took a short holiday, during which Charles went down to Scarborough to spend some time with his folks. He presented his mother with a beautiful handkerchief for her lace collection. The handkerchief had cost £10, a fact which the newspapers pounced upon and converted into the tale that Laughton never used anything for his precious nose coarser than a £10 handkerchief. Charles and Elsa had a good laugh over that story, especially since Laughton's ruling passion at that time was to haunt the old-clothes dealers in Shaftsbury Avenue and St. Martin's Lane. The mustiest and most ragged items in their stock were what Laughton brought home—he was laying in a supply for his part as the tramp in *St. Martin's Lane.* Their apartment rapidly became a veritable rag shop, and smelled like one, too, for no amount of airing and disinfecting could remove the smell from the clothes.

The Mayflower Company began to suspect that they would need at least one box-office hit if they were going to balance their books. They therefore decided to sign up the master of suspense, the genius of the world of shadows, the man who makes movies move—Alfred Hitchcock.

Daphne du Maurier's novel *Jamaica Inn,* with dialogue by J. B. Priestley, was ideal material for Hitchcock. It was a romantic thriller with the salty flavor of England's Cornish coast, set in the lawless days at the turn of the eighteenth century. The characters were a band of outlaws, land pirates who lured ships to their ruin in the Cornish bays for the sake of plunder.

Alfred Hitchcock now became boss. He had won his reputation for suspenseful direction with *The 39 Steps, Secret Agent* and *The Lady Vanishes.* Everyone at Mayflower hoped and prayed that his magic touch would make this last picture a success. Hitchcock was the acknowledged master of the modern thriller. Any picture he made bore the unmistakable Hitchcock stamp.

The rotund director explained his essential formula to his new colleagues, Pommer and Laughton. "I like to build tension, then suddenly throw in comic relief so that the audience can laugh and laugh at the right time."

Hitchcock, like Pommer, had started young in the motion-picture industry. He was nineteen when he took his first job as a film title writer. Before that he had studied to be an engineer, attending the Jesuit college in his native London. From his first film, he stuck to his contention: "A picture must be realistic and believable."

Jamaica Inn starred a new discovery from Ireland, Maureen O'Hara—an auburn-haired beauty still under eighteen. Emlyn Williams, who was to win fame later, also appeared in it, and took occasion to voice the not uncommon dream of actors: "I've always been just going to play Hamlet, and I really want to do it in the end. I'd love to try it with a good director."

If this was a hint to the Mayflower Company, all concerned took care not to hear it. They were in no mood to try anything so delicate and risky as a movie version of *Hamlet.* This was to come many years later, with Sir Laurence Olivier in the title role.

Affairs on the Mayflower lot were not going so smoothly as they might. There seemed to be a certain amount of rivalry between Hitchcock and Pommer. It is significant that Hitchcock, in discussing that picture, has much to say about Laughton's performance but makes hardly any mention of Erich Pommer. As a matter of fact, this film was to be the beginning of the end of the Pommer-Laughton collaboration.

That there were also clashes between Hitchcock and Laughton is evident in Hitchcock's polite remark: "Laughton is a powerful personality, a gifted delineator of colorful types, a magnificent intellect." For all his respect for Laughton's ability, Hitchcock insisted on things being done his own way. Laughton had to redo many scenes. Hitchcock, who depends for effects on surprise and audio-visual techniques, felt that Laughton was inclined to be a little heavy-handed and rhetorical. Said Hitchcock: "I found it a problem in the filming of *Jamaica Inn* to blend Laughton's tendency toward rhetoric into the swift-moving action sequences which make up the story." For Hitchcock, swift motion was everything. For Laughton, sound characterization was the most important factor.

So basic a disagreement demanded compromises by both sides. Hitchcock's final rueful conclusion was his statement to the press: "Directors can't direct a Laughton picture; the best they can hope for is a chance to 'referee.' "

He observed the methods of his temperamental star and gave away no trade secrets when he paid sincere tribute to Laughton's work in any role: "The ease with which Mr. Laughton seems to deliver his lines and gestures on the screen is misleading. No actor ever agonizes more to get smooth results. A Laughton picture is one long battle from start to finish. Laughton versus Laughton. He frets and strains and argues continuously with himself. And he is never satisfied." On another occasion Hitchcock exclaimed: "Charles Laughton is no movie actor—he's a genius." An actor could not hope for greater praise.

One evening Laughton confided to Hitchcock that he did not foresee a bright future for the Mayflower Corporation. The basic idea on which it had been founded was the production of movies for both sides of the Atlantic. But British and American taste in

motion pictures was too different. Laughton was thinking
of returning to Hollywood. He would try to sell his
shares and liquidate his business career in England.

This decision led to the question of Hollywood versus
Europe. The two men started to compare notes and
theories. Laughton listened with interest to what
Hitchcock had to say about Hollywood and Hollywood
glamour, toward which both of them took a critical
attitude. They also knew from their own experience that
no director, producer or actor was stronger than the
system.

Hitchcock pointed out one important difference
between Hollywood and England. "In England," he said,
"we do not try to make our screen actresses conform to
any set standards of beauty. On the contrary, every effort
is aimed at keeping them individual in appearance."
Laughton agreed that this was so. He wished only to
point out that Hollywood seemed to have gathered
together more beautiful women than could be found
anywhere else on earth. "The only pity," Hitchcock said,
"is that they seem to look all so much alike on the screen."

There were no glamorous women in glamorous roles
in *Jamaica Inn, The Beachcomber* or in *St. Martin's
Lane*. This lack showed up at the box office.

Years later, when Laughton again met Hitchcock,
they started joking about their favorite old subject,
Hollywood glamour. "What new surprises have you for
us in the future?" Laughton asked the master of the
suspense film. Hitchcock replied, "I should like to make
a thriller about the United Nations in which the delegate
of a certain nation is denounced by another delegate for
falling asleep in the middle of an important speech. They
go to wake the sleeping delegate only to find him dead
with a dagger in the back."

Laughton was already on tenterhooks, but Hitchcock
coolly broke off the story. "Of course that is only the
beginning," he said.

Chapter 13

HE WORLD was at war again. The blackout fell over London, Paris and Berlin. In London, cinemas and theaters closed down, although by and by many relocated in the suburbs. The Paris opera moved to Nantes. Actors and entertainers sustained as best they could the tradition of "the show must go on."

The Laughtons had been in England for four years. Three months before Hitler's armies invaded Poland they returned to America. Charles had fled back to England originally because he was afraid of being typecasted. He had another picture pending for the Mayflower Company (which the war postponed), but had been lured back to Hollywood with the offer of the part of Quasimodo in Victor Hugo's *Hunchback of Notre Dame*, "Probably one of the greatest parts any actor was ever allowed to play."

We get a good picture of his plans, outlook and mood of the time in the charming letter he wrote to Rose Pelswick, then critic of the *New York Journal American*.

"Dear Rose Pelswick:
"Some little time ago you asked me how it feels to come back to America after such a long absence. Well, it's great; not only for the conventional reason that I like America immensely, which I honestly do; but for the additional reason that this trip will give me the chance to verify a theory which I've had for a long time: that

a man never really gets to know himself until he becomes his own boss.

"You see, for many years—all the time I was on the legitimate stage and in films in England and this country —I used to think of myself as a pleasant sort of chap; a little on the artistic side perhaps, but quiet, under-standing and on the whole pretty easy to get along with.

"But just as I had this mental image of a certain fat man named Charles Laughton fixed in my mind, Erich Pommer, the producer, and I went into business together. We formed Mayflower Pictures in London and right then it started.

"Right away it developed that I had been masquerad-ing under false colors; that I was a dual personality, although I pledge you my word that I had never suspected that dreadful fact before; instantly I split in two, like an amoeba, a herring or a frankfurter roll. From a single fat man named Charles Laughton I turned into a com-bination of Charles Laughton the actor, and Mr. Laughton the businessman.

"The whole thing started out very pleasantly. Erich Pommer, one of my oldest and dearest friends, produced all three pictures which we've turned out for Paramount release to date—*The Beachcomber*, which you've already seen; and *Jamaica Inn* and *London After Dark* which will soon arrive in this country. My wife, Elsa Lanchester, got the feminine lead in the first picture; in *Jamaica Inn* the cast was made up of people like Leslie Banks, Emlyn Williams, Robert Newton and others with whom I've been pals for years, and little Maureen O'Hara, whom Elsa and I have practically adopted as a member of our family. The same thing with *London After Dark*. Prac-tically everyone in the picture, from Vivien Leigh, Ralph Richardson and Tyrone Guthrie down to the extras, has been a close friend of ours for years.

"And in spite of this almost family setup, I started discovering the nasty side of this dual personality—the businessman. He has a sordidly practical nature, that Mr. Laughton, the tycoon of finance. His pockets are always filled with little pieces of paper covered with figures. He scowls constantly at anyone who suggests any idea at all which might cost a little money. He accuses directors of being too artistic and too much inclined to be dreamers. He speaks sharply to his own wife, and when that lady barks back at him with the spirit that she occasionally shows, he sulks disgustingly.

"Worst of all, he has turned out to be a slave driver.

"Each time we finished another picture, we returned to London. We started feeling more like ourselves. Mr. Laughton, fiend of figures, slowly started vanishing. I, his alter ego, began just as slowly to be received back into the good graces of my wife and my friends—until the time when we started the next picture, when the whole routine began over again.

"And that's one of the real reasons why I'm so glad to be back in America at this time. I've come over to make a picture—not for my own Mayflower concern, but for another company entirely, RKO. While I'm here, I don't have to worry about a thing that concerns the business angles of the picture.

"I know that while I'm working on *The Hunchback* I'll be able to be Charlie Laughton as actor all the time. My mind is perfectly at ease about that. But when I get back to London—ah, that's where the rub will come! You see, as soon as I return I'm scheduled to play *The Admirable Crichton*, which Mayflower will make. And that's where I'll be able to see if the 'cure' I will have had in America may be considered permanent.

"If it is, I'll soon know it. But if I backslide to the point where I once more start adding up little collections of pounds, shillings and pence, I'll know there's no hope for me. I'll have to resign myself to looking in the mirror one morning and smiling; and the next to staring at myself and muttering, 'You Scrooge! You Simon Legree!'

"Yours with a puzzled frown on his face. Charles Laughton."

The war changed everything for the Laughtons. Charles was never to do *The Admirable Crichton*, a picture dear to his heart, because for once he would represent a thoroughly decent fellow. It was years, in fact, before he would see London again. At the outbreak of the war Charles and Elsa rushed to the British consul to offer their services and put themselves at the disposal of their country. It was a depressed and frustrated couple who left the consulate. They had been told to stay where they were and continue their normal activities. They were not needed. Laughton did not take kindly to such a negative role. Throughout the war he was oppressed by guilts—he had not been able to do his bit for Britain; his countrymen would misunderstand him; his British audiences would resent his not returning home. It took several years of reasoning before he could overcome this guilt feeling and make the necessary transfer of loyalty to his second homeland, the United States. When America was attacked at Pearl Harbor, he gave himself full-time to the war bond and U.S.O. war effort. In 1943 he applied for American citizenship.

The world was aflame, but in Laughton's words, "Hollywood was still the same ham's paradise." He had come back to California to play another monster, this time the Hunchback of Notre Dame. "Oh, if I could be starred opposite a Garbo or do a picture with Dietrich," he often exclaimed. But there was no chance of that in Hollywood.

He was never to play the young lover even though, at forty, he still looked amazingly juvenile and cherubic and dressed with the same jaunty, negligent air as his own Beachcomber. He knew that staying permanently in Hollywood meant becoming resigned to such roles as the hunchback—monster, fat man, freakish eccentric, the Hollywood concept of "character actor" who takes any wild parts that may come along.

The situation held another danger, though a less obvious one. In international circles Laughton was considered an actor of the greatest magnitude. He had played the leading roles in such fine pictures as *The Private Life of Henry VIII* and *Rembrandt*. But in Hollywood, though he was treated with great respect, directors saw in him only the great supporting actor, not the leading man. Such roles were reserved for young and handsome men. Talented or not, it was they who were assigned the star roles of lovers, happy husbands, war heroes and film idols.

It was years before Laughton realized just what his status was in Hollywood. He could receive the highest weekly salary but still he was doomed to be the uncrowned king of the supporting actors—not the prince of players. He realized that Bing Crosby—who in his modesty has attributed his phenomenal success to plain luck—was right ten times over when, in reply to a question by Oscar Levant as to whether he liked movie work, replied, "It's all right, but you have to watch out for traps like the one I'm caught in—being typed."

And Charles was now typed for the rest of his natural life.

He had hoped to escape the fate of a Hollywood actor by his venture with Erich Pommer and the Mayflower Company. Now he was eagerly waiting to see the American reception of *St. Martin's Lane* which had been renamed *London After Dark* and finally had its American première under the name of *The Sidewalks of London*.

The film was an utter flop in America. "Dullish is the word for it," wrote *The New York Times*. "Laughton is disappointing," was the almost universal verdict. Yet this picture is today cited as one of the great pictures in motion-picture history. In spite of the fact that American

critics did not like it and that it failed completely by
box-office standards, its cast was studded with new,
unknown and highly gifted actors from whom the world
was to hear in years to come. It touched on a theme which
twelve years later was unknowingly adopted and raised
to glory in Chaplin's *Limelight.* Vivien Leigh was the
star, long before she became famous as Scarlett O'Hara
in *Gone with the Wind*; she played the part of a young
dancer called Liberty, or Libby for short. Rex Harrison,
Tyrone Guthrie and Larry Adler were in the same cast.

The picture dealt with the trials and tribulations of
the buskers of London. A busker is a fourth-rate street
entertainer who usually turns up and puts on a show for
the benefit of the queue waiting for tickets outside
London theaters. The gamin Vivien Leigh broke into
this game herself after Charles Laughton, a completely
untalented busker, makes her give up petty robbery and
takes her under his wing. She moves in with him and
becomes a dancer. Eventually Libby-Liberty-Vivien
Leigh becomes a great star while Laughton disappears,
sinking without a trace into the slums of London.

Rex Harrison was one of Laughton's picturesque team
of buskers. This great British actor had started in the
theater at the age of sixteen. He was later to appear with
Ethel Barrymore in *Anne of the 1000 Days*, star in *The
Four-Poster* and even invade Laughton's own territory
and play Henry VIII.

Even then Rex Harrison was the master of the sophisticated manner and the flippant phrase. His particular style
showed up to perfection in the role of a down-and-out
street musician with the suave manners of a Noel Coward
hero. In fact, Rex Harrison put into this forgotten picture
with Charles Laughton one of his greatest characterizations, which may well match his role in *Anna and the
King of Siam.*

Larry Adler, the world's greatest harmonica player,

an artist who has given command performances before the late King George VI, King Haakon of Norway and grand old Gustaf of Sweden, who has made a concert instrument out of the mouth organ, was also in the busker team. It is hard to see how a picture presenting such personalities could have failed as utterly as it did.

Laughton, however, could see that the picture was doomed. Erich Pommer was in America at the time and he too could see that it was a failure. Why, they asked themselves desperately, but no one knew. It may have been the timing—war was crowding the sidewalks of London with air-raid wardens and defense workers rather than with buskers. And as the bombs fell upon just and unjust alike, this great picture was also buried in the rubble.

Vivien Leigh, who was to become Lady Olivier, was also in New York in 1940. She was not so anxious as the rest over the fate of the picture—for she was too deeply in love with Laurence Olivier to care about anything else. "Our love affair has been simply the most divine fairy tale," she said, to which Olivier added, "I don't suppose there ever was a couple so much in love."

Charles Laughton had chosen Vivien Leigh for the role of Libby in *The Sidewalks of London* because he felt that she, better than any other actress, was able to convey the mystery of the psychological development of a young girl into a mature woman. She was born in India and, like Laughton, had been a student at the Royal Academy of Drama. She had also studied at the Comédie Française and had made her debut in 1934 as Anne Boleyn in *Henry VIII*. She played Ophelia in *Hamlet* at the Old Vic in 1937.

Always frail and delicate-looking, she made a wonderful foil for the lovelorn Laughton in *The Sidewalks of London*.

She had worked with Olivier in a few British pictures, among them *Fire Over England*, but no particular

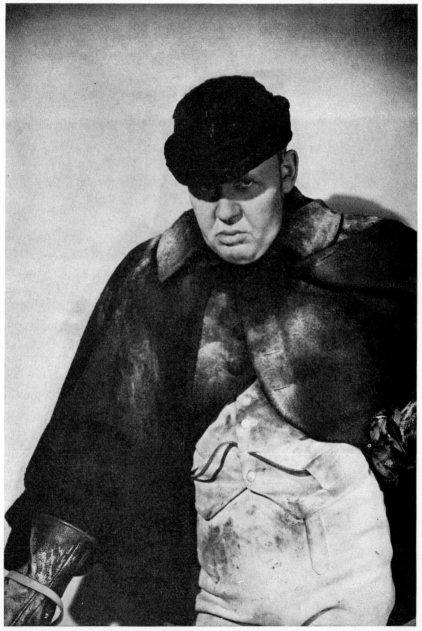

Penguin Photo

Laughton-Javert. "I myself was born in prison . . . I would never fail my duty toward the law. . . . It is my life."

Javert, fanatic agent of the law in **Les Misérables,** looks very subdued in the hands of Valjean (Fredric March).

Three winners of the Motion Picture Academy Award, Laughton, Shearer and March.

intimacy had developed between them. He seemed to stand so far above her, the great actor who had to his credit immortal performances in *Hamlet, Henry V, Wuthering Heights* and *Rebecca*. So it was all the more wonderful to both of them when they discovered each other.

Though there existed a subconscious rivalry between Laughton and Olivier, it never showed in the open. Laughton knew by this time he would never play *Hamlet, Romeo* or *Henry V*. But it was a great and generous actor who admiringly told Olivier after a Ralph Richardson production of *Henry V*: "Olivier—you're England."

Olivier never forgot this great tribute coming unexpectedly from a man whose judgment he always knew as high and fair.

Sir Laurence knew that Hollywood often gave Laughton the edge over him, and that the United States is the bigger country, with many more opportunities for a screen actor. Laughton, for his part, always realized that Olivier possesses features so regular as to make his own seem haphazard. Actually the only actor Laughton probably would want to be—were he not himself—is Sir Laurence Olivier.

One day Sir Laurence's motion-picture agent, Myron Selznick, introduced him and Vivien Leigh to his famous brother, the producer David Selznick. For two years Selznick had been searching for a new face for the leading lady in *Gone with the Wind*. He had not seen *The Sidewalks of London*, but immediately went to have a look at the latest Laughton picture and particularly at Vivien Leigh's performance in it. And he saw in Vivien Leigh all that Laughton had seen. But whereas Laughton's effort to put her across had failed, Selznick succeeded beyond anyone's hopes. With Laughton's leading lady, the Hollywood magnate produced one of the greatest picture triumphs of all time.

There was a certain kinship between the part of

Scarlett in *Gone with the Wind* and the part of Libby in *The Sidewalks of London*. Both pictures called for the portrayal of a lovely and altogether ruthless heroine. But the usual bystanders and wet blankets of the movie capital voiced the routine objections: Vivien Leigh—who was she? She couldn't act; she was a flop in the Laughton picture; she wasn't even an American, much less a Southerner. That meant she was absolutely unfitted for a part in the great Civil War drama. Nevertheless, this one picture raised Vivien Leigh, a talented but unknown young actress, to the very pinnacle of Hollywood success.

Here was another instance of the fickleness of fortune. An actor's career was a gamble. From picture to picture, from play to play—but nowhere more so than in Hollywood. After four years away from Hollywood, Laughton could see this clearly. He had the feeling that he had to start all over again on his climb to fame. It wasn't like starting at the bottom of the ladder, but still it was a long, hard, perilous climb. As far as his position in Hollywood was concerned, the past few years had been wasted. It was now quite obvious to him that American taste was different. His British pictures, in spite of fine scripts, first-rate actors and great directors, could never be popular in America. He perceived, for example, that though Hollywood loves to import "exotics," it had no use for foreign films. Later this situation was to change somewhat, but the rule still held. Foreign personalities were welcome, but they would be exploited the Hollywood way. The list of movie greats was studded with foreign names—Ingrid Bergman, Greta Garbo, Marlene Dietrich, Erich von Stroheim, Conrad Veidt, Raymond Massey, Sir Cedric Hardwicke, Maurice Evans, Dennis King, Fritz Kortner, Eric Pommer, Oscar Homolka, Paul Lukas, Hedy Lamarr, Albert Bassermann and others too numerous to mention. Laughton was only one of many in the legion of foreign actors and directors.

Hollywood took all these people, set them in a niche

and codified their uses. Laurence Olivier was the world's greatest romantic actor. John Gielgud was the greatest lyric actor. Charles Laughton was the greatest villain.

Again Charles was plied with possible scripts. He could take his pick from every variety of murder, terror and brutality. Nothing had changed, and nothing ever would change in this respect.

Laughton was plainly unhappy. There was no point in returning to England where the theater was at a halt. They did not want him for war service. He would never get a chance at any of the great lyric and romantic roles. All Hollywood let him do was to frighten children. Hollywood had decided that he could poison women, or, in a lighter moment, behead a few of them; Hollywood had decided that cruel and unnatural parts were his dish of tea, even though he bored himself and his audience to death. The pictures he had done under the aegis of the Mayflower Company had not changed a thing. With the great war on, he could see himself slated for ever more brutal action, more horror, more violence.

"A few more years of what I've been through and you might have to call on me in some psychopathic ward," he said.

But Hollywood's stereotype answer was, "Why change? No one can play a murderer the way Laughton can."

And Laughton had to admit that this was so. He seemed to have special gifts in that direction. An outstanding Los Angeles psychiatrist once asked him what he really thought of the murderers he has always had to portray. Laughton gave the matter some serious thought. His answer was slow and carefully considered. "The murderer fascinates me," he said. "I like to take him apart, to look in his eyes and dissect him. I like to know what had made him like that. But I have never felt the impulse to murder. My sins are never of aggression. They are always of omission. . . ."

No, Laughton is not a man of violence, though he

knows anger. Without being an opportunist, he is more apt to concede on certain issues than to fight, merely because his character lacks the element of aggression.

In a mood of rather dejected submission to the inevitable, he began work on the new film venture, *The Hunchback of Notre Dame*. This time he was cast as an out-and-out monster—not only a moral monster, but a physical one. This time Laughton refused to go on a diet —he was not going to put himself out to that extent for another grotesque role—so he played the stoutest Hunchback of Notre Dame in screen history.

"My make-up was horrible," he said, "simply horrible. I looked vicious enough to make anyone scream. You have never seen anything as hideous."

This was not an overstatement. The people in the make-up department had really outdone themselves. They covered the left side of his face with a sheet of sponge rubber, concealing his own eye and creating an eye socket lower down. The effect was of an almost unbearable deformity. To top off this hideous countenance, he was given an enormously large hump. Laughton let them do what they wanted, for after all, he was being paid a fee of seventy-five thousand dollars for the picture, with the studios obligated to cover his taxes in both the United States and England.

The Victor Hugo story had all the ingredients of drama, horror, torture and love interest the movies demand. It contained a scene in which three thousand beggars storm the Cathedral. There was shown the torture and flogging of the luckless hunchback. There was the grotesquerie of the "Feast of the Fools" in the Paris of Louis XI, where the idiots and beggars crown Laughton as their king. The drama reaches its climax with the hunchback saving Esmeralda from the hangsman's noose and escaping to the bell tower crying his brutish appeal, "Sanctuary!"

One thing pleased Laughton and that was the picture

offered many opportunities for pantomime. Like all great actors either in the comic or tragic spheres, Laughton relies on his body as an instrument for expression of character and feeling. He knows that he can speak with his body as deeply and as movingly as he can with his wonderful voice. He longs for parts that will give him a chance to practice this art, and delights to quote Leonardo da Vinci on the subject, who said, "The soul desires to dwell with the body because without the unity with the body it can neither act nor feel."

Laughton's greatest parts have always been based on powerful pantomime. That is his master formula for heightening stage illusion—the illusion audiences crave.

The Hunchback of Notre Dame was a smashing success, but when Laughton attended its preview in Radio City in New York, he could not recognize himself in the part and found sitting through the picture a protracted agony. "How could I be that bad?" he exclaimed. Again he made a vow to himself—the yearly vow which he inevitably broke, "I will no longer take unsympathetic roles."

Laughton had also supplied *The Hunchback of Notre Dame* with its leading lady. He brought her from London just before the war had started in Europe. When the *Queen Mary* bearing Laughton and her back to America docked in New York, the reporters who swarmed on board were slightly disconcerted when Charles Laughton presented them with an eighteen-year-old-girl—introducing her as his new leading lady. Everyone knew that he was married to Elsa Lanchester and it seemed more than a little unorthodox for a middle-aged man to be traveling with a young woman as pretty as she was. Suspicions were calmed when the mother of said young lady turned up and was introduced—she was evidently a formidable chaperone.

This was Maureen O'Hara whom Charles had already given a star part in *Jamaica Inn* in 1938. She was an Irish lass, a protégée of Elsa's whom the Laughtons launched on a brilliant career. She had an unearthly kind of beauty, with dark red hair and a white, faintly freckled skin. It was too bad that the fan magazines were to be cheated of the possibility of such an interesting romance. The reporters made up for the loss of a front-page story by writing up every other aspect of the famous arrival. They noted that Laughton's stateroom was fantastically untidy, that he packed simply by pitching his clothes into a suitcase, that the suit he was wearing was unpressed and wrinkled, that his face was so puffed from sleep and seasickness that he looked almost like the monster he was to play in *The Hunchback of Notre Dame*.

Erich Pommer was waiting at the pier and kidnaped Laughton away from the sensation seekers. Laughton threw these parting words at the press: "Don't you know I'm very shy, very shy of audiences. That's why I've done so much picture work."

On to Hollywood, where he plunged into the usual battle with his director, William Dieterle. Laughton had strong convictions on the way the picture ought to be produced. He had planned to do a version of it with Thalberg. "This is the way we visualized it," Laughton told Dieterle. Dieterle tried to explain his views and the reasons behind them, but he finally learned what Korda had learned—that no one can direct Laughton.

Dieterle was at that time and still is one of the top talents in Hollywood. German by birth, he was an actor in his twenties. He played at the famous Stadt Theater in Mannheim; worked with and under Max Reinhardt in Berlin; played Brutus in Reinhardt's *Julius Caesar*, went into movie-making with such important German pictures as *The Saint and Her Fool*. The great Reinhardt came to America as his assistant when they made their fabulous *Midsummer Night's Dream*, in which Mickey Rooney made his spectacular debut as Puck.

Dieterle directed Marlene Dietrich in *Kismet*, Bette Davis in *Juarez*, Paul Muni in his celebrated roles of

Pasteur and Zola, and later on Joseph Cotten in the romantic *Portrait of Jenny*. A good-humored chap, Dieterle was nevertheless Laughton's match when it came to determination. A certain amount of clash between the two was inevitable. Nevertheless, their combined efforts resulted in a fine picture, exciting, colorful and with more than the usual allotment of historical authenticity.

No Garbo, no Dietrich. But still Laughton, the archetype of the villain, teamed with such beautiful actresses as Vivien Leigh and Maureen O'Hara, Claudette Colbert, Tallulah Bankhead, Gloria Stuart, Merle Oberon, Norma Shearer, Mary Boland, Gertrude Lawrence. In his next two films he would add two more to his roster of beautiful leading ladies—Deanna Durbin and Carole Lombard.

The pictures he did with those two charming ladies represented a clean break with his erstwhile sinister roles. For once he was allowed to be human, even likable. He rubbed his hands with glee over his part in *It Started with Eve*, in which he was to play a sort of elderly Cupid, a white-haired, lovable fellow with a droopy mustache, twinkling kindly eyes and only a few albeit forgivable eccentricities. In fact, the whole part was so un-Laughtonesque that his admirers found it difficult to recognize him beneath the disguise.

The leading roles went to Deanna Durbin and Robert Cummings. Laughton played a supporting role only. He did most of his acting lying down in a huge carved bed piled high with down cushions and silk coverlets.

He found the picture a lot of fun. On his birthday Deanna Durbin presented him with a huge birthday cake. He was also handed an enormous bouquet of flowers by an extra, who presented it to him while he was still reclining on his ornate bed. Unfortunately there were some ants on the flowers, and Charles jumped out of the bed as though the silk coverlets had caught on fire.

"There are four things I hate," Charles lectured

Deanna Durbin. "Overacting, seasickness, cigars and ants." Deanna Durbin, the child wonder singer and a discovery of Eddie Cantor's, who later made the grade as an adult star, was not intimidated by his severe tone. "I see what you mean, Cuddles!" she said laughingly.

Deanna was the only one who could call Laughton "Cuddles" and get away with it.

His relationship with Carole Lombard was slightly more formal. Miss Lombard, who costarred with him in *White Woman* and *They Knew What They Wanted*, was one of the highest paid actresses in Hollywood, and one of America's most popular ones. In private life she was Mrs. Clark Gable. Shortly after her picture with Laughton, she set out on a coast-to-coast bond-selling tour and met her death in an airplane accident outside Las Vegas, Nevada. The whole nation mourned her loss, for Carole Lombard came closer than almost any other screen personality to being the sweetheart of America.

But she was missed especially in Hollywood, not only as one of the most beautiful actresses, but as an individual. She was far more approachable than many other stars. There was an earthy streak in her make-up to which everyone was attracted. On the screen this showed up as an intense and irresistible sexiness. In real life she insisted on behaving and being treated as "a regular guy." Because of this, everyone on the set—prop men, carpenters, electricians and chorus girls—adored her.

Charles heard dozens of stories about her—and passed the racier ones on to Elsa. He was charmed by Carole's casual approach to life. According to one story, she had been doing a scene with Bing Crosby, and after a session in very cold water she decided to give herself a rubdown with oil of wintergreen, which happened to be on hand. The oil started to smart her skin and rapidly became so irritating that she ran out of her dressing room, almost naked, and in front of all the people on the set jumped into the cool Catalina water for relief.

Few other women would have behaved so uninhibitedly. Carole never worried about shocking people. She even went out of her way to do so. For instance, she might go into a restaurant, and on spotting a male colleague greet him by saying loudly so that everyone could hear it, "By the way, did I forget my nightie in your bedroom?"

Her behavior was all in good fun. Laughton enjoyed her brand of humor tremendously. The one thing that never failed to amaze him was the way Carole, a member of the "weaker" sex, could actually outswear any producer, actor or truck driver. Her profanity, in fact, was famous. Bing Crosby, who, like Charles, had found it something of a phenomenon, has this to say about it, "Carole could lay tongue to more colorful epithets than any other woman I've ever known, and more than most men. Oddly enough, you never were shocked when she swore. You felt the way you feel when you're with a bunch of men who're fishing or working and one of them bangs his thumb with a hammer or gets a fishhook in his pants. If they swear, nobody pays much attention because they're entitled to let off steam. That was the reaction I had to Carole's profanity. It was good, clean and lusty. Her swearwords weren't obscene. They were gusty and eloquent. They resounded, they bounced. They had honest zing."

Laughton, too, came to accept her profanity as an integral part of Carole Lombard's charm.

In *They Knew What They Wanted* Laughton played an aging Italian winegrower in California's beautiful Napa Valley, and Carole Lombard was his mail-order fiancée. The film was based on Sidney Howard's Pulitzer Prize play. It was produced by Erich Pommer, no longer for Mayflower but for RKO, and directed by Garson Kanin.

Charles, who had portrayed an Italian earlier in his career, did a wonderful characterization of the successful peasant turned landowner, fat, amiable, fond of good living, resplendent in his best brilliant purple Sunday suit, with a handsome black derby hat on his head, and in his hand a pair of new patent-leather shoes "for da feet." "Looka me," he announced. "I'm da most stylish fella in da world."

He wins the heart of the audience, but not of Carole Lombard who as Amy is wooed at long distance by letters but finally marries Tony's hired hand after she arrives at Tony's home. The story takes place during the wine festival when, amid drinking and dancing and gaiety, Tony shows off until he falls from the roof of the house.

When the picture was finished, RKO's publicity staff had a brain storm. Why not send Laughton around with their own Terry Turner on a good-will safari to promote the picture—personal appearances in as many communities as possible. It would sell the film.

So suddenly, without any elaborate planning, Laughton, in the care of a publicity man, left Hollywood and set out to meet his movie audience face to face, like any minor actor out on the road. Elsa heartily approved of the idea. Those days Charles was at home too much, brooding, worrying over England and his family, worrying over the war. Their beloved London apartment had been demolished by bombs. A distraction would do Charles good, she said.

But how would Charles react to the trip, everyone wondered. Did he have the popular touch—could he establish contact with the thousands of average, small-town Americans who would turn up at the motion-picture houses?

Turner telephoned his bosses in Hollywood. "Do you know what he does? The man's incredible! He gets up on the stage and recites The Lord's Prayer, reads the Bible, quotes Shakespeare, reads poetry, quotes from his Rembrandt picture."

"Is it helping the picture any?" the voice on the other end of the line asked.

"Helping? Why, he packs them in!"

"That's all that counts. Let him recite The Lord's Prayer all he wants to."

And Charles Laughton has continued to recite The Lord's Prayer ever since.

Chapter 14

DURING the war I began to feel sorry for myself. I was restless. The movie work was not enough to keep me occupied. Elsa had called me a loafer. Hollywood entertainers were entertaining military hospitals, touring the war theaters of the world—what could *I* do?"

This question gnawed at Laughton day and night. True, he had had his share of active duty. He had been gassed during the First World War; he could remember how slowly and drearily the hours went by in an army hospital in France.

The Armed Forces were closed to him, but surely he could do something to help. He was no dancer, no singer, no instrument player. But wasn't there some other way of bringing a little cheer to the men?

It was then that "I asked out of a clear case of selfishness two boys from the Birmingham General Hospital visiting the studios if they would let me read to them—after all, I was a storyteller."

He was still shy of unselected audiences, afraid the soldiers "might throw ripe fruit at me." But he was ready to risk that chance. Fate in the guise of those two soldiers who had gone sight-seeing to Universal Studio altered Laughton's career for the following ten years and longer.

He had been a great actor and an ambitious producer.

208

He was to shoot nine pictures between 1941 and 1945. But at this time he emerged as the Prince of Storytellers.

One day he turned up without official invitation at the Birmingham General Hospital in the San Fernando Valley, a few miles from Hollywood, asking to entertain the troops for an evening. That night the hospital authorities welcomed him with open arms. It would, they told him, be a treat for the boys to be entertained with excerpts from such famous Laughton roles as Henry VIII or the brutal Captain Bligh.

Every seat in the hospital auditorium was filled, and excitement ran high as the rotund man in the rumpled suit stamped out on the stage, "looking like a bum as always."

"Boys," the sloppy figure started, "I'm going to read to you."

What a letdown! Like a wave a disappointed sigh ran through the auditorium. It took no mastermind to know that several thousand GI's had only one thought: What a bore! One even expressed that thought aloud. "Hell, anybody can read," he shouted. "I thought actors acted."

It must have been an ordeal for Laughton, who is still prone to acute stage fright. He is still nervous whenever he has to face a huge audience in a large and cold auditorium. But he had chosen his material with care; he had the utmost faith in it. He set his big bulk down on the chair in the middle of the platform and waited until the officer in charge of the recreation program shouted, "Let 'er roll." Then he began to read.

He opened with a few limericks, proceeded to James Thurber's version of Little Red Riding Hood, in which the point is made that little girls are harder to fool nowadays. Then he went on to a touching story of a French prostitute, following it with "To His Coy Mistress," the ever-fresh Andrew Marvell poem which is one of the most delightful masterpieces of English verse.

Working with nothing but his flexible voice and expressive gestures, Laughton read on, though he knew that in his audience of five hundred tough soldiers some of them had never read anything but comics.

From Marvell he turned to Shakespeare and Dickens, but as he continued, a nagging question entered his mind. He had no closing piece. Then as he made a few remarks between selections, he interpolated that he had recited the Gettysburg Address so many times that he had all but gone stale on it. As he said this, a blinded flier in the audience called out, "Mr. Laughton, do it now."

"Why?" a bewildered Laughton asked, thinking his point had been missed.

From the flier the answer came back: "I want to see how much it really means to me. I used to wonder, on missions over Germany dropping bombs that killed people, why I was doing it. Then I'd remember how you spoke the Gettysburg Address in *Ruggles of Red Gap.* I used to ask myself, is it just words or does it really mean something."

This was the sort of challenge to which Laughton can always respond. He launched into the address—"And," he said later, "I wasn't stale, I was good, for I had to be good."

He was doubly sure of his success when the applause came—deafening applause increased by the pounding of many crutches against the hardwood floor.

"To me this was a bigger thrill than all the bravos I ever listened to at Drury Lane or the Old Vic," Laughton said.

The soldiers who were able to walk thronged around him on the platform, eager to shake his hand. Others pushed themselves forward in wheel chairs. The boys on stretchers waited patiently for Mr. Laughton to go to their side of the auditorium. He shook hands with each of the five hundred. A corporal spoke for all of them when he said, "Mr. Laughton, I never thought I'd get such a lift out of mere words."

"I'll be back next week," he promised. "I'll read something even better."

Again the applause proved that he was wanted.

Laughton drove through the cool Hollywood night to his home in Santa Monica. He waited impatiently for Elsa to get back home—she was appearing at the Turnabout Theater. He had to tell her how it had gone over. Hadn't Elsa accused him of being a nuisance around the house? Hadn't she told him he ought to find a job? Well, he had. This would be his contribution to the war effort.

Hadn't *The New York Times* reviewer said in a recent article, "We do wish that someone would do something to put his eminent talent to right use?" Hadn't the other New York critics referred to him as a "man overboard"—meaning that so few satisfactory film roles had come his way during those war years?

Reading was a new career. Perhaps it had come to him late in life, but it was the fulfilment of early dreams. He would be a storyteller, a spellbinder. What if he had come to it by accident? What if there was an element of risk in it? What if it meant abandoning conventional acting. "Why shouldn't I switch?" he asked himself. "I knew a man who vowed at fifteen never to take a chance. You should have seen him at forty."

Laughton was not much over forty at that time.

A week later he returned to the Birmingham General Hospital and thanked the men for the wonderful reception they had given him on his first appearance. They had given him more than he possibly could have given to them, he said.

"I would like to be the man who knows all the stories," he began. "I would like to be the storyteller who has on his back a bag full of stories, as bottomless as Santa Claus's bag of toys. But that can never be, because no man could ever know all the stories, even if he were to live to be a thousand years old. Even I shall never know all the stories when I am a thousand years old."

That got a laugh.

But it was basically good therapy for wounded and convalescent soldiers sitting there in their red robes and pajamas, bandaged and with crutches. He wanted to instill in them the will and optimism to live, a vision of life's beauty and meaning—for most of those men were amputees facing a grim, painful future when, after the hospital release, they would return to normal society mutilated war heroes without uniforms and medals. Many were afraid of that return.

Laughton had grasped their mood. He had some insight into their problems, and it was with great gentleness that he said, "I shall never be a thousand years old and I shall never know all the stories in that way I like best—but it is a good thing to want to go on living longer than possible. It is better than wishing you were dead."

There was total silence in the auditorium. His audience was larger than it had been the week before. There were not only more of the men, but also nurses and orderlies. Again he faced an auditorium filled with men on stretchers and in wheel chairs. Everyone was eager to learn what the promised "better program" would be.

It turned out to be the Bible. None of the soldiers had ever heard the Bible read the way Laughton read it, vividly, with dramatic overtones and cadences and inflections.

There were tears in everyone's eyes—patients, nurses and doctors. The greatest praise came from an amputee who had lost both legs in the Pacific. "It's like seeing the Bible in technicolor," he said happily.

The hospital seemed to have turned into a cathedral as the patients and the staff joined Laughton in saying The Lord's Prayer. No one who heard that spontaneous recitation will ever forget it. Laughton spoke the opening words, and without a gesture, without a word, without a signal, every one of the men took up the lines until the massed voices sounded like the pealing of an organ with a plea of humility and hope to the Almighty.

Laughton had never planned on administering such powerful emotional medicine to the soldiers. It was more of a surprise to him than to the people in the hospital.

"How was it possible?" the psychiatrists asked. "That was better psychotherapy you gave them in one hour than we could give them in a month."

It had been done on the spur of the moment. It was another proof of Laughton's astounding flair for what a particular audience needed—the deep instinct of the actor.

"It's the ham in me," he said smiling.

The doctors were not satisfied with that answer. Why had he decided to read the Bible, they wanted to know. Why, that was easy, Laughton replied.

"Stories were told and retold for hundreds of years before they were set down. And these stories are the best stories, the stories which were told before they were written. This is so of the stories in the Bible. As an actor, it is easy for me to understand that they are for the voice. There are places to go loud and places to go soft and places to go fast and places to go slow. The Bible has made a storyteller out of me."

Later hearers, people who are perhaps in a more critical frame of mind than the hospitalized soldiers, have also been spellbound by Laughton's reading of the Bible. As one critic put it:

"Laughton brings to his interpretation of the Bible enthusiastic vigor. He combines dramatic power with true scholarship. Instead of declaiming the words as though they were overfamiliar texts, Laughton reanimates them with fervor and profound passion—the result of years of intensive study—and reads them as though they were a new experience, almost as if they had never been read before. He brings a fresh interest and understanding to the narratives which have always been inspiring but which now take on renewed life and power."

So as fate would have it, it was the Bible and not Shakespeare that opened a new field for Laughton, who up to that time had specialized in unsavory and thoroughly secular characters, such as Captain Bligh and Henry VIII.

Performances at Army and Navy hospitals and mental institutions were not enough for Laughton. The stints he was still doing for Hollywood companies were definitely not satisfying. He must do more, he felt. He suffered from a constant, haunting anxiety about the war. France was already lost. Could Britain go the same way? The whole world was engaged in a battle for survival and he was just acting, just reading. There were days and weeks of great depression and helplessness over his own inadequacies. His physical condition ruled out active service. "I look like a departing pachyderm," he said.

There must be more he could do. The tragic death of Carole Lombard on her bond-selling tour gave him an idea. He must put aside some time to go on a bond-selling tour through all of the United States.

After a sixteen-day bond drive starting in California, he finally reached New York. He entered WEAF's studios at Radio City in a state of complete exhaustion. He looked terrible, his face was puffed with fatigue, his eyes were half shut, his features were distorted and coarsened. The night before he had had only three hours sleep, preceded by a nine-hour script-writing ordeal and a bond rally in Connecticut.

It was 7:45 A.M. on the first Tuesday in October, 1942. He walked into the broadcasting room. A musical program was on the air, but he interrupted it without apology.

"Last night," he said, "I sold war bonds at a rally in Connecticut where I shared the platform with eight

American sailors back home to tell their war experiences and persuade Americans to buy bonds. At sea one hundred and seven days, their ship was damaged in the Battle of the Coral Sea, then bombed and sunk in the Battle of Midway. When these boys got back to San Francisco, they knelt down and prayed, wept and some even kissed the ground . . . and the civilians laughed at them."

His tone changed to one of deep indignation and urgency.

"Ladies and gentlemen, don't fool yourselves. American democracy is the last hope left to mankind, and you are the keepers of the flame . . . and make no mistake about it, that flame is flickering. God help you and your children and your children's children if that flame ever goes out. . . . I'm here on this program today to sell you war bonds. Why don't you call me up at Circle 6-4250 and buy a bond. By the way, I'm answering the telephone myself."

All this was spoken in an impeccable British accent. With it Laughton opened his unheralded one-man war bond drive over a single 50,000-watt New York radio station.

It was actually an endurance contest.

Rushing from studio to studio, he shook his air audience with his powerful voice and skilful histrionics. Sometimes he was friendly and cajoling; but more often he was angry and disgusted, ridiculing, shaming and even threatening the listeners. He delivered snatches of his characterization of Captain Bligh in *Mutiny on the Bounty* and his famous delivery of Lincoln's Gettysburg Address.

But the movie star's microphone work was only part of the day's job. He found time during the afternoon to address station employees. At the end of each broadcast he rushed to a smoke-filled room on the seventh floor, whipped off his coat, and slumped behind a table, facing a battery of six operators handling five telephones and tabulating the bond-pledge totals. Laughton talked to each purchaser, calling back later to congratulate those he missed in the rush. In the few free seconds he downed coffee, milk and an occasional slug of whisky. He tried to lie down on a couch, but those respites lasted less than a minute.

Laughton's first caller was Mrs. Myron C. Taylor, wife of the special envoy to the Vatican, who bought $1,000 worth of bonds. A four-year-old Brooklyn girl took a $25 bond. Another youngster, who said his brother was lost on the *Yorktown,* pledged to buy two $100 certificates. One man waited more than an hour in a telephone booth for Laughton to call him back and congratulate him.

A completely fagged Laughton ended his broadcasting at 11:25 P.M., only to make nearly one hundred calls to bond buyers he hadn't been able to speak to earlier. He finished at 1:15 A.M. As he pulled off the telephone chest transmitter and the earphones, his husky voice, which had been strained down to a whisper by nightfall, failed him entirely.

But the results of the seventeen and a half hours' work spoke for him. He had sold $301,000 in war bonds.

As it turned out, Charles never worked so hard as he did during the war years. He gave all his free time to bond drives and hospital and troop entertainment. But he still found time to work in nine pictures: *Tattle of Tahiti, Tales of Manhattan, Stand by for Action, Forever and a Day, This Land Is Mine, The Man from Down Under, The Canterville Ghost, The Suspect* and *Captain Kidd.*

None of those pictures offered the potentialities of *Henry VIII, Rembrandt* or *The Sidewalks of London.* It was inevitable that Laughton should put more and more of his heart into his public readings. They were one-man shows, one-man theater and one man's great contribution to the morale and spirit of a nation at war.

At that time Charles had his beloved house high on a cliff overlooking the Pacific Ocean at Santa Monica. Visitors would usually find him in the garden, the knees of his pants muddy from kneeling, his hands grubby too. He would beg his visitors not to mind his appearance. "They say every Englishman is born with dirt in his veins. The Nazis are just finding it out," he'd jibe.

If he were not in his garden, he would be indoors, running through a little play for his own benefit. "I'm an incurable ham. Even when I'm alone in a room, I prance about giving a performance for myself. Years of working at my trade only makes me love it more," he'd explain.

The day came when Laughton, grandson of a butler, finally felt that his position called for having a butler of his own. It was an unfortunate experiment and did not last very long. Both Elsa and Charles are unconventional people—the personal habits and style of dress of his master and mistress were a source of anguish to the very correct butler. For example, Charles loved eating in drugstores. One day an important producer called at the Laughton home, only to be informed by the butler: "Mr. Laughton is dining out, sir."

"But it's extremely urgent," the producer persisted. "I have to see him immediately. Do you know where he can be reached?"

In his most icy voice the butler pronounced the dreadful words:

"Mr. Laughton is dining at Schwab's Pharmacy."

Charles's personal life held many satisfactions, but the same could not be said of his professional life. He was sinking deeper into a quagmire of mediocre films. The public readings were a godsend. But as far as opportunities in Hollywood went, things were going from bad to worse.

Even the newspapers noticed the downward trend and asked embarrassing questions. The New York critics were especially cutting. No actor could remain smug in the face of articles which spoke of "Laughton's talent tossed carelessly away," or, "What has happened to Charles? Why is he but a shadow of his former self in everything but size?" Or, "Why has he been permitted to dissipate his talent in arrant mugging within the past few years?"

Laughton knew there was truth in all this talk, but what could he do about it? Had he eaten too much of the Hollywood lotus flower?

All his recent films had been flops; besides, they had never done justice to his great talent and potentialities. *Tales of Manhattan*, for example, was a typical Hollywood "cavalcade of stars," with Charles Boyer, Henry Fonda, Paul Robeson (Hollywood had not yet fired him as a Communist), Rita Hayworth, Ethel Waters, Ginger Rogers, Edward G. Robinson and Elsa Lanchester. Charles played the penniless musician who finally achieves his life's ambition and conducts a concert at Carnegie Hall, only to have his rented tuxedo burst open when he wields the baton. Though it was only a very small role, Charles handled it with something of his old brilliance. When the film's director, Julien Duvivier, congratulated Elsa and Charles for the beautiful way the two of them had rendered their roles of loving husband and wife, Charles said, "I let my wife steal a scene from me once in a while—just to keep peace in the family."

But *The New York Times* pounced hard on Charles again. "In *Tales of Manhattan* as a conductor he was farcical in a fashion which violated the mood."

His next picture got even a worse spanking from the reviewers. He played an admiral in *Stand by for Action* with Robert Taylor and Brian Donlevy. It was a hastily turned-out war picture, the first to deal with the heroism of the Navy on convoy duty. Laughton was totally miscast as an exemplary naval officer. *The New York Times* rightfully remarked, "As admiral, Laughton would not have passed in a third stock company of *H.M.S. Pinafore*."

Forever and a Day, the picture that followed, was even flimsier stuff than *Stand by for Action*. All that could be said for this picture was that its American profits went to a good cause, the National Foundation for Infantile Paralysis. The publicity department boasted that it had taken seven directors, twenty-one authors and seventy-eight players to make the picture. The reviewers naturally noticed that it was a case of too many cooks spoiling the broth.

Laughton had higher hopes for the anti-Nazi picture, *This Land Is Mine*. He welcomed the chance to play the part of a schoolteacher in occupied Europe. "My role stood for countless thousands of bewildered little people of Europe who have to face a master they hate and cannot understand."

Once more he played opposite his former protégée, Maureen O'Hara. In supporting roles were the suave George Sanders and the incredible Walter Slezak as Gestapo chief. One of France's great directors, his friend Jean Renoir, was in charge of the proceedings.

But it turned out to be a somewhat trite and superficial picture about occupied France. Laughton was lambasted by the reviews.

"As the timid and blubbering patriot, he was plainly grotesque . . . a gargoyle," said *The New York Times*.

When Laughton appeared in *The Man from Down Under*, as an Australian veteran who comes home after World War I with two French war orphans—who eventually fall in love and get married—*The New York Times* and many other papers frankly exploded over what Hollywood producers were doing to a fine actor. But they blamed Laughton too. Why, they asked, did he undertake such roles, when he had always stood firm against compromise?

Was this the same man who had won the Academy Award for *Henry VIII*, they asked?

The Man from Down Under was "a naive story,

clumsy, oddly lifeless," said the *Times,* protesting vigorously against the sort of roles Laughton was being given. "He was outlandish in *They Knew What They Wanted* a few years back," the newspaper said. "He was miscast as the old grandpa in *It Started with Eve."* In its mood of indignation, the critic even denounced Hollywood for Laughton's part in *Jamaica Inn*—which Laughton had done on his own in England.

Summing it all up, the moderate *New York Times,* which does not usually indulge in rash statements, concluded that Laughton had not been seen "since *The Beachcomber* in a really fine performance."

Those were damning words. Laughton did not answer them, though he was deeply hurt. He wasn't blind—he could see that the movie industry had geared itself for the war boom and was concentrating on quick turnover rather than quality production. He knew that his name had a value on which the studios wanted to capitalize. No one was interested in letting him have creative roles. He received fabulous salaries, but his roles were only supporting ones.

What could he do? What should he do?

He tried to find other outlets—poured more of himself into his readings and spent as much time as possible in hospitals. He even took a hand coaching amateur groups, encouraging young actors. He spoke before drama clubs and societies. He accepted invitations to read before church groups. There was a kind of pathos to those gropings, that search for a new audience. He was trying to find a way to make his art meaningful again.

His next film, *The Suspect,* was released at a time when the criticism against him was at its peak. Again he played a murderer, this time with Ella Raines, under the direction of Robert Siodmak. It did nothing to enhance his badly damaged reputation. It was a Grade B thriller, destined to be forgotten along with so many others.

His index took a sharp rise when he played a ghost with such verve and originality that the role won universal acclaim. The picture was *The Canterville Ghost,* with gifted Margaret O'Brien, then only six years old, and Robert Young. Laughton was not the star, but it was a big part, and most important of all, a part with possibilities.

The ghost in question was the restless spirit of Sir Simon de Canterville in Oscar Wilde's famous story. In 1624 Sir Simon had shown cowardice during a duel and was doomed to haunt the earth until a descendant of his would commit an act of great courage and bravery. Then and only then would the ghost of Canterville find peace.

Laughton was a lovable and whimsical spook. For his big speeches he insisted on using the original text of Oscar Wilde, which he delivered with all the eloquence and style of his old manner. He was being himself again. He had staked something of himself on this role and he put up a stubborn fight for his conception. He would act it the way he thought right. For instance, he refused to wear a wig. "This is absurd," he protested. "Whoever saw a ghost with a wig on?"

He was no longer passive, but opinionated as of old. He harangued the director and the make-up department. "What is a ghost like? You don't know. It's wholly a matter of imagination. Others in the cast would have to imagine they are seeing a ghost. How then am I to make up? And how does one behave like a ghost? Usually the question with an actor is to make what he is doing seem lifelike. But in my case as a ghost, it is necessary to make the character quite the opposite of lifelike. I will wear no wig and will not be flying around."

The director gave up, as Korda and Hitchcock had given up. For a spectral coiffeur, Laughton let his hair grow for three months, and appeared on the set with a very comical mustache that looked like a cat's whiskers.

The make-up man had never seen anything like it

either on the MGM lot or anywhere else. "I have never seen a mustache grow upward, Mr. Laughton. Only downward."

"Ah," Charles gloated, "have you ever seen a ghost's mustache?"

But no ghost ought to weigh two hundred and twenty-five pounds, and Laughton had to lose weight. Again he put himself into the hands of masseurs, and steamed himself in Turkish baths, where he was heard muttering:

> "O! that this too too solid flesh would melt,
> Thaw, and resolve itself into a dew . . ."

The Canterville Ghost was a total triumph for Laughton—it received good reviews and a good box office, as it met the general need for a lighter war story. The way was now open for Laughton's most popular role of all—Captain Kidd.

Here was a sort of Henry VIII scoundrel cast in a marvelous sea story, full of adventure, drama and fun for the general public of all ages. Captain William Kidd was the notorious seventeenth-century pirate who, after a swashbuckling career as a privateer in the pay of King William III of England, was hanged in chains in London—not for piracy, but for the murder of a member of his mutinous crew.

One of the most spectacular personalities of a gaudy era, he was presented by Laughton as the most picaresque villain who ever brandished a cutlass, ruled with an iron hand over a crew of ruffians, or buried stolen treasure—his legendary hoard included sixty pounds of gold, a hundred pounds of silver, brocades, rare muslin and diamonds. As far as is known, the treasure was never found, and historians estimate that it would be worth two million dollars today.

The film was such a huge success that it rated a comic

take-off entitled *Abbott and Costello and Captain Kidd,*
with Charles Laughton running around in long under-
wear and gorging himself on food à la Henry VIII. For
some reason directors and producers always feel compelled to introduce a water scene and an eating scene
into a Laughton picture.

One of the young actresses in *Captain Kidd* was the
daughter of a Methodist minister, the Reverend Adna
W. Brantingham of Long Beach. The young lady in question, Barbara Britton, had been brought up on the Bible
and even taught a Bible class on Sundays. She was sure
she knew her Old and New Testament well until she
met Charles Laughton on the lot. Charles, whose religious schooling was far in the past and whose earlier
adult life had been given up to more sophisticated reading matter, quickly discovered that Barbara Britton could
join him in his new-found enthusiasm. They had many
a Bible session together between scenes. To show her
appreciation, one day she brought him a pastry of her
own creation and gave it to him for lunch. A man of
hearty and discerning appetite, Laughton prepared a
pitfall for her.

"It's surprising," he observed offhandedly, "how many
things you can find in the Bible. Such as a description
of a hangover."

"No!" cried Barbara, shocked.

"No? I'll wager you a dozen of those little cakes of
yours that I can."

She rashly took the bet. He thereupon read from Proverbs 23:29-35, ending with the words, "I will seek it yet
again," this being a reference, in Laughton's interpretation, to the hair of the dog. Barbara paid off.

One day she took the notion of asking the pastor of
the North Glendale Methodist Church in California,
"How would you like to have Mr. Laughton read the
Bible at our church?"

"We would all be honored," was his answer.

And this is what Reverend Ezra Ellis had to tell about bringing Laughton to the Glendale Church:

"Barbara arranged that my wife and I visit her on the set where she was the only woman in the cast of *Captain Kidd* which Mr. Laughton was making. During one of the scenes she took us to Mr. Laughton's dressing room, and he was very gracious in agreeing to come to our church. However, his coming was not to be advertised. He said, 'I do not want a lot of people just interested in seeing a movie star. I want to read the Bible only for your people.'

"Several weeks later the Sunday evening arrived and so did Charles Laughton. In my study before the service he was very nervous. 'Do you know,' he said, 'at the radio studio this afternoon where I was rehearsing for a play to be broadcast on Lux Radio Theater tomorrow night, I was nervous as a cat. Someone asked me if the thought of broadcasting to so many millions of people made me nervous.

" 'Heavens no,' I told them. 'I'm nervous because I'm reading the Bible in church tonight.'

"When we were in the sanctuary he remarked that he was there because Barbara Britton had rolled her eyes at him and he could not resist. Then he added, 'And so last week what happens? She got married!'

"He asked me what he should read and I told him that he could read anything that was in the Bible. 'Anything?' he said, raising his eyebrows. 'Do you know some of the Bible stories?' I assured him he could read anything he desired from the Bible.

"So eloquent were his presentations of the words of David and Goliath, the Nativity story and passages from Proverbs that many church members went home that night to look up their Bibles. They found new meaning in the old stories.

"Perhaps this is the open secret of the Bible which

Charles Laughton found in his new adventures with the Word."

This was, of course, the cue for church after church, synagogue after synagogue, Army chaplain after Army chaplain, to ask Laughton to read the Bible. Laughton was at best a little alarmed at the way the movement gained ground.

"The idea of a movie villain discovering the Holy Scriptures intrigued the ministers, and I had to make clear to them that I was appearing as an actor and not to deliver a sermon."

He was still Captain Kidd the pirate when he was invited to speak before a group of forty-eight ministers in the home of Dr. Remsen D. Bird, the alert and popular president of Occidental College at Eagle Rock, California.

He arrived thirty minutes late, breathless, still in stage attire, and apologized:

"Sorry to be late, Dr. Bird. Captain Kidd—you know, the picture—and I've not even had time to remove my make-up."

The session that followed has made history. Seated in Dr. Bird's spacious drawing room were forty-eight ministers of the Gospel, some of more than local reputation, representing a rather comprehensive cross section of Christian Protestant belief, and all of them men with a practical grasp of the problems of workaday Christianity. The Old Testament in the hands of a skilled portrayer of emotion and mood lends itself wonderfully to dramatic interpretation. Under the magic of Laughton's soothing inflections, the magnetism of his voice, the artful interplay of ocular and facial expression, the familiar Biblical stories came vibrantly alive. He read the narrative of Noah and the Flood, of Tobias and the angel, the drama of David with its interesting supporting cast of Saul and Jonathan, Goliath and Uriah and Bath-sheba.

To undertake Bible reading to the outstanding ministers of California was a daring enterprise for anyone.

Laughton was quite elated by his success in what he called "my venture before the clergy."

He was currently making $100,000 or more a picture and was offered equally impressive fees for public readings. But he declined all offers and continued to read before church groups. Among his most striking pieces was the third chapter of Daniel. His vocal virtuosity found a wonderful outlet in reading about the grim and bloodthirsty King Nebuchadnezzar. He was also fond of reciting Psalm 139, lending dramatic climax to the verse, "Search me, O God, and know my heart: try me, and know my thoughts."

After hearing it, the Reverend Dr. Graham Hunter of Cathedral City, California, commented, "Mr. Laughton, we ministers make a fetish of the Bible. You turn it into a dramatic, earthy tale of real people."

Laughton was grateful for the tribute. Clarifying his reasons for reading the Bible, he said:

"Reading the Bible gives me a feeling of great responsibility. I don't want to be an authority on it or on ecclesiastical matters. That's for the clergy. I want to read it only for its richness and beauty."

Laughton's Bible reading had opened up new vistas for him. He was discovering that he could sway and stir any crowd and that he had more power over an audience with a short silence than he had ever had with a recited line. Bible reading was a spiritual activity from which he derived comfort and strength during the trying war years.

The crisis was personal as well as world-wide, for the studios still offered him only mediocre scripts. He was depressed, angry and helpless. Once he burst out to an actress, "These — — —— think they can have everything their way."

"Charles, you use such bad language," she said in a shocked tone. "How do you presume to read the Bible to all those people?"

He looked abashed. "I won't ever use such language again," he vowed. "And please don't give me away—I'll learn."

As time went by, the Bible became more and more of a spiritual adventure for him. However, he did not try to go beyond his sphere; he kept insisting he was merely a reader, not an evangelist, even when he was invited to religious workshops, conferences, etc.

One day at a church dinner to honor veterans from Korea a chaplain read the Twenty-third Psalm. The chaplain finished the psalm, but no one was particularly moved. Then he said, "Now let's listen to Charles Laughton. He can read it so much better . . ."

Laughton began to read. As the beautiful words "The Lord is my shepherd" came from his lips, there was complete silence in the vestry. People were moved to tears. When he stopped, a loud applause broke out.

Laughton was bothered by the applause. It was unkind to the chaplain who had read the same text. He rose again from his chair, waved his arms to stop the applause, and said softly:

"Ladies and gentlemen, you have given me this applause because I have reached your eyes and ears and know how to read the psalm. But he, our chaplain from Korea, he *knows* the Shepherd."

Soon Laughton's Bible readings were known everywhere in America.

Finally Decca, the recording company, asked him to make some disks of his most famous readings. Through as simple a thing as this, Laughton became a missionary with unparalleled force; some hundreds of thousands of his Bible recordings were distributed the world over, to tell again the greatest stories ever told in the voice of the greatest storyteller of our day.

Chapter 15

I CAN NEVER quite get things straight in my mind," said Laughton, playing coy for the benefit of *The New York Times* correspondent. The statement obviously had to be taken with a grain of salt, for it is a well-known fact that Charles always knows what he is doing, and why. He was putting on an act when he gave the correspondent one of his shy, innocent-novice looks. He had not forgotten what they had said about him only a few years earlier. Now they sang a different tune, acclaiming his new career as storyteller. With the end of the war people came by the thousands to hear him read. He could pack any auditorium from an urban town hall to a college chapel and a woman's club meeting room. In the Hollywood studios people were saying that Laughton had done the impossible. He had made himself independent. His *one-man theater* was the greatest platform phenomenon in America since the days of Mark Twain. Here was one theatrical personality who had broken free from the commercial contingencies of Hollywood and Broadway.

"Mr. Laughton, when did you think of these public readings for the first time?"

He smiled. "I'll tell you," he said.

But where had the idea originated, people wanted to know. From the soldiers at the hospital? From the

Long before her Scarlett O'Hara in **Gone with the Wind,** lovely Vivien Leigh starred with Laughton. *(Partners of the Night.)*

Laughton, as Papa Barrett, drives his daughter Elizabeth (Norma Shearer) into permanent invalidism.

In the arms of Bacchus and Geertke Dirx (Gertrude Lawrence), Rembrandt (Laughton) seeks solace from the death of his beloved wife.

As the artist Rembrandt van Rijn, Laughton portrays careless good nature to cover up despair.

Charles looked so long at self-portraits of Rembrandt he made his own one eye look smaller than the other.

churches? From Paul Gregory, his dynamic new manager? Or had he thought it up all himself?

"The first experience I remember with readings was on a Swiss lake. Basil Gill had been reciting Shakespeare [it was Cassius' aria from the first act of *Caesar* and Hotspur's speech about the cream puff on the battlefield]. We had rowed some distance from the shore because we were shamefaced about reciting poetry out loud. Then Basil talked of the Greeks and how they stood in a row and used nothing but their voices. Basil had been with Beerbohm Tree for years and liked spectacle but had had a stomachful of it. He wanted to hear the words again. I did not understand his anger then, because, like all my generation, I had been brought up to look at the expense of listening. That is not fair either, because looking is almost as important as listening, but at gestures and not at millinery and paint and stained beams of light. So years afterward I became angry and understood Basil Gill's anger and set to work.

"If I ever said to a brother actor I did not understand what was going on on the American stage, he looked at me as if I were a menace to the Constitution. So I stayed in Hollywood and, out of misery I think, I studied. I studied every day including Sundays. I felt like the lunatic who said he was a poached egg and had no piece of toast to sit down on. There was no organization to go to and I knew from experience that I could not organize a rabbit hutch.

"Then I started reading to odd friends what I had been studying. They didn't particularly want to listen.

"And then I couldn't hire a hall, or rather the people that were advising me, advised me that this was not the kind of thing to hire a hall for. I am no organizer and, having had experience with what happens if I try to organize, I gave up.

"Then things took a turn for the better. As I said, I can never get things quite straight in my mind. I am not

sure how I happened to be doing a piece out of the Bible
on a television show. I know they tried to talk me out
of it. They said for one thing that you couldn't read
on television. You had to learn the lines, as it was a
camera and you could be seen. I replied that you could
photograph a man reading a book. That I remember.
And it must have been in the contract that I was to read
and so I did and the following morning Paul Gregory
turned up and said 'I am the organizer.'

"He was head of the Music Corporation of America
Concert Department at the time. I had better go back
so that you will know something about him.

"He is now thirty-one years old and he was born in
Des Moines, Iowa. The first thing he organized was a
show in a henhouse where he and the rest of the gang
acted out the comics. He acted Li'l Abner. Then he
organized the Iowa Young Artists League. Then a Gilbert and Sullivan company. He also organized audiences
for these things. Then he was with MCA and he came
and told me there was a market for my readings. And
was I open for organization! I forget to say he once organized a film test for himself for MGM but he didn't think
he looked like that and got the heck out."

Queries to Paul Gregory will bring us his side of the
story. He will tell you it all began when he was enjoying a short beer at an obscure bistro and saw Laughton
reading the fiery furnace chapters from the Book of
Daniel on television. Gregory was immediately struck
by the fact that a full evening of Laughton reciting the
Book of Daniel and other Bible readings would be of
great interest to other audiences. He telephoned Laughton, made his suggestion and offered to book a tour.

"It was Laughton who really started me as a producer," Gregory will say, "and also got me a new auto-
mobile. I now have a very elegant convertible which
Laughton gave me as a present. Years ago I had a flivver
which wasn't much to look at but it was a very good car

and serviceable. I hocked that flivver to get a few dollars cash to start out as a theatrical producer. My first presentation and my first star was Laughton doing his readings from the Bible."

Gregory had a personal enthusiasm for Bible readings based on his own experience. When he was a student at Drake University, he gave Bible readings in a radio broadcast from Des Moines.

Six feet tall, dark and handsome, Paul Gregory might well have gone on the stage himself. Instead, he preferred to be Laughton's manager and to go into his own highly unorthodox form of production. The shows he sponsors are not plays; they are not musicals and they are not concerts or lectures, but they retain elements of all four groups.

Laughton says Gregory "has a reputation for being difficult, and he can be *extremely* difficult." The saving factor is that the two men work well together—their business relationship is practically a partnership. When Laughton says, "Gregory is a temperamental fellow, he likes to take risks," he is picking out what is perhaps Gregory's most congenial trait. Laughton is also temperamental and has likewise, in the past, followed the lure of the "risky proposition" and found that it brought him luck.

Gregory's idea of reading the Bible proved to be an inspiration. During the past ten years Laughton has traveled some five hundred thousand miles and given over a thousand performances. His audience has amounted to some hundred million. On his tours he has used every conceivable and available means of transportation, including planes, ships, trains, cars and busses. Legend has it that he will resort to skiing, riding horseback and hitchhiking when other means of reaching his destination fail. His accommodations have ranged from the swankiest hotels to the lowliest one-horse-town inns. He has sweated at temperatures of a hundred and ten in the shade in Nevada, and frozen at fifty below zero in Minnesota and the Dakotas.

Laughton has broken every previous platform record in the United States. Mark Twain netted $228,000 from his tours. Whereas Wendell Philipps was paid $500 per lecture and Winston Churchill rated $2,500, Laughton receives up to $4,000 a night. Henry Ward Beecher gave 1,261 lectures in his lifetime. John B. Gough earned $40,000. In 1896 America's greatest orator, William Jennings Bryan, traveled 18,000 miles and gave 952 talks heard by an estimated five million people. At Gettysburg, Abraham Lincoln spoke to 15,000 people. The President of the United States reaches some twenty-five million through radio and television. But thanks to Paul Gregory and his spirit of enterprise, Laughton has outdone all his predecessors and rivals.

Bennett Cerf, publisher and columnist, has compared Laughton's phenomenal drawing power to that of Charles Dickens, who also made a fortune with dramatic readings. "The success of Charles Laughton recalls the triumph scored by Charles Dickens when he visited America in 1862. He appeared at the old Steinway Hall in New York, and the line of ticket seekers was so long that many brought mattresses with them and rested on their way to the box office. Opening night tickets fetched twenty-five dollars apiece—and those were days when a dollar was worth a dollar, too! George Dolby, who presented Dickens to the American public, discovered that there was such a thing as too much success. An irate citizen who had been unable to buy a ticket cornered him in his office, waved a gun under his nose, and wouldn't let go until Dickens himself, hearing the furor, came in and read a story on the spot. 'Charles,' said Dolby later, 'I'm sure that if you hadn't scored a hit, our friend would have all by himself.' "

It is interesting that some of Laughton's most popular

pieces are selections from Dickens' novels. But no matter
what the selection, to watch Laughton on the platform
is a pleasure in itself. He is inimitable, outrageous, unconventional and thoroughly charming. He is so obviously enjoying what he reads that it is impossible for his
hearers not to enjoy it too.

There may be some slight doubt in the listeners' minds
when they first see a tall, prodigiously fat man on the
platform. He does not look like a celebrity. He may not
even be wearing a tuxedo, and since he has adopted blue
shirts for his television program, he is apt to wear this
type on all occasions. Typically, he will open a program
with the words:

"I hope you'll forgive me, but the studio has ordered
me to lose fifty pounds and I have lost only thirty, so
my evening clothes do not fit. And until I have lost the
other twenty pounds, I cannot afford to buy new ones."

Naturally this quip brings a laugh. And once the audience has laughed, it is in his power. Charles loves to talk
and is rarely at a loss for words. He comes by this loqua-
ciousness naturally. He warms his audience up, makes
friends with it. In his stage appearances he displays the
same naturalness of all great actors, from Danny Kaye
to Laurence Olivier. As for his dress, once he begins to
speak, his clothes and appearance are all forgotten. He
is obviously a man who is superior to such trivial things.

After a while he gets down to business. "I love the
music in words or prose," he begins. He shifts the weight
of a dozen or so volumes he is carrying and takes his
place in the center of the stage, with the lights on him,
facing the darkened theater. He fumbles with his books,
and his blond forelock slips down over his brow. He
breathes heavily, puts one hand into a pocket and brings
out still more books. "These are my little treasures," he
explains. These prize volumes look timeworn; their bind-
ings are torn, their pages are dog-eared. Some have lost

their covers. Inside—if anyone could examine them that closely—they would be seen to be filled with penciled scrawls and marginal notations. Some pages have typewritten slips pasted onto them.

"I know them all by heart," he explains, and this gets a second laugh. With an artless, apologetic air, he says, "You know, I like to leaf over the pages as I speak. It's automatic with me now."

He reaches into his breast pocket, takes out a spectacle case, puts his glasses on and then takes them off. He paces up and down the stage several times, cleans his glasses, clears his throat, dons his glasses, and starts his program.

He leans forward on the two end tables stacked one next to the other; the glasses slide down to the end of his nose. His eyes are half closed as the words are released, seemingly uncontrolled, from the cavern of his mouth. Even if he has started the evening looking spick and span in a dark blue serge and light blue shirt, elegance is at an end once the recitation begins. As soon as the words start to roll forth, the ends of his shirt collar are somehow activated. They curl up to meet his chin.

His hair, at first plastered to his head, rises in revolt from its forced order. The neatly arranged white handkerchief in his breast pocket wilts from the thunderous heavings of the man's chest. The double-breasted jacket now climbs around the actor's middle and becomes a bulging sack.

Laughton is lost in a world of words. Petty words, such as "neatness" and "tidiness" and "order" have been stampeded by the soaring words that pour out of the mountain.

He chats and chuckles with his listeners, then launches into another piece where he whispers, cajoles, roars and hams as only Laughton can. Every piece he "reads" has the Laughton touch through and through—whether it be the exploits of Shadrach, Meshach and Abednego or

Abraham Lincoln, or a few jingles and fairy tales mod-
ernized by James Thurber.

The romantic parts and love speeches he does beautifully, but not without a bashful preamble that they are
"soupy but nice." A howl of appreciation usually greets
an excerpt from Confucius: "The superior man knows
what is right; the inferior man knows what will sell."

Laughton was recently asked what his "program" for
a particular evening would be. "I don't know," he replied. "I may be on-stage all of ten minutes before I learn
the spirit of the audience. Sometimes they're in a mood
for the toughness of *Caesar;* sometimes for the delicacy
of *Midsummer Night's Dream;* sometimes for the lusty
story of David and Goliath; sometimes for the solemnity
of the psalms; sometimes for one of Dickens' Christmas
stories, sometimes for one of his melodramatic passages;
always for James Thurber and old Aesop, and stories and
poems of romance never fail."

His readings have taken him through all forty-eight
states of the Union, through Canada and even his homeland, England. His voice, through these platform appearances, as well as through television and recordings, is
famous wherever English is spoken.

When *Life* magazine asked him in 1950 which of the
poems he had read in childhood was still most vivid to
him, he surprised everyone by naming not any passage
from Shakespeare, but Longfellow's *Song of Hiawatha—*
as American as apple pie. "I remember Longfellow's
Hiawatha Song from my childhood," he said, "and because of it I made a point of visiting Minnehaha Park
when I was in Minneapolis, reading at the University of
Minnesota not long ago, to see the falls which had been
made so vivid to me by Longfellow. I remember it was
like a festival day. The park was crowded with families
in a holiday mood and it seemed to me that everyone
was excited to be near the running water. Afterward
I went to a bookstore and looked up the poem again.

" 'In the land of the Dacotahs,
Where the falls of Minnehaha
Flash and gleam among the oak-trees,
Laugh and leap into the valley.
   There the ancient Arrow-maker
Made his arrow-heads of sandstone,
Arrow-heads of chalcedony,
Arrow-heads of flint and jasper,
Smoothed and sharpened at the edges,
Hard and polished, keen and costly.
   With him dwelt his dark-eyed daughter,
Wayward as the Minnehaha,
With her moods of shade and sunshine,
Eyes that smiled and frowned alternate,
Feet as rapid as the river,
Tresses flowing like the water,
And as musical a laughter:
And he named her from the river,
From the water-fall he named her,
Minnehaha, Laughing Water.' " [1]

The visit to the park evidently made a great impression on Laughton. As James S. Lombard, director of the Artist Course at the University of Minnesota, said, "He went about in a trance." He gave a reading to an audience of three thousand at the Northrop Auditorium and concluded his program with *The Song of Hiawatha.* Since then that poem has become a staple item in his repertoire in the Northwest, and he uses it as his final piece "the way Marian Anderson finishes with 'Ave Maria.' "

The happy family practice of reading aloud from books had gone out with the last century. Nothing has quite taken its place—neither popcorn parties, card games, not even the folks sitting around and watching television. Laughton has filled a deep-seated need in American life. He has aroused a nostalgia for the values inherent in family reading. Almost everyone in the smaller and larger communities tried to hear him, see him. After one of

---

[1] From *The Complete Works of Longfellow.* Published by Houghton Mifflin Company.

his recitals, almost everyone wanted to shake his hand and tell him he was doing a wonderful thing.

How could one man, unaided except by his excellent manager, conquer a country as large and as diversified as the United States, with nothing more impressive than a reading repertoire? Many a manager who lacked the vision to launch any such enterprise has asked this question of Laughton. Many an actor has asked him for the secret of his success, for Laughton has extraordinary modesty about his achievements as a reader and is perfectly willing to share his discoveries.

"I have been asked about the techniques of reading aloud," he says. "I had better tell you something of my experiences in the hospitals when the men came to me and asked me to teach them to read love poems to their wives or Mother Goose rimes to their children. They would first of all start by imitating my English accent. I had to get them back to speaking in the accents of the place they came from. People always speak most beautifully in the accents of their home towns. Then they would go downtown to some store and make recordings of their voices. I would have to tell them they had to learn to tell stories or poems to another person, and that if they wanted to learn to read aloud well, they must learn to seek the response in somebody else's eyes as they read; and so I would get them reading to each other. After that it's a question of practice, a lot of practice."

To become a teacher was a new phase in his career. He took to it with ardor—much to the despair of Paul Gregory, who foresaw Laughton wasting his time and talent reading gratis to literary clubs and amateur players. Finally he formed his own nonprofit Charles Laughton Players, a dramatic group for the training of young actors.

Letters poured in from universities and dramatic teachers, asking for help. Mothers moved heaven and earth to enter aspiring daughters into the Laughton group. But Charles admitted only top-notch talent, and he was hard to please. Once the drama critic of a large city newspaper came to see him. "I'd like to send my daughter to you," he said.

"Can she act?" Charles asked.

"Not too well yet, Mr. Laughton."

"Then you'd better not send her to me." The critic took this refusal as a personal insult.

"Don't you know *who* I am in this city?"

"I know you write reviews about me, but your daughter will only come to the Laughton Players if she can act."

And that was the end of it.

This sort of thing happened all the time. Actually Charles has always been a most generous man and will do a great deal for young actors who strike him as promising. On the other hand, he can be almost brutally curt and rude toward people who are trying to take advantage of him.

Later he incorporated Shakespeare into his reading repertoire. He could not resist the Bard of Avon. Even though he had never been a success as a Shakespearean actor, he could *read* Shakespeare magnificently. Here is his own account of a reading:

"Not long ago I read passages from Shakespeare's *Twelfth Night* to a group of college English teachers. Afterward a young instructor confronted me. 'That wasn't quite fair, you know,' he said. 'You edited those passages to make them livelier.'

" 'But I didn't skip a word,' I protested and opened my book to show him the unmarked pages I had read from. When he seemed convinced, I asked him, 'Whatever made you think that?'

" 'Well,' he replied simply, 'this is the first time I ever really liked the play.'

"I won't take credit for explaining Shakespeare to a scholar. I feel certain, however, that his new appreciation of the play was inspired mostly by the enjoyment of hearing it read aloud."

Again and again, as audience reaction testified to the entertainment value of such readings, he made a plea for more people to "get into the act"—to take up where he left off. "I plead for more reading aloud. It is a friendly, quiet and thoroughly refreshing thing to do. It makes us participants rather than spectators. Instead of sitting by to let the professionals amuse or enlighten us, *we* can get into the act, make contact with new ideas, exercise our imaginations. More than that, it is a shared experience which draws people closer together. Husbands and wives, families or groups of friends can enjoy the comfortable satisfaction that comes from laughing together, learning together—from doing the same thing at the same time together."

After any performance, dozens of people would come to Laughton to ask whether he had any suggestions as to how the average family could revive the forgotten custom of family reading. This idea inspired him to work out a formula. "You don't have to be an orator," he counseled. It was less a question of old-fashioned elocution than of sincere desire. As published in a family magazine, his suggestions are as follows:

"LAUGHTON'S FIVE TIPS ON FAMILY READING

"1. Choose a book you *want* to read. Reading aloud is simply a way to share something you like with someone you like. A book read because you feel you should read it will impress no one and bore you.

"2. Don't make it an endurance contest. No book need be read doggedly from start to finish. Be selective if you like. Experiment with several different books at once.

"3. Go at your own pace. This is the schedule I prescribe: read until you are ready to stop, read as often as you would like, don't worry whether it takes a week or a year to finish a book.

"4. Be natural. Straining for effects sounds affected. Your normal speaking voice will be your best reading voice. Your own interest will lend the best emphasis to the story.

"5. When you stop reading, begin talking. Reading aloud is fun in itself, but it is better yet when it prompts lively conversation after you've put the book aside. That is when it truly becomes a shared experience and a rewarding one."

The only carping voice in the chorus of congratulations came from Elsa. After one of his big performances she told Charles: "You were terrible. You went on much too long with your Dickens. No one could hear you in the back rows. Why don't you learn your lines properly?"

Charles did not take such criticism meekly. A lively squabble ensued, but in the end, as always, Charles acknowledged that he might have done better. He strove each time for a better performance.

Few realize what a tremendous strain such tours can be. By this time Charles was a seasoned trouper and in many cases endured very trying conditions. In one town he had to share the only hall with a visiting circus. His reading was punctuated with a medley of peculiar noises made by the circus menagerie stowed away in the cellar. In another auditorium he could hardly be heard over the noise of the heating fans. The management decided to stop the fans. After a while Laughton noticed that his audience was shivering with cold. He broke off his reading to ask them what should be done. The unanimous vote was that he should go on without the competition of the heating system. The audience preferred hearing him to keeping warm.

From the success of those tours it would seem as though

Laughton monopolized the whole field of entertainment. As a matter of fact this was not the case. A Laughton appearance might be the chief attraction for the night in any small town, but it was by no means the only attraction. Towns had a way of scheduling night football matches, baseball games, prayer meetings, dances, vaudeville shows and even Tallulah Bankhead when those events competed with a Laughton engagement.

Tallulah Bankhead, also an experienced lecturer, likes to boast of what tough competition she gave Charles in Texas. At her Dallas appearance she danced the Charleston, mimicked Katharine Hepburn, mugged, clowned, emoted, recited, chain smoked and blew kisses to her audience. She stopped to sip water from a glass and quipped: "I bet you think this is gin. I wish it was."

Naturally, the Dallas audience hated to give her up. If they had had their way, she would have gone on all night. Finally the chairman brought the program to a graceful close with the words: "There is no doubt that Mr. Charles Laughton, tonight's 'lecturer' at McFarlin Auditorium has what vaudevillians call 'a tough act to follow.' "

As was expected, Charles faced an empty hall that night. Perhaps that was inevitable under the circumstances, but the parting words of the Bankhead show reached Charles's ears, and he never forgot that unsportsmanlike dig.

The tours went on through snow and rain, ice and sleet, heat waves, dust storms, plane cancellations and common colds. Charles traveled lightly, never taking more than three suits, a few shirts and some books with him. Most of the time he was accompanied by a male secretary. Elsa seldom joined him on his travels, as she was kept busy with her Turnabout Theater in Los Angeles.

For Charles, the tours meant a new town every night, an unpredictable new audience. We can assume that every night he experienced the same sinking feeling in the pit of his stomach which is the lot of the actor. In darkened halls Laughton could not see the facial expressions of his audience. How would the people react to his readings? What he had to offer was an entirely different matter from acting: Words without stage illusion or drama. First of all he had to establish human contact with the people in the audience. He projected his voice into the dark, fought for rapport, and every night a miracle took place. Before he had time to realize it, the audience had been warmed up and was ready for whatever he wanted to read.

Such tours were a tremendous undertaking. There were schedules to be considered, itineraries to be planned, interviews to be arranged. The Gregory office sent out advance posters to the towns, attended to the advertising campaign, handled the ticket sale and reservations. There were weeks of work to be done by many people before Laughton walked out on the stage with a few well-worn books under his arm.

Nearly every city will give celebrities the visiting fireman's welcome. Charles Laughton was a celebrity, so they rolled out the red carpet. They wanted to take Mr. Laughton around to show him the town. The committee members who were responsible for his being there wanted to monopolize his company. The bigger town halls gave special luncheons for celebrities, and there Charles was plied with questions. "When did you begin acting?" "Should Shakespeare be taught in the high schools?" "What is your opinion of *The King and I?*" "What was your greatest role?" "Why doesn't your wife travel with you?" "Are you lonely on the road?" The local society ladies gushed over him. And almost invariably they broke the happy news that they had a party arranged for him. "After the show the two hundred members of our Oshkosh Woman's Club are waiting to meet you. We are all so thrilled," etc., etc.

Such a party is an ordeal that one has to go through oneself to appreciate properly. Laughton did his best to dodge such affairs. Most of the time he succeeds, but if he does, hurt feelings are the result. In one case he arranged to have a taxi waiting at the stage door. As soon as he had finished his program, he and his secretary dashed out of the hall and drove to the airport without even saying good-by to the committee or receiving the check. The fugitives were on their way to the next town as two hundred guests waited in the town hall for their "Charles Laughton Surprise Party."

Chapter 16

A YOUNG MAN sat opposite Charles Laughton in the actor's sumptuous living room. "I only came, Mr. Laughton, because you are the one person I can turn to," he pleaded. He was a young GI from Oregon who had heard one of Laughton's hospital readings. The war was over but Bill Cotrell lingered on in Los Angeles. The fact was, the young man was stage-struck.

Shyly, he explained his predicament. His dramatic ambitions were nothing new. Even before the war he had been chairman of the Oregon Shakespeare Association. Now that he was in Hollywood, the idea had occurred to him to form a small Shakespeare reading group. He had inserted an advertisement in the newspaper inviting joiners—hoping that in this way he would, perhaps, get in touch with ten other kindred spirits. Instead, there were 1,500 replies to the ad. That was why young Bill Cotrell had gone to see Laughton. Surely they could form a worth-while group out of all this raw material. Would Laughton please help them get started?

Laughton listened, amused and intrigued. A boy like Bill Cotrell inevitably reminded Charles of his own youth. He too had cut his teeth as an actor on solitary readings of Shakespeare. He too had thrilled over a part

244

A portrait of Elsa Lanchester. She never looks the same way twice.

Significant silhouettes. Charles Laughton gives David Wayne some sound advice in *The Cop and the Anthem*.

in a fourth-rate amateur production. Great thing could come of such enthusiasm, he knew.

"I'll think it over," he told the young man. "I must consult Elsa and my manager, Paul Gregory."

Gregory gave the idea a lukewarm reception. Charles next turned to Elsa. The way he put it was: "Cotrell touched the rock and the Mississippi fell on him. So he has asked me to take it on."

Elsa proved to be more sympathetic to the project than Gregory. "Why, it sounds just fine," she said.

She did not know what she was letting herself in for. Before she knew what had happened, their peaceful Santa Monica house was taken over as a drama workshop. Four evenings a week, when Laughton was in town, and two evenings a week when he was otherwise engaged, the place swarmed with young actors. There was hardly a quiet corner in it for Elsa. As for Gregory, his worst fears were confirmed. Charles was so taken up with his students that he had little time for the new ventures his faithful manager had been dreaming up.

Laughton, however, was having a whale of a time. "I consider it a healthy condition when actors work just for the sake of working," he said. And there was no doubt about their disinterested motives in this case. "There is no financial profit to be expected from performing Shakespeare," Laughton commented.

The group was about seventeen strong. Among its hand-picked students were Margaret Field from Texas; Carol Brenan from Baltimore; the ice-skating star Belita; Maria Bazzi, an Italian actress; Bob Anderson, Florida born, but a graduate from the Royal Academy in London; Hal Bokor from Ohio; Richard Lupino, a Londoner; Jed McKee, with a background in vaudeville; Victor Perrin, with a background in radio; and naturally—the moving spirit of the whole thing—Bill Cotrell. It wasn't long before those young protégés of Charles began to arrive. Soon many of them were taking important parts in the movies. Shelley Winters, for example, an Academy Award nominee a few years later, was perhaps his star pupil of the original group.

Ask any of them what kind of teacher Laughton was and they will say, "Fabulous, sincere, lovable." From Charles's description, relations between teacher and students were apparently highly democratic. "My pupils always insisted that I read my next day's lines to them," he said. He was working on some movies at the time. "Just so they could tear them apart. But I didn't mind. I considered them my best critics—besides Elsa."

Visitors to the Laughton house found the living room full of young people. They occupied all the sofas and chairs. Some sat on the floor. Each one was equipped with a copy of the Shakespeare play he or she was currently engaged on. Any visitor also would be pressed to take a copy and join in the rehearsal. One day Edward G. Robinson dropped in unexpectedly. His host was sitting in the midst of a widely assorted group of young actors, all concentrating on their books. "Shut up and sit down," Laughton greeted Robinson, as he handed the actor a copy of the play. "Here," Charles commanded, "you can read the part of the king."

Robinson was slightly discomfited. Veteran actor though he was, he had specialized all his life in tough gangster and detective parts. "I can't read Shakespeare," he protested. "What are you trying to do to me?"

"Read it!" Laughton said obdurately. Robinson soon got into the spirit of the setting. "Shall I read it in English?" he asked.

"I don't care what language you read it in," Laughton snarled. Robinson, America's hardest-boiled "tough guy," chain cigar smoker, art collector extraordinary, millionaire actor and speaker of eight languages, spent the evening reading Shakespeare with a roomful of hopeful youngsters. "I enjoyed every bit of it," he admitted later.

But it was not long before the tempo speeded up, for the Charles Laughton Players had decided to come out of the parlor and produce a play. Their choice fell not on Shakespeare, but on Chekhov's *Cherry Orchard,* one of the milestones in Charles's own career. Charles confined himself to a minor role, but his part in the production was far from minor. He adapted the script, directed, was stage manager and lighting engineer. Stout as he was, he was here, there and everywhere, lying on his belly to judge the effect of the footlights, bustling to the back of the theater to see whether the voices carried. The group had hired a small hall which seated only 200. Salaries were set at ten dollars a week, with any profits to be shared equally at the end of each month. The modest venture proved to be a smashing success. The hall was sold out night after night and the play enjoyed a nineteen-week run. Everyone in Hollywood was interested and curious about the venture. As one critic put it, "They were clever kids and Laughton handled them as though they were his marionettes."

This was not strictly the case. Laughton was a difficult taskmaster, but an inspiring teacher. His pupils remember the stiff rehearsals, the perfectionist approach, but they also remember the enormous amount of moral encouragement he gave them. He would urge the actors whose parts were only subsidiary, but who had done their best, to go out and take their bows just as the leading actors did. "Go on out and take applause," he'd whisper. "You deserve it."

One evening the leading man did not show up at curtain time. Laughton leaped into the breach. He appeared before the curtain and announced, "Our lover boy has not shown up. He is delayed, probably in Los Angeles traffic. So with your indulgence I will entertain you until Ivan arrives." He launched into his usual repertoire of limericks, poetry, Shakespeare and the Bible. By and by the curtain was tweaked aside behind him and a head bobbed out to whisper, "Bill's here." Laughton started to wind up his recitation. Two hundred voices objected. "No, no. Go on." But Laughton refused to take unfair advantage. Bowing, he retreated into the wings and the curtain rose, as it did every night, on *The Cherry Orchard*.

A young drama student at Syracuse University recalls the time that Laughton stopped in town to present a reading program. It was winter—Laughton bundled up in his overcoat, with an enormous muffler draped about his neck, reminded the students of a Dickens character. He had come only to give a recital but, taking a fancy to the students, he went back to talk to them and ended by devoting three days of his very busy life to communicating his love for the theater to this bunch of young people, none of whom will ever forget the experience. Laughton was full of bounce, overflowing with enthusiasm. He talked to them about his own dramatic group— the Charles Laughton Players, back in Los Angeles. He discussed the problems his group had encountered with their current reading of *Twelfth Night*. Using the students present, he went through one scene of this play. He demonstrated his method for teaching spontaneity to actors. The way he did it was to throw a ball around in a circle. As each actor said his lines, Charles threw the ball to the actor whose lines came next. He himself was practicing the "Friends, Romans, Countrymen" speech from *Julius Caesar*, and he gave the group a preview of the way he was going to do it. Apparently he did not fervently admire Winston Churchill, so he imitated Churchill's oratorical manner with devastating effect.

The Laughton Players had become Charles's ruling passion to such an extent that it was disrupting the life of everyone around him. He was throwing all his time and energy into the group. Both Elsa and Paul Gregory warned him that that state of affairs could not continue.

An experimental theater was all very well; helping young actors and actresses was all very well—but Charles was a professional actor who had to forge ahead with his own career. Reluctantly Charles disbanded the group, and once more turned his thoughts to the solution of his own problem.

Hollywood movie stints were not enough for a man of his drive. He was much in demand by the studios, but again only in supporting roles. The so-called big pictures they wanted him for were based on inferior scripts, on uninspired, hackneyed stories that were being turned out on the assembly-line basis. How could he escape the treadmill? He thought he saw his great opportunity in a play by the German dramatist, Bertolt Brecht.

The play was *Galileo*. Its technique was experimental and its theme was important. It was being done under the auspices of the American Experimental Theater, a noncommercial enterprise with followers in Los Angeles and New York. Charles plunged into the project with his characteristic excitement. He took over most of the work, translated the play, cut and adapted, did the staging, supervised the rehearsals, coached the members of the cast. His salary was eight dollars a week, but again he was happy because he was doing something close to his heart. He hoped to build the group into the American equivalent of the Old Vic.

At first the play seemed headed for success. The New York drama critics hailed Laughton's performance and admired the skill with which he had adapted the original text, which was rather ponderous and wordy, into a fast-moving and stirring drama. However, the production soon ran into snags.

The trouble lay in the political affiliations of the playwright. Bertolt Brecht, for all his talent, was a dyed-in-the-wool Communist. On the point of being deported from the United States for his Communist activities, he escaped, and appeared in East Germany, where he became the Soviet's pet author, supervising the literary life of the Soviet-controlled zone and turning out odes to Stalin on the various state holidays. The musical score for the play on Galileo had been composed by Hanns Eisler, another convinced Communist who had composed many propaganda songs, including "The Comintern March." Some of the actors in the cast also turned out to be Communists.

Laughton had gone into the project in complete innocence of the situation. He had, more or less, been "kidnapped" by the Communists, who were very happy to have a person of Laughton's stature to lend prestige to one of their propaganda fliers. The figure of Galileo, torn between his own convictions and fear of the Inquisitors' rack, had been twisted to serve the ideological purposes of the Communists. Laughton had added new dimensions to the role, but his performance was not the whole play. The tone of the production reeked of Communist influence. To ears that could hear, the Marxist message was evident. Papers such as the *Daily Worker* hailed it as the greatest thing on the American stage. "Laughton went beyond Stanislavsky," they said, according him the highest praise they could think of. But praise from such sources was of dubious value. When the facts of the matter were put before Laughton by his manager, Charles saw that he was playing into Communist hands. He had fallen into bad company. There was nothing for him to do but to withdraw from the production of *Galileo*.

Once again he was left with no outlet but the movies. Hollywood had won out once more. Troubled and defeated by what seemed to be equally ugly alternatives, Laughton returned from New York to the West Coast. A part was awaiting him in *The Paradine Case*. After his brief career as Galileo, the iconoclastic seeker after truth, he was to assume the part of a merciless British

Lord Justice of whom everyone, including his own wife, was in mortal terror. Laughton did a conscientious job of it. His lines in the courtroom, when he addressed the counsel for the defense whom he believed to be in love with the defendant, were properly bloodcurdling. "I'll hang her if I must," he said, "but she is too lovely to destroy."

The Lord Justice's wife, Lady Harfield, was played by Ethel Barrymore. It was a great experience for Charles to play opposite the undisputed first lady of the American theater. The two became good friends. Like Charles, Miss Barrymore is an overwhelming personality and has only to enter a room to dominate the atmosphere completely. Both she and Charles tacitly agreed that *The Paradine Case* was not one of the greatest movies ever made. After its release, the play was mentioned at a party and Ethel remarked suavely, "You know, I've never seen that picture. They tell me it was pretty good, too." Laughton also never bothered to see the completed version of the film.

Veteran trouper that she was, Ethel Barrymore had spent many years on the road. She and Charles swapped experiences, and Charles permitted himself a few minor gripes on the difficulties of playing to a different house every night. Miss Barrymore, however, said she did not mind. "Now, now," she chided in her famous deep voice, "I don't know what people mean when they complain of the rigors of the road. Good Lord, Charles, neither you nor I are faded lilies." To her, the road had more color than any Broadway appearance. "Touring—I love it," she said. "I always look forward to it—the drafty dressing rooms, the rats, everything. It's all in the game."

Laughton has since toured many months every year. He knows well the hardship of sleeping every night in a different hotel, of meeting new committees nightly and of going through receptions given by total strangers.

While he was talking of the wear and tear of trouping, someone knocked on Ethel Barrymore's dressing-room door and called:

"Miss Barrymore, there are three ladies outside who want to see you—they say they are classmates of yours."

"Classmates?" smiled Ethel Barrymore at Laughton. "Classmates?—Well, wheel them in . . ."

Charles's next assignment was *Arch of Triumph*, based on the novel by Erich Maria Remarque. The famous author of *All Quiet on the Western Front* had written a bitter tale of refugee life in Paris. Charles was slated for the part of the Gestapo man Haake, whom the hero, a refugee doctor, who suffered much at the hands of the Nazis, finally murdered in retribution for his evil deeds. The refugee doctor was Charles Boyer, and the love interest was represented by Ingrid Bergman. As a film, it never really succeeded in capturing the atmosphere of Paris or of refugee life. Boyer and Bergman were miscast, and Laughton with his Prussian accent and monocle was only a stereotype of a Nazi. It was another sad instance of a film missing out on a great theme.

However, it was the beginning of a vital friendship between Charles and Ingrid Bergman. The beautiful Swedish actress had been a lifelong fan of Laughton's. They found they had a lot in common in that they were both thoroughly disgusted with the Hollywood way of doing things. Ingrid Bergman particularly disliked being traded around from one studio or producer to another. Like Laughton, she was a demon for work and burned for the opportunity to take challenging roles. She could not bear the frivolity and mercenary outlook of Hollywood. "They make me feel like a race horse, the way they trade me around," she confided to Charles. "I'm so eager to work that the producers have to hold me back. When I'm interested in a play, I can work day and night without feeling any need for sleep. Here in Hollywood people laughed at my arriving on the set ahead of time."

She still remembered her early bad experiences in Hollywood. She had put up the photograph of her daughter Pia in her dressing room, only to be ordered to remove it. The studio wanted to underplay the fact that she was married and had a child. They even wanted to change her name. But she put her foot down. She had won recognition in Sweden as Ingrid Bergman and Ingrid Bergman she would stay. Angrily, she told them she could always go back home where she could go on being Ingrid Bergman.

Once Charles courteously attempted to open the door for her, only to have her burst out: "Heavens, don't be always spoiling me. What a life! I'm not even allowed to open my own doors or carry a small parcel. Imagine such a life for a girl from Sweden, where even princesses carry things and learn how to cook for their family. What about my making a cup of coffee for you someday—just on the sly?"

Once Charles and Elsa were invited to a party given by Ingrid Bergman when she was a part of the Lindstrom home. Both knew that the affair was given in honor of Rossellini, who had come from Italy to Hollywood. Neither of the Laughtons said a word about what they observed. But soon the world knew that Ingrid Bergman had decided to leave her husband, Dr. Lindstrom, quit Hollywood and go to Italy with the man she loved and with whom she seemed to have so much in common.

Later Charles was always to remember the actress's pathetic fight to preserve her integrity. Her great talent was going to waste in Hollywood. After the crisis in her personal life, her flight to Italy to Rossellini and the semi-official ban on her pictures, Charles was to say with the late Eugene O'Neill: "Ingrid Bergman made a place for herself in the history of the theater in the United States. We will remember her as a great American actress."

Charles was next involved with *The Big Clock*, a picture of no particular merit. Again he was slated for a thankless supporting part as the tycoon of a vast publishing empire who had tried to pin a murder on an innocent man.

The Girl from Manhattan gave Charles a chance to play a bishop—a change, at any rate, from the usual villain parts. Dorothy Lamour and George Montgomery were the stars. The cast also included a baby, little Bertram Devlin, with whom Laughton was briefly but memorably involved. It happened that one day the baby started crying on the set. It cried and cried, and no one could do anything with it. Its nurse tried to soothe it, and then Dorothy Lamour took over, but still the baby continued to cry. At last Charles picked up the baby. He took it in his arms and sat down in a corner with it, whispering something into its ear. After a few minutes the baby calmed down and fell asleep. Everyone was mystified.

"How'd you do it, Charles?" they wanted to know. "What was it you whispered?"

Somewhat diffidently, Charles explained, "I just recited the Gettysburg Address. You know, it has such a wonderful rhythm to it."

The public reading tours still kept Charles going. Without them he would have been a very miserable fellow. The movie studios were willing to pay him fabulous salaries, but the roles they offered became smaller and smaller, duller and duller. In the movie *The Bribe* he was allowed to play an unsavory character who hangs around a hotel lobby and offers $10,000 to a Government agent. In *The Man on the Eiffel Tower* the tables were turned and he played a French detective. Much of the picture was shot in Paris, but this was its sole distinction.

His next film, *The Strange Door,* was definitely Grade B. It was a typical horror film with Boris Karloff, and abounded in rattling chains, bloodstained knives and spooky seventeenth-century settings. It was based on a

story by Robert Louis Stevenson, but had been made
into a mediocre melodrama about an effete and evil
nobleman who kept his brother locked in a cellar for
twenty years. Laughton played the part of the sinister
nobleman, but he could not rise above the crude and
unbelievable histrionics of the script. *The New York
Times* again inveighed against the folly of Hollywood in
wasting Laughton's time on such a picture. Of Laughton's
performance it said, "His oily, petulant and flamboyant
nobleman struck us as more farcical than evil."

Perhaps Laughton had played the part with his tongue
in his cheek. He had enjoyed watching the practiced
antics of Boris Karloff, who had played more ghouls and
monsters than any man alive. Frankenstein-Karloff to his
fans and William Henry Pratt to his intimates—Boris
Karloff is actually a soft-spoken Britisher who likes
nothing better than to play Santa Claus at his friends'
Christmas parties. But whenever Hollywood decides the
time has come for another chiller, they call on Karloff.
His name has become synonymous with morbidity and
horror. Strangely enough, Karloff does not mind. As
psychiatrists would say, he has made a satisfactory adjust-
ment to his career as a ghoul. "I'm perfectly content to
be the villain," he told Charles. "It means that I always
know what is expected of me. Once in a while I've played
straight parts in pictures, but they did not turn out well.
The audience kept expecting me to do something terrible.
I think they were deeply disappointed when I didn't.
That's what happens when you get typed."

But Laughton was hatching a plan. He said nothing
about it at the time and filled in the interval with a small
but interesting stint in the movie *The Blue Veil,* starring
Jane Wyman. The script by Norman Corwin was unusual
and concerned a war widow who lost her child and compensated for the loss by dedicating her life to the care
of other children. It was a heart-warming and loving film.
Laughton played a widowed manufacturer who proposed

to Jane Wyman, but who finally married his own secretary.

There was a role worth playing and Laughton made the most of it—projecting the character of the small businessman in all his loneliness, kindliness and decency. Jane Wyman was spellbound by Charles's acting as well as by his conversation. "Laughton is the most learned man I ever met," she declared. "To sit and talk with him is an intellectual bath. I learned more about acting from him in ten days than I had learned before in ten years."

But such parts did not happen very often. Besides, Charles was not so constituted that he could be happy indefinitely in supporting roles. He was too gifted, too powerful a figure. Hollywood had not given him a major part since 1935, when he had dominated the scene as Captain Bligh in *Mutiny on the Bounty*. His *Rembrandt* went back to 1936. His *Henry VIII* dated back to 1933. It was 1950, high time for a comeback. His reading tours were still electrifying audiences, but he craved something more dramatic, a thunderclap of some sort which would satisfy his need for bold, creative action.

The germ of the idea which later became *Don Juan in Hell* came from Dr. Albert Rappaport, one of the chairmen of the San Francisco Town Hall. After listening to a Laughton reading, this gentleman approached Paul Gregory and inquired about the possibilities of a drama quartet, four people, like Laughton, to read a whole play.

Gregory considered the idea. The more he thought about the suggestion, the better it sounded. At last he broached the idea to Laughton. The two men were driving up to Canada for some readings. Laughton thought the suggestion rather intriguing. The question was, what play would lend itself to such treatment? Laughton had a brain storm—what about George Bernard Shaw's *Man and Superman?* What about the third act, which was a self-contained entity and was never performed, on account of its length?

The first step was to get G.B.S. to approve such a production. Laughton wrote one of his masterful, persuasive letters to the old and eccentric dramatist. He even ventured to remind Shaw of the time many years before that he had played Higgins in Shaw's *Pygmalion* and had been given a stiff scolding by the illustrious author of the piece.

After weeks of waiting, the answer arrived. With his phenomenal memory, the old man recalled the incident in the dressing room of the student theater. "I have a vivid memory of checking you years ago in Gower Street because you played everyone else bang off the stage. I spotted your future."

Shaw was not terribly keen, however, on the possibilities inherent in the "Hell scene." "It is such a queer business that I can't advise you to experiment with it," he cautioned, and went on to cite various occasions when other people had tried to do it, with signal unsuccess. "I don't see why you want to do the thing on the stage. It's nothing but a packet of words." To this Laughton, nothing daunted, replied, "Ah, yes, but what words!" and the old dramatist's heart was won. "I enclose a memorandum of my terms," he wrote. The play was in the bag.

There was then the question of rounding up three actors besides Laughton to form the quartet. "We wanted not necessarily the best actors, but the best voices in America," Laughton said, "and we found them." He recruited his old friend Sir Cedric Hardwicke, an experienced and courtly veteran of the stage—"a born actor who knows how to speak an author's lines as if they were fresh from his own brain"—Agnes Moorehead, first discovered by Orson Welles—"she could act any kind of female at the drop of a hat"—and Charles Boyer.

Boyer had worked with Laughton in *Arch of Triumph.* French by birth, he had behind him all the early training and mature experience of the classic theater in Paris. As

Laughton observed, "Boyer is a master of the *tirade* and as such is invaluable in our play—not every actor can handle that difficult form of dramatic speech." It was not easy to sign up Boyer for the venture—he was afraid his ineradicable French accent might spoil the long Shavian speeches. But Laughton was firm. "All right, Charles," he said, "please recast the show for me and find someone else to do Don Juan." At last he succeeded in dispelling Boyer's misgivings.

His warm, fascinating and intimate voice made Boyer a natural for the Don Juan role. Besides, he had the reputation of being a great lover—Hollywood had long before typed him for all sophisticated, romantic parts. Twenty years earlier, when he had first come to Hollywood, he was hailed as France's gift to American women. He is one of the most attractive males to hit Hollywood since the days of Rudolph Valentino. Boyer is past fifty, about the same age as Laughton. His hair is growing thin and he has to wear a toupee, but his air of experience, his magnetic spell, his slight weariness, all fitted in perfectly with his role of Don Juan in the afterlife.

A difference of opinion arose between Laughton and Paul Gregory as to the way the quartet should operate. Gregory saw four stars standing up like musicians in "soup and fish." Charles's mind ran to fancier arrangements. He saw the four perched upon high stools such as tennis scorers sit on, and wearing heavy cloaks which would drape from the pedestals in four pools of color, scarlet for the Devil, orange for Don Juan, white for the statue and mauve for Donna Ana—mauve was Agnes Moorehead's favorite color. Gregory vetoed this idea—he had set his heart on evening attire. Laughton clung stubbornly to his colored cloaks. Eventually, however, Laughton was won over to the four musicians idea. "It got so that I could not hear Shaw's music soar except in soup and fish," Charles admitted.

Gregory scored a victory for simplicity. There were

to be no sets, no costumes, no props other than the music stands which held copies of the play and carried out the musical idea of the production. This Spartan simplicity was to prove highly practical when the production got under way. The actors had to perform in all kinds of places, ranging from gymnasiums, concert platforms, churches, and temples to basketball courts, with no props other than their music stands, no costumes but their evening clothes. The quartet was a highly mobile unit.

But first the show had to be whipped into shape. Laughton, as usual, assumed complete charge of the direction. The business end was handled by Paul Gregory, who reported that bookings were going along swimmingly. Charles made some alterations in the script, but kept as close as possible to the Shaw original. He was very conscious of the playwright himself watching from across the Atlantic. At rehearsals, Laughton took pains over every word, every gesture and every nuance of his fellow quartet members. He was like a Toscanini conducting his orchestra. He knew the score by heart. He would tolerate nothing short of perfection. Every mannerism mattered, every pause, every raising and lowering of the voice. He himself would lie on his belly to see how the quartet looked from that angle. As Charles Boyer remarked, "I was exhausted just watching him.

"Don't you ever rest, Charles?" Boyer teased him.

"Why rest—there's all eternity to rest in," Laughton answered in the true Shavian spirit.

It was a wordy play and a daring interpretation. No one involved suspected that the group had a smashing success on their hands. They did not even consider opening in New York, but took *Don Juan* on a nation-wide tour. Finally they risked a New York appearance in Carnegie Hall. The reception was so overwhelming that they moved into a Broadway theater. Charles had done the unpredictable and the impossible. Four people in evening dress stood before music stands and read a fifty-year-old play without story, consisting purely of intellectual and philosophical discussion. Yet *Don Juan in Hell* was a record-breaking hit, both in New York and on the road. In some cities it grossed more than did *South Pacific*. The company played 52 cities in 42 states. In one Kansas town, with a population of 15,000, the quartet drew an audience of 4,000. It was not unusual for them to gross from seven to ten thousand dollars in a single evening. Their average weekly profits on the road were 30,000 dollars. *Time* magazine reported:

"Audiences throughout the U.S.—in Oakland, New Orleans, Salt Lake City, Syracuse and Williamsport, Pa. have been eating it up. Businessmen and bobby soxers, college students and clubwomen have jammed theaters and auditoriums and high-school gymnasiums to hear the Devil and Don Juan swap epigrams and arguments. As the grosses mounted, the show-business weekly, *Variety*, headlined: 'STICKS OUTSHINE BROADWAY.' "

Finally Charles took his little company to England, where they lent the luster of Shaw's *Don Juan in Hell* to the gala mood of the Festival of Britain.

Charles could well be complacent over a success such as that. "Contrary to what I have been told in the entertainment industry," he said, "people everywhere have a common, shy hunger for literature."

What was *Don Juan in Hell* all about? The author, George Bernard Shaw, had this to say about it: "I have thrust into my perfectly modern three-act play a totally extraneous act in which my hero's ancestor appears and philosophizes at great length with the lady, the statue and the Devil." It has as its basis the Don Juan legend which is also the source of Mozart's opera *Don Giovanni*. But more important, it is an exhibition of the most brilliant wit and exciting talk ever to be heard on a stage. There are marvelous speeches on such diverse subjects as pregnant women and creative evolution, supermen and dictators, war and sex. It sparkles with epigrams and

Penguin Photo

With a bevy of telephone operators and tireless energy, Laughton solicits war bond sales in a round-the-clock radio campaign.

Penguin Photo

Face lined with fatigue, he snatches a few free moments from the bond drive for a cup of coffee.

Charles Laughton, Inc., with very few shareholders besides the two.

paradoxes such as, "Hell is the home of honor, duty, justice, and the seven deadly virtues. All wickedness on earth is done in their name. Where else but in Hell should they have their reward?"

Donna Ana, played by Agnes Moorehead, is one of the unfortunate ladies who falls victim to Don Juan's amorous wiles. Now she expresses surprise because she feels no pain in Hell—which affords Don Juan, played by Charles Boyer, an opportunity to say that this means she was made to live there. Sir Cedric Hardwicke, the querulous statue, complains that Hell is full of English-men who are there only because they think they owe it to their position.

But the star of the evening was, of course, Laughton's Satan. Charles had not appeared on the United States legitimate stage since 1933. For seventeen years he had been playing one movie villain after another. His Satan was, in a way, those many villains rolled into one. Laughton's Satan is consummately realistic and consum-mately intelligent. He is a diabolic force with a very good opinion of himself, who can say with a knowing smirk, "The world cannot get along without me."

In speech after speech he defends the existence of the Devil. Moon-faced, stout, wearing a respectable tuxedo, with reading glasses on his nose, Laughton turns in an outrageously original presentation of man's eternal enemy. At the beginning he is almost lovable as the Devil —shy, slow of speech, diffident. He keeps his head bent so low that his chin brushes his shirt collar. He has a funny little smile and an impish little giggle. Surely there's no harm in the fellow, everyone thinks. But after a while he gains courage, becomes bolder. Before the audience knows it, he is a full-fledged Devil, thundering forth the wonderful lines Shaw wrote for him:

"Have you walked up and down upon the earth lately? I have; and I have examined Man's wonderful inventions. And I tell you that in the arts of life man invents nothing;

but in the arts of death he outdoes Nature herself, and produces by chemistry and machinery all the slaughter of plague, pestilence and famine. The peasant I tempt today eats and drinks what was eaten and drunk by the peasants of ten thousand years ago; and the house he lives in has not altered as much in a thousand centuries as the fashion of a lady's bonnet in a score of weeks. But when he goes out to slay, he carries a marvel of mechanism that lets loose at the touch of his finger all the hidden molecular energies, and leaves the javelin, the arrow, the blowpipe of his fathers far behind. In the arts of peace Man is a bungler. I have seen his cotton factories and the like, with machinery that a greedy dog could have invented if it had wanted money instead of food. I know his clumsy typewriters and bungling locomotives and tedious bicycles: they are toys compared to the Maxim gun, the submarine torpedo boat. There is nothing in Man's industrial machinery but his greed and sloth: his heart is in his weapons. This marvelous force of Life of which you boast is a force of Death: Man measures his strength by his destructiveness. What is his religion? An excuse for hating me? What is his law? An excuse for hanging you. What is his morality? Gentility! An excuse for consuming without producing. What is his art? An excuse for gloating over pictures of slaughter. What are his politics? Either the worship of a despot because a despot can kill, or parliamentary cockfighting. I spent an evening lately in a certain celebrated legislature, and heard the pot lecturing the kettle for its blackness, and ministers answering questions. When I left I chalked up on the door the old nursery saying 'Ask no questions and you will be told no lies.' I bought a sixpenny family magazine, and found it full of pictures of young men shooting and stabbing one another. . . . I could give you a thousand instances; but they all come to the same thing: the power that governs the earth is not the power of Life, but of Death. . . . The plague, the famine, the earthquake,

the tempest were too spasmodic in their action; the tiger
and crocodile were too easily satiated and not cruel
enough: something more constantly, more ruthlessly,
more ingeniously destructive was needed; and that something was Man, the inventor of the rack, the stake, the
gallows, the electric chair; of sword and gun and poison
gas: above all, of justice, duty, patriotism, and all the
other isms by which even those who are clever enough to
be humanely disposed are persuaded to become the most
destructive of all the destroyers."[1]

The nationwide tour was an adventure the four will
not soon forget. Paul Gregory accompanied them to cope
with the practical crises as they came along. A temperamental fellow himself, he had many a spat with his
equally temperamental quartet. But those episodes were
forgiven and forgotten. Gregory knows that actors are a
spirited lot. "I have never known a writer," he says, "or
an actor or a musician, designer or producer who was
worth a darn who was not temperamental. I have known
a number of authors and actors and musicians and
directors and designers and producers who were not
temperamental, but they were not worth a darn."

In this spirit of somewhat strained tolerance for each
other's eccentricities, they covered the continent. Boyer,
for example, is a great hypochondriac. During most of the
tour he kept constant check on his temperature with two
thermometers. Sometimes he even sneaked one on-stage,
concealed it behind his hand and took his temperature
between lines. Once Agnes Moorehead threw him a
sudden cue and Boyer had to sputter the thermometer
out of his mouth before returning to his role of the Great
Lover.

The tour has had its heights of triumph, its awkward
moments and its burst of comedy within a comedy.

One of these occurred when the quartet was putting

---

[1] From *Don Juan in Hell*, by Bernard Shaw. Used by permission of The Society
of Authors and The Public Trustee.

on its show at the Music Hall in Cleveland. Charles had just spoken his line, "I hear heavenly music," when suddenly the pure notes of a flute were heard in the auditorium. Satan's mouth fell open. His confreres looked at him in consternation. This was too much of a good thing. It was a little like having gremlins. The mystery was soon solved, however. It seemed that the Cleveland orchestra was scheduled to rehearse in an adjacent hall—and the flutist had come early and was running over some trills. For once in his life Charles took stern measures. He stopped the show and sent a messenger over to the next room to order the flutist to cease and desist.

Cedric Hardwicke has given his personal description of what the tour was like from the point of view of the four participants.

"The four of us—Charles Laughton, Charles Boyer, Agnes Moorehead and I—have shared many adventures and much excitement. Our discomforts are forgotten in the fun of rushing to catch a train or returning to our hotel, scraping together what supper we can find in small towns at that hour; packing and unpacking (wonderful light entertainment if you care for that sort of thing)— and particularly solving the problems of laundry. Boyer and I have a contest as to how long we can make our dress shirts last between laundries. Miss Moorehead, being the only woman, naturally has a rough time of it, but she more than holds her own. I don't have to tell you that one woman is vastly more clever than any three men.

"We have had so much confirmation of our own faith in the public that it has acted as a tremendous tonic to us. But our pleasure has not been limited to the discovery of new audiences; it has been largely the pleasure of performing this play each night in different surroundings before different audiences and sharing our pleasure in it with them. The performance of this play by four people

who know each other as well as we do—and if I may say
so without being immodest, as experienced and skilful as
we have learned to be—has all the excitement of a game
of tennis.

"We shoot lines at each other in an unexpected way—
just as a tennis player will shoot a ball at you and you get
the thrill of making the right return. It must not be
assumed that we try to defeat one another—it is just the
fun of inventing new readings and trying to give fresh
meanings to the superb wit and wisdom of G.B.S. Never
for an instant have we been bored; nor have we failed
to be stimulated in performing this play, although it
involves the greatest strain that actors can be put to—
which is listening to each other! Each night when we
return to our hotel rooms or to the trains, we discuss our
performance—perhaps why we didn't get a certain laugh
—and we criticize each other's readings. This is not an
occasional experience—it is a nightly routine. In my
opinion it is one of Shaw's greatest qualities that he
challenges both the actors and their audiences to discover
new depths in his works."

True, they sometimes wondered whether they would
ever be able to stand one another's company after the tour
was finished. It was no fun practically living together for
a year on end. "We all stipulated in our contracts that
we should never be cast in the same movie," Laughton
said. And Cedric Hardwicke quipped, "I saw Laughton
on the other side of the street one day. I made an effort
not to catch his eye."

They made jokes about each other's egotism. "Sometimes we have to stop Laughton from doing the Gettysburg Address right in the middle of Don Juan," Sir
Cedric would confide.

"Cedric feels he has to carry on this way all the time,"
Laughton would reply witheringly. "He's as boring as
any comedian."

Cedric, quick on the trigger, would snap back, "Any time Laughton or Boyer is not talking on the stage, it's very refreshing."

Agnes Moorehead would pretend to pour oil on the troubled waters. "It's wonderful to be with Charles," she would say placatingly. "It's like a real education. The trouble is, I can't enjoy myself on the stage because the others are always jawing."

In spite of those difficult personal relationships, a good time was had by all. As for the audiences, for whom after all the whole thing was being done, their response was heart-warming. As Charles said, "People are ready to listen to the best stuff in large quantities. Ours is not a fashionable success. The audiences are very proud to be offered great drama or great comedy. We have noticed this. They go out of the theater in a proud mood."

Chapter 17

"WHY, YOU FAT DOG!" said Elsa one night after she had gone to hear the quartet perform *Don Juan in Hell*, "you have learned the very best thing an actor can learn: how to talk to an audience as if they were people in a room." This sounded like high praise coming from Elsa, who had not been too lavish with compliments. "Charles," she then said with wifely concern, "you look very tired—and fifteen years younger."

Everyone who knew Charles remarked on the change in him. The critics, too, noticed his air of happiness since he had found fulfilment for his creative energy as reader, as "concertmaster" of the drama quartet, as actor, director and adapter. Said one San Francisco critic, "Laughton on the stage looks and acts like a balloon held captive. He enjoys himself as much as the audience does."

As for the audiences, informed critics wondered where Charles had produced them. Charles maintained that he had done nothing special. It was not a question of magic. "They seemed to come out of the ground," he said. "I don't really know who my audience is or where they come from. They are farmers and teachers, businessmen and teen-agers, clubwomen and soldiers. All I do know is that there is a vast and culture-hungry audience untouched by radio, television or the movies."

Laughton's success was the talk of Hollywood. At an

important executive meeting a producer who had worked with Laughton in an unsuccessful picture said: "We imagine that our research departments and public opinion polls keep us in touch with the pulse of the nation. Yet here we are losing money. Over six hundred movies have shut down. Thanks to television, we lost seven million movie-goers in 1952. Then along comes Gregory and puts Laughton into the saddle. They go on a reading tour and gross more than a million and a half dollars. What can you make of it?"

Hollywood loves to capture and capitalize on successes that others have created. Now that Laughton's star was on the rise, the studios suddenly began to take a new interest in him. The movie moguls, threatened by television, were throwing all they had into grand spectacles which television could not match. They now made room in their plans for major roles for Charles Laughton.

But in the meantime Paul Gregory thought up a television project for Laughton, and found a sponsor for it. Television was a relatively new medium for Charles—he had read the Bible on TV and had appeared as a guest artist on Ed Wynn's program but now he had his own show, "This Is Charles Laughton."

What was he going to do with it? Would he play safe and adopt one of the current television formulae? Said Charles, "Others keep advising us that we must be careful. By this they mean that we must copy what has already been found successful and that we do not want to do. For that, as we can see by looking about, is Death, and, what is worse, Damnation."

The average television screen does not allow for much movement. The actor is centered square on the screen. Any program is preceded and followed by stories of gory murders and hair-raising mysteries. All in all, the situation presented a challenge to Laughton, who had to learn to put himself across on the small screen and to concentrate his fire into twelve uninterrupted minutes.

As in his nationwide platform appearances, Laughton is presented on a bare stage in his own TV show. His only prop is a lectern for his books. The commercial is restricted to a short announcement at the beginning and at the end of the program—he will not tolerate interruptions. As in his readings, he depends on nothing beyond the extraordinary force of his personality and the rich, melodic timbre of his voice. His only material is world literature—from the Bible to Dickens, from *Don Juan in Hell* to James Thurber. Some of the pieces are serious and some are funny. When he first started he had some troubles which have since been smoothed out. On reading tours Charles would fashion his own program according to the mood of the evening. In movie work no director, neither Korda nor Hitchcock nor De Mille, had ever been able to tame him. But now he found himself facing the studio clock—an absolute dictator. The clock was to become Charles Laughton's first boss. At times he was so conscious of racing against its hands that his breath would start coming loud and hard, as though he were actually running. But Laughton is fast to learn, and in a few weeks he seemed to be an old hand at television. He kept his natural and informal approach to his selections. For example, he will speak of a Chinese fellow he wants one to meet, and then he will read some poems by Lao Tse. He speaks jokingly of current events, such as elections, and finds pieces that fit in with such occasions.

As he cannot pace around on the stage and has to consider the limitations of the TV screen, his mannerisms have multiplied by the dozen. He is a great fidgeter—stands up, sits down, removes and polishes his glasses, rubs his eyes, puts his hands in and out of pockets, chafes his chin and nose. As far as his personal appearance goes, he has made no concession to television. He is as negligent of the way he looks as ever—so much so that Erskine Johnson, columnist of the *Los Angeles Daily News*, was prompted to write:

"Aside to Charles: It would be nice if you would have your suit pressed before appearing in front of the TV cameras."

But rumpled or not, Charles makes his one person do for three and four, thanks to his voice, which runs the gamut of emotions, and ranges from soprano to basso.

Laughton had set out to prove to himself and to others that the motion-picture industry, which was geared for entertainment pure and simple, was on the wrong track. Given the right slant, art could speak to millions who were tired and bored by standard romance, adventure and gore. And prove it he certainly did.

Laughton's name alone was magic again. A new edition of the Shaw play sold by the thousands. Booking agents who had counted on a hall in a small town holding 800 people had to transfer to a larger auditorium with a capacity of 3,000 when Laughton appeared. Laughton was big box office now, for everyone but Hollywood.

The movie studios decided that this was an untenable situation. If there was that much appeal to Laughton, they wanted him back. They knew they could lure him with a good fat role. So MGM decided to do *Salomé*. The Hollywood version was to be a technicolor extravaganza starring Rita Hayworth, just back from her Aly Khan venture. What an idea, to have an ex-princess for the part of Princess Salomé! Judith Anderson would be Queen Herodias. Stewart Granger was cast as Claudius, and Sir Cedric Hardwicke as Caesar Tiberius. Charles Laughton would be perfect as King Herod. Would he consider it? It was an important production, based on one of the great Biblical incidents, with a script by none other than Oscar Wilde.

The Oscar Wilde *Salomé* was a short play, poetic in language, moody in tone. Early in the present century it assumed the form by which it is best known. Richard Strauss, the composer, seized the Wilde play and used it in toto for an opera libretto.

In the play and in the opera John the Baptist is at large in Galilee. He denounces Herod for taking to wife the widow of a brother he has murdered. She is Herodias, and asks for the execution of the Baptist on the ground that he incited the masses against her.

Herod, fearing the public, refuses. Herodias' daughter is Salomé, who has fallen in love with John the Baptist. The holy man, however, rejects her advances.

At Herod's birthday party Salomé agrees to dance, removing her seven veils one by one in the most celebrated of strip teases. Herod, lusting for his stepdaughter, promises her anything up to half his kingdom if she will remove the seventh veil. She asks the head of John the Baptist on a salver. Herod is terrified, but having promised, orders the Baptist beheaded. One blow of the ax, and Salomé and her mother were satisfied.

She places her lips against the Baptist's mouth and cries, "I have kissed thy mouth, Jokanaan." Herod, horrified, stalks off, ordering his soldiers to "kill that woman."

The movie version treats the legend quite differently. Rita Hayworth as Salomé dances the dance, but as a price for Jokanaan's freedom. The plan miscarries and the prophet loses his head anyway. Salomé and her Roman lover, Claudius, are converted to Christianity by the tragedy. They flee to the wilderness to follow Him whom John the Baptist presaged.

The movie differs from its illustrious predecessors not only in its outcome, but in its whole approach. Rita Hayworth in her Seventh Veil Dance, reminded one more of a burlesque dancer than of a Biblical princess. There was nothing the matter with her allure, though. Laughton was not at his best in this version of *Salomé*. Only in the scenes where he is shaken by fear, tortured by superstition and hungry to "return to God" did he rise to any heights. But for the most part he overacted—just as everything in this colorama was overdone. Having secured Laughton,

Hollywood committed its usual mistakes with him. For example, producers consider an enormous eating scene a must in any Laughton historical picture. Charles always does a wonderful job with such scenes, but by this time they are unbearable clichés. On the whole, *Salomé* was a stupid film studded with beautiful costumes and expensive sets. The reviewers were not deceived by the roster of big names. On the West Coast Tom Ormsby put it succinctly in a one-word movie review. He wrote:

"For *Salomé:* Salami."

A few other disrespectful voices were raised. Another critic wrote:

"Laughton is getting so obese that he looks obscene. I will make a prediction that his robes must have been fitted by Omar the Tentmaker. If you ever stuck a knife in this fellow, it would take twenty minutes to walk from one side of his spine to the other. I take nothing away from his acting ability, but there is enough of him to cause an eclipse of the sun."

The film definitely did not cause any eclipses in Hollywood. After its completion Laughton was coaxed into another assignment. He was to play Henry VIII, a role which had come to be his exclusive property. He had received the Academy Award for his full-length portrait of the Tudor monarch; he had played Henry VIII in the Shakespeare play in London. Now he would bring Henry VIII to life again in *Young Bess,* a picture to be released at the time of the coronation of Queen Elizabeth II. It was a splendid and well-planned picture, and the people in charge saw it as a golden opportunity to bring Laughton to the screen in his most famous role.

And so, twenty years after the Academy Award, Laughton again turned his thoughts to the character of the much-married king. *Young Bess* was meant for a new generation of movie-goers who had been too young for the earlier film. For their benefit, Laughton did a thumbnail sketch of his favorite monarch:

"Henry is being pictured as lusty and gusty as ever, and he was quite a bum, too. But he did have his good points, even though nobody seems to pay any attention to those these days. For example, the best authorities indicate that he prided himself on a strong sense of responsibility to his kingdom and his people. They agree, too, that he was an outstanding statesman and that he started the British Navy on its way to rule the seas.

"He was noted for a tremendous drive in everything he undertook and was an exceptional athlete. He excelled in tennis, archery, jousting and riding until well into his forties.

"You'd never guess from the way we picture him today that he had a keen appreciation of painting and literature, or that he was extremely interested in schools. People are amazed, too, to learn that he was a skilled musician. In fact, the research for *Young Bess* revealed an old ballad written by him. It was good enough to be used in the film's music score."

Laughton thought that Henry would not be troubled by his portrayal. "He'd be the first to admit it's good showmanship," Charles said. "He was quite a showman himself—just look at the pomp and glitter he surrounded himself with."

Laughton got wonderful reviews for his work in *Young Bess*. Encouraged by this, he signed up for one of the five sketches in O. Henry's *Full House,* in which he again stole the show—his scene being the best in the entire picture. He played a Bowery bum who is arrested at the very moment he undergoes a change of heart in church. It was a masterly bit of character creation in a film that came and went all too fast.

In the summer of 1953 Laughton, attracted by the idea of returning to England to see his family, accepted an offer from Sir Alexander Korda to play with Robert Donat in *Hobson's Choice.* He tried to whisk through his readings so as to get to England as soon as possible.

His mother was ailing. The reunion, however, was not
to be. Mrs. Eliza Laughton, at eighty-four, passed away
without seeing her celebrated son again.

The famous drama quartet was on tour with *Don Juan
in Hell* when Paul Gregory suggested that they do *John
Brown's Body* next. "I did not like the idea at all,"
Laughton said. "I even opposed it for a long time. I had
done some broadcasts from it, and the poem had been
revised so that it looked like a Leftist tract. I knew only
those excerpts, until Paul got me to read the whole thing.
Then, of course, the big question was how to do it?"

Hours of discussion ensued. A three-hundred-fifty-page
epic needed things done to it. It wasn't even a play. Its
main attraction was readability, "as a backbone I wanted
to stick to our platform drama," Charles explained.
"There are millions, nationwide, who have an appetite
for the best stuff, who have not the facilities for a physically heavy show."

Slowly the project began to fall into shape. The company was still on tour with Shaw's play, coping with the
manifold stresses and strains of the road. But Charles
found time while traveling, waiting or in hotel rooms,
to work on *John Brown's Body.*

Both as artist and showman he realized the necessity
for simplicity and a somber style in adapting the poem
to his purposes. The Stephen Vincent Benét Civil War
epic had to be brought alive, to be made into living
drama through nothing but the spoken word. Charles
himself would not be able to take part in it—he had too
many other commitments. But short of acting in it, he
attended to every detail of the production, regulated and
rehearsed every movement, every step, every raising of
the voice, every whisper. His guiding idea was the Greek
drama—he wanted to re-create this epic in the style and
mood of the ancient Greek theater. Nothing of the sort

had ever been done on Broadway, which would add to
the surprise value of the production.

The presentation was again to be highly unconventional. The sole prop was to be an "acting bar," a three-
foot-high rail against which the principals would sometimes sit, sometimes lean, while they recited Benét's
stirring lines into microphones. Charles conceived of a
chorus of about twenty, to stand in the background and
speak lines in unison as a collective fourth actor. Perhaps this chorus might even sing, thus welding music
and drama the way the Greeks had done.

While Laughton huddled over the script, editing and
cutting the poem to one-sixth its twelve-hour reading
time without adding or changing a word, Gregory started
to cast it. He met Tyrone Power at the 20th Century-
Fox lot.

"The moment he suggested that I participate in *John
Brown's Body,* there was nothing further to discuss," said
Power. "I was eager to get back to the stage, and, having seen *Don Juan,* I knew it would be a wonderful
opportunity."

After signing Power, Gregory went to New York to
see Raymond Massey.

"I guess I had been kind of envious when I'd heard
that Ty was signed for *John Brown's Body,*" recalls
Massey, a gentle, Lincolnesque figure. "So when Gregory
offered me a part, I accepted immediately, even though
I had no idea how they were going to do it."

The feminine role was the hardest to cast, but Laughton came to Gregory's assistance.

"Charles and I were together in *Salomé* at the Colum-
bia studio," Judith Anderson recalls. "We talked about
Don Juan, and this young man Gregory, who had the
imagination and the audacity to give us pure theater with
no trappings of costume and scenery. Charles talked, too,
of *John Brown's Body;* and I found myself wishing there

were something in it for me. The first thing I knew, I was in."

For weeks the composer, Walter Schumann, listened while Laughton read the edited script, then he spent days in Laughton's home in Hollywood trying to work out the sort of musical accompaniment that would fit the heroic tale. What resulted was not background music, but a chorus with a folk-song quality that carries the dramatic action forward as it did in the ancient Greek theater.

For years Tyrone Power had been Hollywood's choice for dashing adventure roles. Audiences knew him as a deft swordsman and a general daredevil. They were now amazed at his magnificent voice and enormous dramatic prowess. Sixteen years in Hollywood had never given him a chance to express his potentialities. As he himself explained it:

"You go to the same studio every morning. You get the same kind of part. The costume will be different and the leading lady different, but you find it hard to get much more of a change than that. When Charles Laughton asked me to do this, I'd have gone through almost anything to accept. Fortunately for me, and unlike some other people I know who want to do the same thing, I had no contract to keep me from accepting. The only thing I had to worry about, and I did worry, was about playing with Judith Anderson and Raymond Massey, because there is an inevitable comparison when you play with actors such as they are."

Laughton understood the particular problem which an actor such as Tyrone Power faced in making his change-over from the screen to the theater. He had the situation analyzed. "When you come out on the stage," Charles warned, "you will be the fellow who is going to recite some stirring lines and portray some interesting characters in Benét's very much admired literary work. But you will also be the monster, made up of all the

characters you have played on the screen. Many people
will come to see that monster. You must go out there
and dispose of him with a little speech which demon-
strates that you can talk and breathe and move, and then
you must draw the people along to an interest in the
story we are going to tell."

But Charles had confidence in the man he had chosen.
"Tyrone Power is a storyteller, where Laurence Olivier,
for instance, is not. He can say, 'Once there was a princess,' and you feel at home. You don't need the panoply
of the theater."

Again Charles was staking everything on the power
of the spoken word. Whereas *Don Juan in Hell* had been
a battle of wits, *John Brown's Body* was a symphonic
composition depending on the lyrical interweaving of
voices.

Don Juan in Hell was still running, which meant that
Charles had two shows going simultaneously. Critics had
a hard time deciding which of the two was the more
challenging—or which of the actors took the palm. Raymond Massey was doing a superb job as Lincoln. "He
took Lincoln's picture off the penny," said some of the
critics. Judith Anderson, with immense versatility, carried off all the female parts—from that of beautiful Sally
Dupré to the naive Melora and the strong-willed, proud
plantation mistress. One of America's great actresses, she
brought fire and drama to her climactic scenes.

With Broadway still shaky ground for anything but
a musical, Paul Gregory could total up 200,000 dollars'
worth of tickets in advance sale before the "trio" even
started on its tour. Their première took place in California and they worked east, stopping at every major city
and many smaller ones, so that all America might have
its chance to hear *John Brown's Body*. It was an enormous undertaking and sometimes a gruelling one. Judith
Anderson has told her story of some of their mis-
adventures:

"We were supposed to travel by bus, and the chorus did, all the way," she recalled. "But the principals varied this confining, shaky and tortuous method by air hops, train trips or hiring private automobiles when they could, so they could benefit by a little extra rest time before the performance.

"Somewhere up in the Northwest—I can't remember just where now—we ran into a real blizzard. I was pretty sick at the time, and couldn't face the bus trip, so I hired a driver and piled into his car, with plenty of blankets, hot-water bottles and pills. It was a wild ride through a blinding snowstorm on a narrow, icy highway. Finally, on a curve, we skidded, turned completely around and landed in a ditch. The driver couldn't budge the car in spite of chains, so I told him to watch for the company bus which was trailing us by an hour or so, and hail it.

"The bus showed up eventually and they wanted me to board it, but I was stubborn and demanded that they pull us out of the ditch so we could proceed on our own. They finally hooked up a chain and pulled us up on the pavement again. We were headed in the wrong direction, and had to drive on a quarter-mile or so before we could turn around. When we passed the scene again on our way east, there was another car in the same spot in the ditch.

"We drove on for another hour, with the weather getting worse and worse. Finally, out in the middle of nowhere, the driver stopped, turned around and said: 'Miss Anderson, I don't know how much you value your life, but I know how much mine is worth to me. I ain't going no further.' I looked around at the howling blizzard, with no building in sight, and pointed out that he certainly couldn't just stop there and freeze to death. 'Take me into the next town,' I said. 'The bus will be stopping for lunch, and I can join it.' So with much grumbling he proceeded; we made the next town, I paid him off and he headed back home without even waiting for coffee."

By the time the troupe reached Cleveland, Miss Anderson had a high fever and pains in her left side. It was just a few days before the scheduled opening on Broadway, and the situation looked bad. Charles Laughton and Paul Gregory were tiptoeing around the room, questioning the doctors, trying to get some reassurance. Finally the actress was carried onto a plane for a quick hop to New York, where her doctor met her at the airport and took her in charge. "Pleural pneumonia," was his diagnosis, and he ordered her to remain in bed. That was Thursday morning. The New York opening was set for Saturday evening.

"Will she be able to go on?" Laughton and Gregory hounded the doctor.

"Can't say; depends on how she responds to treatment," he replied.

"Well," Miss Anderson says, "Saturday night I went on. My legs were weaving and my voice came from I don't know where—I was so full of medication I scarcely knew what was going on."

Once in New York and settled comfortably in a hotel for weeks, she finally regained her usual good health. But then came the disappointment. The New York critics had been somewhat divided in their reviews, although Brooks Atkinson and several other leading reviewers had been enthusiastic. The New York audience responded well, but not in so large numbers as had been hoped. Paul Gregory was astute enough to see which way the wind was blowing. He decided to close the show while it was still doing well, rather than to risk a gradual slowdown. The New York run lasted only eight weeks. Then they doubled back on their tracks to cover points in the South and Southwest.

Laughton was in New York at the time, staying at the St. Moritz Hotel. On his rare holidays from one-man

readings in and around the New York area, he was a
backstage guest at *John Brown's Body,* which was as dear
to his heart as *Don Juan.* In fact, one day in April, 1953,
actually saw six Laughton productions running simultaneously: Charles was making a platform appearance.
John Brown's Body was running at Central Park. *Salomé*
was being shown in a Broadway movie house. A small
house was running a revival of *The Private Life of Henry
VIII.* The radio featured his recording of *Moby Dick.*
And to top it all, Charles was to be seen on his regular
television show.

Laughton had never been happier. He liked the multi-
plicity of his activities. He was proud that he had been
swimming against the stream of Hollywood and Broadway and done extremely well. When Mary Margaret
McBride—the grand lady of America's air waves, met him
in New York she said abruptly, "Charles, you are different. What's happened to you?"

"I'm happier, that's all," he replied. "It's the readings,
I think. The stage wasn't enough. Hollywood wasn't. It
seems to me they required about a quarter of the man
I wanted to be. And, after all, there are only a certain
number of parts for my type of person. I'm a fat, middle-
aged man. But in my readings I can be anything. I can
be a little girl or an old woman or a handsome young
adventurer."

He was still the same old romanticist.

Charles paused and smiled, as he added, "I might as
well admit it. I'm much nicer now to have around the
house."

It really seemed as though Charles had cornered the
theatrical market. No Broadway or Hollywood actor
could point to a similar record. Charles outshone them
all. Yet at the height of that incredible success one New
York critic raised his voice to protest. The critic was
Eric Bentley, author of many books on the theater and
a man of unquestionable intelligence. "Fancy lighting,

fancier words, grouping and movements, trios and quartets, don't make up for *real* theater," he wrote. "But my real complaint is that it is for this artist [Laughton] not good enough and my hunch is that it is an evasion. An evasion of the theater. Mr. Laughton walks round and round the theater like a dog that cannot make up its mind to sit down. He tries the movies. He reads in hospitals. He reads the Bible in schools, or on TV. He invents the drama quartet. He trains a drama trio. Meanwhile he falls in love with literature and therefore with Thomas Wolfe. It is all an evasion."

This could be dismissed as the inevitable faultfinding of the high-brow intellectuals who see something wrong in any great success. But the fact remains that Laughton has not appeared on Broadway in real legitimate theater since 1933. Why? *Galileo* did not count—it was an experiment, and an experiment that failed. Why has Laughton never appeared in a real play? Now the question was being raised, and Laughton could feel its justice. He had achieved unheard-of success by daring experiments. What about the most daring experiment of all— a full-scale Broadway play?

Was the failure his or was it Broadway's, which had never taken him into its bosom? Realizing what was on Charles's mind, a close friend of his, a millionaire, spoke up. "I will buy a Broadway theater specially for Laughton," he announced.

"I might buy one myself," grinned Laughton. "Who knows?"

Gregory, as usual, kept his ideas to himself. But only a few months later, on July 30, 1953, Paul Gregory announced that Charles Laughton would star in *Lord Pango*, the story of the late art collector Joseph Duveen, adapted by S. N. Behrman from his own story which had appeared in *The New Yorker*. The following year would be the year of decision in Laughton's life.

The decision came, but in a rather surprising way.

Of course Laughton always loved to surprise his audiences and critics. He went to Broadway only indirectly.

He became a full-fledged producer for the theater, and his magic touch gave Broadway *The Caine Mutiny Court Martial*. This production surpassed his *Don Juan in Hell* and *John Brown's Body*. It was theater at its best.

Herman Wouk, author of the novel *The Caine Mutiny*, which has sold more than one million copies and was translated into many languages, tells of his bewilderment and amazement at what happened to him and his book.

His play was born out of an unsuccessful attempt to persuade Paul Gregory and Charles Laughton to give a dramatic reading based on the trial in his novel. This was shortly after Wouk had seen *Don Juan in Hell*. Laughton gave the idea some consideration and then advised Herman Wouk that *The Caine Mutiny* was not suited for readings.

Laughton suggested, however, Herman Wouk "ought to try to write a legitimate drama" based on the *Caine Mutiny* trial. Finally, Paul Gregory got Henry Fonda to accept the part of Lieutenant Greenwald in a *Caine Mutiny* play. It was in July, 1953.

Of course, the play bears the touches of Charles Laughton, as the performance shows his genius as director. Wouk dedicated the new play to Laughton "in admiration and gratitude."

The play first toured the West Coast with Henry Fonda and Lloyd Nolan and John Hodiak. It took them actually two months to reach New York.

When it was shown in Wilmington, Delaware, Laughton, between his own reading-tour engagements, sneaked in to the Playhouse there. He took his place among the standees and watched throughout the performance. A few feet from him stood Herman Wouk the author. Both knew this was the last chance before the New York opening. Would they have to revise the play? Did they need cuts or a new scene? Both men were tense.

But the audience gave it a thundering approval.

Laughton said later, "This play expresses Wouk's respect for authority. It's an affirmative play. It took a patriotic American to write *The Caine Mutiny,* a man with deep feeling for his country. This is Wouk's concept, but them's my sentiments, too, and I'm glad to write 'em on the wall. I get so awfully sick of debunkers."

Before *The Caine Mutiny Court Martial* went into rehearsal, Laughton met with Wouk over a period of three months, discussing with him how he could tell the whole story of the *Caine*—the men, the battles, Captain Queeg's persecution of the crew, the typhoon, the mutiny —in the framework of a courtroom, and how other playwrights had solved that problem before. After long, arduous work, Wouk brought a huge and heavy script to Laughton which the latter cut to pieces. Page after page was thrown overboard, sentences edited and changed.

"When Laughton gave me back my script," Wouk told a friend later, "I felt like saying, 'Look, you fat so-and-so, you can't do that to me.' But actually I knew his editing was the thing. He took the script and made it into a play. It was educational for me but, like education, very exasperating."

There was a great understanding between Wouk and Laughton. But in spite of their friendship, Laughton was hesitant to take over the direction of the play. This was an American naval play. Laughton had only recently become an American citizen. Just two years before he had felt an American ought to direct the picture.

Paul Gregory signed Dick Powell as director, but after two weeks Mr. Powell withdrew. Laughton then took over completely and proclaimed, "Wouk is a wonderful person to work with, a bottomless well of fine lines. You know, about eighty per cent of the play is new material. Herman couldn't merely lift his dialogue word for word from the novel. He had to write specifically this new creation, this drama, *The Caine Mutiny Court Martial.*"

"Captain Queeg's crack-up on the witness stand at the court-martial is less than a page in the book," Wouk told a reporter. "In one sentence I just said, 'Queeg went on for eight or nine minutes in this way.' But in the play, Queeg's breakdown had to be explicit. The eight or nine minutes had to be written, word for word."

Queeg is not a sympathetic character in the novel or in the play; he is a typical inhuman and cruel commander who drives his crew to the limits. Some called him even "paranoic."

"That's it," explained Laughton, "Queeg is really the victim. He shouldn't have been superseded as commander of the *Caine*. When a war breaks out and authority is stretched thin, these are the only people that can be in authority because they have the training. The men who mutinied against Queeg were concerned with their comfort. Comfort isn't the most important thing. What do you do when you get a Queeg? Barney Greenwald, the lawyer at the court-martial, answers this. 'You fight the war,' he says. Cruel or not, Queeg was essential, for if he hadn't been there to fight—as Greenwald points out—'the Nazis and the Japs might have been shaking hands at the Mississippi.' "

Seymour Peck gave *The Caine Mutiny Court Martial* a penetrating review in *The New York Times* and discussed the various changes made in the novel:

"A significant change Wouk has made is that whereas in the novel the action was seen through the eyes of young Willie Keith, in the play everything is seen through the eyes of Barney Greenwald. 'Greenwald has the long wisdom of the Jew in him,' said Laughton. 'He has the depth, the age of the race in him.' Does author Wouk speak through Greenwald? 'All good writing must be autobiographical,' Laughton replied. 'You can find Shakespeare in any of Shakespeare's plays, pick a number.'

"In *The Caine Mutiny Court Martial*, Greenwald is a Jew who has come to respect authority deeply, who has grown up to know there may be a time for 'rebellious youth' but the time is over now. And certainly aboard a Navy ship in World War II there is no time at all for 'rebellious youth.' As a Jew, Greenwald pays tribute to Queeg, for Queeg helped keep Greenwald's mother—and other Jews—from being melted down for soap by Hermann Goering. 'Herman Wouk's a very strict Jew, you know,' said Laughton. Doesn't Wouk teach at the Yeshiva University, Laughton was asked. 'You're telling me,' said Laughton, 'you're telling me. In fact, I had an awful time getting him away from his classes to work on the play.' "

At the end of the Wilmington performance, the lights went on in the theater and Laughton hurried backstage, tears streaming down his face after the final speech by Henry Fonda, who acts the part of Greenwald, about Hitler and the destruction of the Jews. "I can't help it," said Laughton. "That scene always makes me cry." Backstage everyone seemed jubilant about how the play had gone with the new material in it. "I think I've done all that I can do," said Laughton. "I think it should just be left to cook now."

Chapter 18

FOR MORE than twenty years Charles Laughton had used the spoken word to bring him closer to the American multitudes. That day back in 1950 when he received his American citizenship, his name was a byword in America and a familiar concept over several continents. He belonged to the very small group of actors whose career had covered a span of almost three generations. He had won supremacy on the stages of London and Broadway in the twenties. He had given the generation of the thirties and forties his rich and original screen characterizations. More recently, he has been aiming his fire at a brand-new college generation whom he introduced to world literature. For this generation he was building a bridge from the past to the present day by his bold productions, *Don Juan in Hell, The Caine Mutiny Court Martial, John Brown's Body,* and others. With the years his art had gone on growing, widening and deepening. To his gifts as an actor he was now adding the mature powers of a great director.

Signs of his full promise had appeared on the horizon long before. In the thirties the late Alva Johnston, one of America's great publicists, had called Laughton "A great man who accidentally became an actor."

Charles's physical endowment made him ideally suited

286

for an actor. The Ringling Brothers side show used to exhibit a rubber-skinned man and a human telescope. They were a remarkable pair who could do almost anything with their bodies—could stretch their joints or contort their features beyond recognition. It was all a question of the pituitary glands. Laughton certainly could compete with any of those side-show characters, when it comes to physical elasticity. He has an amazing capacity to transform himself. His face can change within a split second. His body swells or shrinks like a sail. His loose jowls and slack muscles can take on any shape at will. Without make-up or costumes, he can represent a vast array of physical types.

With this talent, there was always the temptation to become the world's greatest ham. But Laughton was saved from this fate by his superior intelligence, his enormous amount of work, self-denial and self-discipline.

Charles has more than his share of contradictions and eccentricities. For example, his main quarrel with Hollywood productions is that they oversentimentalize everything they touch. This statement sounds odd coming from Charles, who has been a lifelong sentimentalist and romanticist. In real life his eyes fill with tears whenever he is deeply moved. On the stage, however, he does not rely on his natural facility, but can manufacture tears by some tried and true stage tricks. Fellow actors have seen him put both hands around his neck as if he were going to choke himself. He starts coughing and gasping for breath and soon is weeping copiously.

He brings passion to every part he takes. It doesn't matter to him that he has so seldom played the lover on the stage. His passion was and is acting—that is the only real "romance" he has known, despite the fact that his marriage has lasted longer than many Hollywood marriages. He has always put his art higher than anything else in his personal life. Elsa, too, has followed this principle. Both of them are amazingly free of jealousy and possessiveness. This allows them more opportunities to dedicate themselves more completely to their work.

"I believed in myself," Laughton once said, "and have let no one destroy that belief." Like most great artists, Charles has never ceded his independence to anyone. He is his own master, his own ultimate judge. In his artistic life he trusts no one but himself.

The significance of Laughton's art lies in the fact that it cannot be classified. As an actor he has taken for his field the human race. He is the personification of theatrical versatility. His lack of ordinary good looks makes it convenient for him to play maladjusted villain types. He has portrayed beggars, vagabonds, outcasts and criminals. With his astoundingly beautiful voice he can put across the highest, the most noble poetry. He can be comical or tragic, terrifying or preposterous, as Nero, Henry VIII or the Devil himself.

From start to finish he has been an actor entirely possessed by his art. He lives most intensely when he is playing a role—even in private life he is lost and unhappy unless he is carrying off some role or other.

He can play anything you want him to play and things you never expected him to play—at the snap of your fingers.

He has never personally felt the lust of King Herod, the brutality of Henry VIII, the sadism of Captain Bligh. These are borrowed emotions, assumed for the moment and then cast aside. Yet while he is portraying them they are more real than so-called "real" feelings. For Charles, fiction is more important than truth.

"My own family," he once remarked, "never knew me when I acted. For example, if I were supposed to die on-stage, they were glad to find I was alive afterward. They would ask me repeatedly, 'You're sure you are all right,' and I would answer, 'Don't be silly, of course I'm all right.'" After one of his convincing movie scenes, a distant relative came to him. "You know, Charles," he said, "you played that scene so beautifully your insurance agent must have fainted."

When evaluating Charles Laughton's acting, it is important to grasp the simplicity that marks his art. He has been represented as heavy, high-brow, long-haired; but in essence his approach is very simple. He interprets the great eternal emotions of man—a quality that under-lies his vast popularity. When he slips into what seems like vulgar buffoonery, we might recall that this is a tradition going back to Aristophanes, Shakespeare, Rabelais and Molière. Always inventive, Laughton gives even low comedy his own peculiar twist. As an actor, he is a humorist of the first order.

He is as many-sided and mysterious in his art as Hamlet. His pantomime is the finest since Chaplin. As audience after audience testifies, he can convey the deepest emotions with the most disarming sincerity. Thanks to his superior voice and able mimicry, his one-man readings have done more to introduce the American public to poetry than anything else in the cultural scene today.

Laughton serves no one—not the Hollywood studios, nor the managers, nor the press, nor the critics. His only duty is to himself and to his audiences.

He is proud of his art and has the firm conviction—contrary to the belief of the late G. B. Shaw and most playwrights—that it is the actor and only the actor who brings a play to life. Until he, Laughton, speaks and moves, the play is a closed-in thing, an interesting piece of literature, but not a dynamic experience.

He puts all his faith in the power of the actor. He will point out that the Greek theater, and Chinese theater and the classic French theater succeeded without scenery and props. During the shooting of *Arch of Triumph*, John Orlando, one of the veteran prop men, said to him:

"Well played, Mr. Laughton, but where would you have been without the German riding crop I found for you."

"My dear fellow," replied Laughton, "take the props from an actor and he can still act. Remove the actor from the props and they are helpless."

In many respects Laughton has done for the American stage what Louis Jouvet did for the French stage with his famous Théâtre de l'Athénée.

Both Jouvet and Laughton have realized that the conventional play form has become obsolete. The well-made, realistic play of Ibsen has dominated the European stage for about fifty years, but its conventions and devices no longer satisfy the modern audience. Both Jouvet and Laughton have branched out in new directions. They have both sought older and more fundamental approaches to the drama. They have restored poetic reality in place of the tedious superrealism of Hollywood and the conventional stage.

It is not generally known that Laughton is greatly indebted to the Japanese theater. He astounded his Shakespeare class one day by delivering a lecture on the art of the Japanese.

Every time he passes through Chicago, he stops at the Art Institute. He usually makes a point of wiring to the curator to request certain Japanese portfolios he wants to see. He will then spend hours in the Japanese Print Study Room.

One time he spent six consecutives hours with portfolios of the prints of Hokusai, which he studied for the vigorous power of observation and the attitudes of the great Oriental's figures. Laughton said, "I would not dream of going into a play without first consulting the miraculous brush of Hokusai. In every little figure, every line, there is an abundance of life. Look at that figure walking against the wind. See this one bent under a load; see the stance of this pompous nobleman. You can learn about acting by studying Hokusai. As for the composition, the stage, after all, is a living interpretation of the plastic arts."

Laughton not only loves this artist's works, but he has made it his business to acquaint himself with the painter's life. He regards Hokusai, who was known in his lifetime as "The Old Man Mad with Painting," as one of his masters and likes to quote the words of the eighty-nine-year-old artist, who, on his deathbed, said:

"If the gods had given me only ten years more—only five years more—I could have become a really great painter."

On another visit to the Museum Laughton devoted himself exclusively to the works of Sharaku, whose prints were hung on the walls of the gallery. As he went from picture to picture, he acted out each position and facial contortion that Sharaku so caustically depicts of the popular dancers in eighteenth-century Japan. Two other visitors in the room stood entranced and did not utter a word at this unexpected treat.

As he went through the gallery assuming the different expressions of the various prints, Laughton would say, "There was a man—vitriolic. There's hatred in every hairbreadth of a line. Can't you just see that he despised these depraved female impersonators? Note the small gesture of the finger, the position of the wrist—the turn of the head or even the foot. Everything suggests his feeling toward these people. I think he was the greatest genius of them all—so damn penetrating and such wonderful ability."

How many actors go this deeply into their studies? Perhaps the secret of Laughton's greatness is that he stepped off his pedestal, cast aside his laurels and continued to study, to learn, to explore new vistas in the field of art.

"Once, when my good friend Jean Renoir and I were discussing art, we decided that the only reason we dreaded dying was because we would not be able to learn any more about the arts. Everything worth knowing is in them."

The dozens of Laughton imitators in cabarets and on television have no conception of this side of the actor Laughton. The picture they give of him is that of an overgrown clown. There is something about Laughton that invites comic take-offs. Top performers have borrowed the Laughton accent to make audiences roar from Maine to Mozambique. In Australia a comic named Sam Slowings became famous for his imitation of Laughton as Rembrandt. In England a comedian named Tom Wells "murdered" the audience in the music halls doing Laughton as Henry VIII. In Mexico City Juan Garcia clicked with an impression of Laughton as a beachcomber.

"At first it was annoying," Laughton confessed. "Everywhere I went I seemed to hear a caricature of myself. Imitation may seem to be the sincerest form of flattery, but it got to such a point that waiters in restaurants served me both soup and an imitation of Captain Bligh."

But after a few years of such caricaturing, Laughton grew tolerant. By and by he actually started to enjoy the routine.

"Objectively, I realized it was a kind of compliment. I became so detached that I didn't identify them with myself at all. I even began to understand, remotely, of course, why audiences would like these imitations."

The students in Laughton's Shakespeare Group used to have fun imitating him, too. But since they knew him better than presumptuous comedians, they were always aware that no one can really imitate this man who is a man of a thousand faces. Some of his students took a leaf out of his book and started visiting art galleries. They discovered how much there was to be learned from the great portraitists of the past, from Japanese prints and Dutch paintings. It is no accident that Laughton is one of the great art connoisseurs and art collectors of our time. For him, paintings supplement the more perishable art of the actor.

His home is filled with art treasures, ranging from primitive Tahitian sculpture to such highly developed painting as Renoir's "Judgment of Paris." The latter is a large, rose-colored canvas, one of the masterpieces of the artist's last years. When Laughton shows the picture to guests, he remarks, "I spent every cent I had and borrowed two thousand dollars to get it."

Laughton credits many of his insights as an actor to "the great artists who reveal the God in man. It's in the pictures of Morris Graves. It's in my Rouault 'Satan.' That, like all Rouault paintings, came straight out of Chartres. And Chartres is where I feel it more than anywhere on earth. I first went to Chartres when I was twenty-four. I didn't know much about the Cathedral, so I asked a little old man I saw standing there if he could tell me about any of the figures and windows. He showed me everything. It was three days before I learned that he was Étienne Houvet, Guardian of Chartres and probably the world's greatest still photographer. I looked him up just recently in France. He's eighty, but he remembered everything he had shown me and in exact order."

Charles will go on to say, "There is a tenderness, a spiritual quality about real art. I never felt it in Picasso. Guernica seems cruel to me."

Laughton is not the usual type of art collector who buys what is fashionable or highly esteemed at the moment. He trusts his own judgment, chooses anything that will bring him happiness, inspiration, joy, or satisfies his sense of beauty. There may be a lovely small Mirox, a white wonderfully spaced Cézanne water color; a Horace Pippin painting, "Cabin in the Cotton" ("makes you realize that Uncle Remus was written by a white man"); "The Marne," one of the most beautiful Raoul Dufys, in blue, pink and green; or a tiny color study for La Grande Jatte by Seurat.

A painting always means something to Laughton personally, whether it be a charming portrait of Elsa Lanchester as Mistress Prue in Congreve's *Love for Love,* or a typical Utrillo street scene like his Rue St. Eluethere. Laughton had a strange experience one time in Paris. He was having a drink with a cab driver when he happened to look up. There before him was his Utrillo in brick and stone, seen from a different angle. Laughton commented, "It was frightening, like a dream."

Like the great art patrons of the past, he discovers artists on his own. For example, he owns "The Firebird: Disintegrated and Reanimated," by Morris Graves, now acknowledged to be one of the great masterpieces of the modern American school. How did he happen to become so interested in Morris Graves?

"It was during the war. I was in Seattle, on a bond drive, when I saw some pictures by him. I fairly shouted, 'Who did those? Where is he? How can I meet him?' "

The answer was the typically offhand one about a home-town painter. "Oh—a crazy artist who lives around here somewhere."

"I found him," said Laughton, "and we sat up till seven in the morning. Morris Graves is a great religious artist, one of those people who come along every two hundred years or so." Laughton esteems this painter not only as an artist, but as a great man.

Laughton's interest in painting has accelerated the trend in Hollywood toward more and more private art collections. This means a new interest in contemporary American painting and a new market for living art.

Just as he has furthered the cause of painting in America, so has he influenced book reading. It is significant that the Committee of Reading Development, sponsored by the American book publishing industry,

has met with Laughton to thank him for what he has
done for books. His nationwide reading tours have
stimulated book sales appreciably and awakened the wish
to read in a country where television has darkened many
a living room.

Fame and glory have not hurt Charles Laughton. Many
other artists conquered the buffetings of adversity only
to be ruined by the glitter of success. Laughton has con-
sciously set out to withstand the perils of fame. Instead
of becoming self-complacent, he tries to be tolerant,
humble and kind.

But he is almost outrageously demanding when it
comes to his own art. He is constantly on the lookout
for new faces, new roles, new interpretations, new productions. He is determined never to repeat himself and
to prevent himself from becoming one-sided.

Today, when Laughton has achieved perspective on
his childhood, he admits it was perhaps not quite so bad
as he used to think it was. But he knows that he entered
the world of culture starry-eyed, and aimed from the
very beginning at higher goals than the almighty dollar
and the din of applause.

Perhaps Laughton had left Hollywood in time. The
glamorous city had never fully used his talent. Laughton
had chosen to be a director, producer, one-man theater
performer at a time when Hollywood faced the hard facts
of television's progress and its challenge of the films.

The age of the big-money star was over and Laughton
recognized it, thanks to Paul Gregory.

A few years before there had been a thousand screen
writers living in Hollywood. In 1954 only thirty-three
worked full time for the motion-picture industry. At one
time a major studio alone employed thirty-four hair-
dressers. In 1954 they employed one.

Hollywood with the aid of cinemascope and other
future inventions will have its comeback again, but the
art of the theater is eternal.

Laughton never regretted returning from his tours to Hollywood as a producer and director. The man who had made, in four coast-to-coast tours, over two million dollars, just by his readings, went back to Hollywood as a victor at a time when the whole industry was still in a fog and its future was full of uncertainties.

Every actor in America or England, it now seemed, was suddenly ready to work for Laughton and Gregory. They drew such names as Marlene Dietrich, Charles Boyer, John Hodiak, Tyrone Power. In 1954 Laughton was at a new peak of his career, with no end or letdown in sight. He had come a long way, indeed, for a "gifted amateur." *The Night of the Hunter* will see him as new producer and director in Hollywood.

Someone once asked him, "What has given you the greatest thrill of your acting career?"

He had to think for a long time before he finally answered, "The most beautiful thing of all is the complete stillness of an audience so intent that it scarcely breathes."

At such a moment he knows that *he* is the master of the audience—and this is the greatest thing that can happen to him.

He allows himself not a trace of petulance, impatience or fatigue while at work. He never takes an "upstage" attitude toward any of his co-workers. In fact he would be the darling of the studios and rehearsal halls were it not for his fanatic craving for perfection. He wears out even the most conscientious of directors. Once a director who could not take it any longer blurted out, "You finish it on your own—I'm going home now." Laughton stayed and finished it alone—and the result was to everyone's satisfaction.

His energy is phenomenal, but he has learned to hoard his strength jealously. He will not tolerate distractions or interruptions. Once on the set during a scene, an outsider asked him where she could find a friend, the actress

Miss X. Laughton knew perfectly well where the actress was, but he was not going to have their forthcoming scene held up. "Never heard the name," he muttered. "Don't know the woman. You've come to the wrong place."

He was following one of his fundamental principles. "I have always felt very strongly about those disturbing visitors coming into a dressing room during a performance," he says. "I never liked it. I never tolerated it, rarely permitted it and never understood why anybody thought he had a right to come."

When not at work, Laughton loves his privacy—and nowadays has Paul Gregory to watch over it like a bodyguard. Charles's personal friends are few, but his loyalty to those is boundless. Once one of his Shakespeare students tried to approach him to ask help in securing a role. Gregory, who knew that Charles did not want to be bothered, kept fending her off. The young woman was very determined. At last she achieved her purpose, saw Charles and immediately started complaining of the way she had been treated by Charles's manager. "Gregory is a cold and calculating fish," she said, "a man without heart—a business machine . . ."

Laughton lost his temper. "How dare you talk about my friend that way? Don't ever speak that way about Paul Gregory in my presence or elsewhere!"

He will not stand for any detraction of his friends. In the same way his friends will come to his defense if anyone speaks against him in company. This sometimes happens, as Laughton naturally has jealous rivals, envious colleagues and people who are prejudiced against him— mostly without ever having met him. A man in his position inevitably makes enemies. He cannot be obliging to everyone, and it takes only a minor incident to make an enemy for life. For example, a world-renowned pianist gave a party to which he took care to invite Laughton. The guests were treated to a surprise after dinner: The pianist's son and his young friends performed a two-act play. The son was eager to go on the stage. When the amateur theatricals were over, Laughton told his host, "I've never been fortunate enough to have any children. But if I had had a son, I wonder what you'd say if I invited you to a party and had him play the piano for you."

Such a remark is hard to forgive. On the other hand, Laughton has to guard against being exploited. He cannot sponsor the hundreds of aspiring actors who come to him, and he is particularly unwilling to be bribed into such sponsorship.

Superpatriots in America suddenly lashed out at Laughton for his stand regarding Chaplin, whom he called "the greatest of comedians." It took courage in such times for Laughton to declare publicly, "Chaplin is not only the greatest theatrical genius of our time, but one of the greatest in history. Criticize him, yes, but on his own level. One has a tremendous responsibility when writing of a man of his stature."

The upper hierarchy of Hollywood were not particularly pleased by Laughton's further remarks. "There is no doubt in my mind," said Laughton, "that the finest actor in Hollywood has never been honored by an Academy Award. I think it is because we all take him so much for granted. If I were to recall the three greatest performances I've ever seen on the screen, all of them would be performances by Charlie Chaplin. He's yet to win official recognition."

To see some real, robust, old-fashioned clowning, one has to visit the Laughtons at home. As among many people of great accomplishment, the atmosphere in the house is relaxed and informal. He and Elsa have learned how to live in a way best calculated to preserve their gifts. Charles says, "A talented man has a responsibility to himself. I have a little talent with which I have to struggle and toil as best I can. I really work."

For more than a decade Elsa appeared almost nightly as *diseuse* at the Turnabout Theater, an intimate little place where the audience turns its seats around—the seats are discards from the Pacific Electric Company's street cars—as the puppet show stops playing at one end of the theater and the music hall revue starts playing at the other.

"What about you and Charles going on a husband-wife radio program—all you have to do is chat to each other," a shrewd radio promoter asked Elsa.

"Good gracious, no," Elsa said. And with her usual wit added, "We do not want to be known as Ma and Pa Kettle of the kilocycles."

She did not even consider putting the proposal to Charles. Even if she had, she would not have had the chance to do so. For on a spring evening in 1953 she was rushed from the stage to St. John's Hospital with a case of acute appendicitis. Charles was two thousand five hundred miles away in Philadelphia. All he could do was to phone her from the stage. Elsa could still hear his audience applauding his exit.

A few weeks later she was well and able to join her husband in New York, "to renew our romance before Charles goes off to England," she said.

"How does it feel to be the wife of a great man?" This question has been asked Elsa at least a thousand times. Rudyard Kipling supplied the answer to a question such as that years ago. "The silliest woman can manage a clever man, but it needs a very clever woman to manage a fool," he wrote.

"Oh, Elsa—she has sex appeal," Laughton once told a woman reporter. "I wish someone would say that about me."

Elsa, overhearing the comment, remarked, "He is a born mocker, isn't he?"

After many years of marriage, Elsa still loves her husband deeply. Her eyes were sad when she said: "I haven't seen Charles for seven months—he is touring so much. But the future looks better, for he will be in Hollywood more often and he will stay longer as he will now direct pictures."

Elsa glows with warmth and kindness for the people she likes and appreciates. When I, as the inquisitive reporter, asked her recently after a performance in the Turnabout Theater: "Do you believe marriage to a great man has handicapped your own career?" she looked at me quite bewildered and answered carefully: "Who knows? Without Charles I might be a salesgirl in a Woolworth store. Our marriage has its advantages and disadvantages." And she added, "So many people try to play up to me in order to reach Charles—even Alexander Korda did—and having achieved what they want, they forget me quickly. It is quite a nuisance, really."

The two Laughtons have very much in common, for both are actors through and through. Both love their independence, guard their own freedom and are proud that neither of them knows the word "envy."

Of course Charles has steered some roles in Elsa's direction. He knows that she will never turn in a disappointing performance. However, other actresses will grumble, "Laughton would have given me the role if Elsa Lanchester hadn't happened to be his wife." In this they are absolutely wrong. Charles is one of the fairest-minded actors; he does not go in for favoritism.

This does not mean that Elsa has had any easy time living with this theatrical genius. But she knows all his problems, all his moods. From the tone of his voice she can guess what is secretly bothering him. She has learned that he eats most heartily when he is emotionally upset. Elsa has never been able to cure him of his Henry VIII eating habits. He still loves to eat steak with his fingers, and even in a fashionable restaurant will be unable to resist tasty morsels that he notices on his friends' plates. No one minds, however.

Laughton may embarrass people, may quarrel with them, may rehearse them until they are exhausted, may disturb friends in the middle of the night, may break hearts, may drive people crazy, may ask the impossible of them—but he will always remain first and foremost a genius of the spoken word.

By his own standards he has had from life all he has ever wanted. He has soared to the clouds, and he has touched the bottom of despair—and he carries on. He acts because he must. The drive is stronger than he is. There is a gigantic vitality and life force within him, a passion to act which cannot be explained by reason alone. As long as he lives, there will be this rapport between himself and his audience.

He is the actor who fulfills the unspoken needs of men to see the richness of human nature deployed on the stage.

Two thousand years ago, in ancient Greece, people were saying the theater was on the downgrade. Well, it never was and never will be. The theater is still a place of miracles. People will always want to see stage plays. It is the healthiest art there is.

As for Charles Laughton, he will go on acting, as he himself says, "as long as they want to have me."

Index

303